A SHORT HISTORY OF
DISTRIBUTIVE JUSTICE

A Short History of
Distributive Justice

Samuel Fleischacker

HARVARD UNIVERSITY PRESS

Cambridge, Massachusetts

London, England · 2004

First Harvard University Press paperback edition, 2005

Library of Congress Cataloging-in-Publication Data

Fleischacker, Samuel.
  A short history of distributive justice / Samuel Fleischacker.
    p. cm.
  Includes bibliographical references and index.
  ISBN 0-674-01340-9 (cloth)
  ISBN 0-674-01831-1 (paper)
  1. Distributive justice. I. Title.

HB523.F58 2004
340'.115—dc22   2004040517

In memory of Jerry F. De Witt

SINE QUO NON

Contents

Acknowledgments

It was in the course of a review of Charles Griswold's book on Adam Smith that I started to think about changes in the meaning of the phrase "distributive justice," and Charles's response to my comments was not only a model of scholarly generosity, but an extremely helpful prod to further reflection. Our exchange on this subject then led to a chapter titled "Distributive Justice" in my *On Adam Smith's Wealth of Nations: A Philosophical Companion* (Princeton University Press, 2003), which I draw on in parts of Chapters 1 and 2 of this book; I am grateful to my editor at Princeton, Ian Malcolm, and Princeton University Press for permission to do that.

David Waldman and Leon Kojen, in their extremely well-informed and thoughtful way, raised a number of objections to the arguments in my chapter on distributive justice, and in answering their objections—at which point the original chapter began to balloon to more than seventy pages—I began to think I had a book here. I started work on the book during a year's leave at the Institute for the Humanities at the University of Illinois, Chicago; I thank Mary Beth Rose and Linda Vavra for making the Institute such a welcoming place and fostering an atmosphere that encourages scholarship. I also want to thank my colleagues at the Institute that year and the audience at the Institute lecture where I first presented this material for their comments. Sonia Michel and Deirdre McCloskey were particularly helpful, and they directed me to some useful sources on the history of welfare policies. I then learned a great deal from the experience of teaching this material as a graduate class in the Philosophy Department at the University of Illinois, Chicago—many thanks to Andy

Blom, Tina Gibson, Barbara Martin, Chris Martin, and Ben Haines, whose enthusiasm and rich insights were extremely valuable.

I owe a similar debt of thanks to those who responded to presentations of this material at the 2001 meeting of the Eighteenth Century Scottish Studies Society in Richmond, Virginia, and at the Eighteenth Century Seminar at Northwestern University in 2003. I thank Richard Sher and Jerry Muller for their role in setting up the former and Judith Schwartz Karp and Bernadette Fort for their invitation to the latter. Richard Kraut gave me especially rich suggestions at Northwestern. A lively Chicago Political Theory workshop with Ike Balbus, Stephen Engelmann, Paul Gomberg, Michael Green, Charles Mills, and Justin Schwartz contributed significantly to my revisions of Chapter 3. Others whose comments have been helpful include Eric Schliesser, Leonidas Montes, Jeff Weintraub, Tony Laden, Ciaran Cronin, and especially Dan Brudney. Andy Blom has done a terrific job as a research assistant, and Tina Gibson efficiently and cheerfully prepared the index. My thanks go to all of these people, but my even greater thanks go to my wonderful family—Amy, Noa, and Benji—who make life worth living every day.

Abbreviations

The following works are referred to in the text by the abbreviations listed here; full publication details for them can be found in the bibliography. If I cite a text several times in a row, in a single paragraph, I use its abbreviation the first time but just give a page number for subsequent citations.

ASU   Robert Nozick, *Anarchy, State, and Utopia*

DJ   John Rawls, "Distributive Justice," in *John Rawls: Collected Papers*

DPE   Jean-Jacques Rousseau, "A Discourse on Political Economy," in *The Social Contract and Discourses*

E   David Hume, *Enquiries*

ED   Adam Smith, "Early Draft" of the *Wealth of Nations,* included in Smith, *Lectures on Jurisprudence*

FSD   Jean-Jacques Rousseau, *First and Second Discourses*

G   Immanuel Kant, *Foundations of the Metaphysics of Morals.* (The first word of this title is better translated as "Groundwork": hence the "G." Citation will be given to the Akademie pagination as well as the translation.)

LE   Immanuel Kant, *Lectures on Ethics,* trans. Louis Infield

LJ   Adam Smith, *Lectures on Jurisprudence*

LNN   Samuel Pufendorf, *The Law of Nature and Nations*

LWP   Hugo Grotius, *The Law of War and Peace*

MER   Robert Tucker, ed., *The Marx-Engels Reader*

MM   Immanuel Kant, *The Metaphysics of Morals*

NE   Aristotle, *Nicomachean Ethics*

NJ   Istvan Hont and Michael Ignatieff, "Needs and Justice in the *Wealth of Nations*"

SI   Frances Hutcheson, *A Short Introduction to Moral Philosophy*

SMP   Frances Hutcheson, *A System of Moral Philosophy*

SS   Herbert Spencer, *Social Statics*

ST   Thomas Aquinas, *Summa Theologiae,* Blackfriars translation

T   David Hume, *Treatise of Human Nature*

TJ   John Rawls, *A Theory of Justice*

TMS   Adam Smith, *Theory of Moral Sentiments*

Tr   John Locke, *Two Treatises of Government.* (Any edition will do: references specify I or II, for First or Second Treatise; chapter number; and section number.)

WN   Adam Smith, *An Inquiry into the Nature and Causes of the Wealth of Nations*

A SHORT HISTORY OF
DISTRIBUTIVE JUSTICE

Introduction

"Distributive justice," also called "social justice" or "economic justice," is a phrase on many people's lips these days. Demonstrators against globalization invoke it when they decry the evils they associate with multinational corporations; people who oppose capitalism altogether have used it for much longer than that. Many assume that the phrase, and the complex of ideas it represents, is an ancient one, one with which human beings have for time immemorial evaluated their societies. But this is a misimpression, albeit a misimpression that circulates widely, even among scholars. Consider the following:

> The theory of distributive justice—how a society or group should allocate its scarce resources or product among individuals with competing needs or claims—goes back at least two millennia. Aristotle and Plato wrote on the question, and the Talmud recommends solutions to the distribution of an estate among the deceased's creditors.[1]

This little summary is not precisely false. Aristotle did write about something he called "distributive justice," Plato did write on how property should be allocated in an ideal society, and the Talmud, like other ancient legal texts, contains discussions of competing claims to property. But we are getting a misleading picture here, as we can see when we recall the following additional facts:

1. Aristotle never put the problem of how to "allocate scarce resources" under the heading of distributive justice, nor did he regard need as the basis of any claim to property;
2. Plato did not recommend his communal property arrangements for an entire society, nor did he see them as demanded by justice; and

1

3. The problem of how to distribute an estate among competing cred-
itors is not normally a question that depends on the principles a
society or group uses to allocate its collective resources or product.

So while it is true that people have long seen conflicting property claims
as a matter for justice, and while it is also true that philosophers have
long been concerned with societal principles of resource allocation, it does
not follow that these two kinds of issues have long been brought together.
And, in fact, they have not been. Until quite recently, people have not
seen the basic structure of resource allocation across their societies as a
matter of justice, let alone regarded justice as requiring a distribution of
resources that meets everyone's needs.

It is this last object to which distributive justice in its modern sense is
directed, and in this sense the notion is little more than two centuries old.
In its original, Aristotelian sense, "distributive justice" referred to the
principles ensuring that deserving people are rewarded in accordance with
their merits, especially regarding their political status. To get from the Aristotelian to the modern notion, we need minimally to explain why everyone might merit a life free from need. But it was widely believed for a long
time that certain kinds of people *ought* to live in need, that they would not
work otherwise, or that their poverty was part of a divine order: "God
could have made all men rich, but He wanted there to be poor people in
this world, that the rich might be able to redeem their sins."[2]

In this book, I want to begin telling the story of how we got from the
Aristotelian to the modern sense of "distributive justice." One reason for
telling this story is simply that it is interesting, and there is no book-
length treatment of it. But the fact that there is no such book suggests
another reason for one. It is very possible that there is no such book
because people do not generally realize that the meaning of "distributive
justice" has changed, or that for most of human history practically no
one held, even as an ideal, the view that everyone should have their basic
needs satisfied. Socialist historians used to teach that some such ideal has
been around for all human history, at least in the West. Books with titles
such as *From Moses to Lenin* (a real volume) can be found in any library
that retains its holdings from the 1940s and '50s. The just-so story in
such books goes like this:

> Once upon a time, decent but religiously befuddled leaders such as
> Amos, Isaiah, and Jesus taught the equality of all people and the right

of all people, consequently, to life without suffering. Their teachings were distorted and suppressed by oppressive powers in a variety of class struggles, but they were at least held up as an ideal until the eighteenth century. Then came modern economics, with its healthy purging of religious and other superstitious notions about how economies work, but with, as well, an amoral valorization of selfishness that drove out the old respect for the poor. The bourgeoisie now threw off the cloak of morality that had hidden the class struggle in feudal times, which was an advantage in that workers came to understand their true situation but a disadvantage in that the suffering of workers increased enormously. Finally, scientific socialism appeared, which provided a synthesis between the prophetic and the modern attitudes, uniting the norms of premodern religious teachings with a science stripped of the confusions and fatalism that had made it impossible to translate concern for the poor into practice.

This story satisfies the dialectical inclinations of many socialists, as well as their dislike of the cautiousness and hard-boiled realism of eighteenth-century social science. It also fits the facts about Christian teachings, on the one hand, and the harshness of the Industrial Revolution, on the other, well enough to appear convincing. But it is radically mistaken in many ways, and especially in its nostalgic fondness for premodern attitudes toward the poor. The nostalgia derives, I believe, from a wish to see modern capitalism as a wrong turn in human history, to maintain that a kinder, gentler human nature, and view of human nature, existed before capitalism and may, therefore, return. Coupled with this hope is an unwillingness to accept the possibility that the very modest reforms held out by David Hume, Adam Smith, James Madison, and the like are really the most that can be expected from the political realm. If one can show that a set of corrupt *moral* views—about, for instance, the role of selfishness in human life—and not merely an astute grasp of the way economies work, lies behind the much-vaunted realism of the classical political economists, then one may be able to remove the scientific mantle from their policy proposals. If the eighteenth-century social scientists were led only by class prejudices to their view of human nature, then perhaps their low expectations of politics were also just prejudices. Perhaps it is possible, contrary to their teachings, that the political realm can transform the economic one.

So socialists have ideological reasons to project the history of distributive justice backward into the distant past. But laissez-faire ideologues often endorse much the same account of that history, for opposite ideological reasons. Promoters of free markets often like to see themselves as proud modernists, separated by the advent of science from the superstitions and muddy thinking of the past. It goes well with that view of oneself to embrace the supposed cold realism of eighteenth-century science even as socialists reject it. Hume and Smith, one can say, made modern economics possible by freeing themselves from the foolish "just price" notions of the Middle Ages. The laissez-faire ideologues are then happy to agree that these thinkers did something new in rejecting an ancient notion of distributive justice. The ideologues simply welcome that rejection instead of condemning it.

My point is that the history going into both these views is confused. Eighteenth-century social scientists did not reject "distributive justice" in the way we today use that phrase because that notion did not yet exist. Once we recognize that fact, we will be able to see that, far from being cold amoralists who delighted in a realism that ruled out state aid to the poor, they helped lay the groundwork for such aid. The history of distributive justice should thereby help us understand the eighteenth century better, but it should also help us better understand ourselves and our own debates over aid to the poor. Only when we disentangle the modern from the premodern notion of distributive justice can we see precisely what the modern one involves, what new—often, but not always, admirable—shifts in human thought have enabled it to arise.

"Distributive justice" in its modern sense calls on the state to guarantee that property is distributed throughout society so that everyone is supplied with a certain level of material means. Debates about distributive justice tend to center on the amount of means to be guaranteed and on the degree to which state intervention is necessary for those means to be distributed. These are related issues. If the level of goods everyone ought to have is low enough, it may be that the market can guarantee an adequate distribution; if everyone ought to have an ample basket of welfare protections, the state may need to redistribute goods to correct for market imperfections; if what everyone ought to have is an equal share of all goods, private property and the market will probably have to be replaced altogether by a state system for distributing goods. Distributive justice is thus understood to be necessary for any justification of property rights, and such that it may even entail a rejection of private property. A small but influential minority of citizens and theorists, believing that protecting property rights is the central job of justice, question whether distributive demands belong to justice at all. Robert Nozick's *Anarchy, State, and Utopia* is the primary philosophical source for this dissenting view.

But even Nozick does not doubt that the phrase "distributive justice" has always been understood to apply to the distribution of property, by the state, and for the needy. In its Aristotelian sense, however, "distributive justice" called for deserving people to be rewarded in accordance with their merits, was seen as bearing primarily on the distribution of political status, and was not seen as relevant at all to property rights. At least at first glance, then, the ancient and the modern meanings of the phrase are very different. Above all, the ancient principle has to do with distribution according to merit while the modern principle demands a distribution *independent of* merit. *Everyone* is supposed to deserve certain goods regardless of merit on the modern view; merit making is not supposed to begin until some basic goods (housing, health care, education) have been distributed to everyone. We can be quite sure that this is not what Aristotle had in mind when he wrote about political status being distributed in accordance with social or moral status.

How, if at all, can we get from the Aristotelian to the modern notion of distributive justice? Perhaps we should retreat from this to a more primitive question: how does distributive justice, in either of its senses, come to fit under the general heading of "justice"? Well, what is justice, generally speaking? As a formal matter, justice has usually been understood to be a particularly *rational, enforceable,* and *practicable* virtue. Unlike, say, wisdom or charity, justice has been understood across cultures and historical periods to be a secular and a rational virtue, whose demands can be explained and justified without appeal to religious beliefs; to be a virtue that governments can and should enforce, and that indeed ought to be the prime norm guiding political activity; and to be a virtue that, if only because politicians need to organize their plans around it, ought to take as its object practicable, readily achievable goals. Thus promoting belief in Christ or enlightenment via the Buddha has never been held to be a project for justice because the goodness of these projects, if they are good, cannot be explained in purely secular and rational terms. Thus warmth in friendship, while a good thing according to almost everyone, is not considered an object of justice because it depends on the uncoerced feelings of individuals. And thus guaranteeing to everyone freedom from illness has never been included among the objects of justice because, so far at least, it seems to be impossible.

Moving from formal to substantial features, justice in general is usually understood to be a virtue that protects individuals against violence or dishonesty at the hands of other individuals, and against demands by the wider society wantonly to sacrifice their lives, their freedom, or their property. "Wanton" is a vague term, of course. It is hard to say for what causes, and when, individual interests might legitimately be sacrificed. Perhaps individuals can be asked to sacrifice themselves for any cause they share; perhaps they can be asked to sacrifice themselves only when the survival of their society is at stake; perhaps they should never be asked to sacrifice themselves. Some religious and political figures have argued that individual interests should never be allowed to get in the way of the greater human good. But those who hold the latter view have also tended to have little regard for justice, or to redefine it in virtually unrecognizable ways; people who respect justice (or *ius* or *recht* or *haqq* or *tzedek*)[3] tend correspondingly to take the importance of the individual very seriously.

Again, what constitutes respect for individuals can be a difficult and controversial matter, but some kinds of acts are universally held to violate such respect. Physically harming our neighbors or defrauding them is supposed to be something that everyone, regardless of religious or cultural beliefs, recognizes as wrong; and preventing such harm is generally recognized as something governments must do, whatever else they do. So the prevention of harm clearly belongs to justice. Some call this "negative" or "commutative" justice and say that that is all there is to the virtue. But justice has also long been considered to have some bearing on the distribution of goods and status. Justinian famously opens his *Digest* by declaring that "[j]ustice is giving to each person what is due to each." This formulation is supposed to cover both commutative and distributive justice. What is due to our neighbors is that we not kill, beat, or otherwise physically harm them and that we not take things that belong to them. What is due to people who violate these minimal standards of justice— to criminals—is a punishment fitting to their crimes. What is due to people with whom we have a contractual relationship is that we deliver on our promises or make good for our failure to do so. And what is due to people who make great contributions to society is some sort of reward—something that "fits" their achievement. Thus distributive justice is just one case of giving to each person what is due to each. Note, however, that this suits only the Aristotelian concept of distributive justice, where goods are distributed in accordance with merit. To get to the modern concept, we need to explain why it might be "fitting" to the poor that they receive housing, health care, education, and so on. Perhaps such goods are due to every human being, just by virtue of being human. But where then would the merit lie, to which such a distribution would be fitting? In any case, as we will see, it takes a very long time before anyone suggests that any distribution of goods is due to all human beings, just in virtue of being human.

In summary, then, given the general meaning of "justice," we need at least the following premises to arrive at the modern concept of distributive justice:

1. Each individual, and not just societies or the human species as a whole, has a good that deserves respect, and individuals are due certain rights and protections in their pursuit of that good;
2. Some share of material goods is part of every individual's due, part of the rights and protections that everyone deserves;
3. The fact that every individual deserves this can be justified rationally, in purely secular terms;
4. The distribution of this share of goods is practicable: attempting consciously to achieve it is neither a fool's project nor, like the attempt to enforce friendship, something that would undermine the very goal one seeks to achieve; and
5. The state, and not merely private individuals or organizations, ought to be guaranteeing the distribution.

These five premises are closely linked, but it is particularly important, and particularly difficult, to get from Aristotle's distributive justice to my premise 2.[4] To say that a person "merits" a certain thing suggests that he or she has some excellent quality or has performed some excellent action to which that thing is fitting, while to distribute a thing to all people implies precisely that they deserve that thing *independently* of any special character trait or special action they have performed. From the point of view of the Aristotelian tradition, this makes no sense. Moreover, to most premodern moral and political thinkers the poor appeared to be a particularly vicious class of people, a class of people who *deserved* nothing.

Even those who believed strongly in helping the poor regarded such help as undeserved: it was to be bestowed as a matter of grace, an expression of the benevolence of the giver.

I use the word "grace" advisedly. Most premodern proponents of charity, or of the communal sharing of wealth, based their views on religious grounds that violate premise 3. The apostles' community in the New Testament, in which "distribution was made unto every man according as he had need" (Acts 4:35), was a sort of priestly order, keeping the faithful from being too involved with material goods, rather than a solution to political or social problems. It had descendants in the monastic order established by Francis of Assisi, in the Anabaptist kingdom in Münster in 1534–35, and in the Diggers' community of 1649, all of which were premised on a belief in radical self-effacement in the presence of God rather than on any secular, purely rational belief in the equality of human beings.

Nor were the other premises I have listed widely held. Premise 1 was controversial in Aristotle's own time: Aristotle regarded Plato as having unjustifiably placed the good of societies over the good of their individual members. Whether or not Plato is guilty of this charge,[5] he certainly inspired many later thinkers to hold such a view. Premise 4 is still much debated, and its negation was taken for granted in almost every society until the late eighteenth century. The "poor will always be with you" sums up the conventional wisdom until quite recently. Finally, premise 5 is something one does not hear at all until "Gracchus" Babeuf's conspiracy at the end of the French Revolution. Premise 5 really depends on all the others. The state is an entity that is required to protect individuals against each other and against larger groups; that dispenses what is owed to people and not what it would merely be nice for them to have; that, at least in the modern world, is supposed to abjure religious justifications for its actions; and that aims at feasible goals. So only if people deserve some set of material goods, if they do so as individuals and not merely as segments of a larger class or community, if they do so for reasons that can be explained without appeal to religion, and if it is a practical and not a far-fetched goal to give them what they so deserve, can it be reasonable to expect the state to take upon itself the distribution of these goods.

I can hear an objector complaining that people have long believed in human equality and therefore must have implicitly believed in distributive justice. People have indeed long believed in human equality. What they have not long held is that the equal worth of humanity entails equality in political and social goods—much less in economic goods, as premise 2 requires. The notion that all human beings are in some sense equally deserving of a good life can be found in many societies, across human history. Even Plato justifies his hierarchical republic, in part, by the fact that the hierarchy will be good for those in its bottom echelon. Aristotle similarly says that slavery, when properly conducted, is good for the slaves.[6] Again, Hindu caste hierarchies have been defended by the claim that the suffering that comes with a life at the bottom of the hierarchy will help those who endure their lot uncomplainingly to gain merit by which they can rise to a better life in their next incarnation. But by such arguments it is possible to represent the most inegalitarian society as serving egalitarian ideals. It is an encouraging fact that, as seems to be the case, most cultures have regarded all human beings as equal in some fundamental sense. It is a discouraging fact that this belief does not mean very much as far as equality in social, economic, or political status is concerned. Any of the following assumptions will block the inference from the equality in principle of all human beings—metaphysical egalitarianism—to a presumption that efforts should be made to equalize people politically, socially, or economically:

1. Poverty is a punishment for sin—hence the poor, in principle equal to the better-off, have done something to forfeit that equality;
2. Poverty is a natural evil, like earthquakes or sickness, which cannot be overcome by human efforts;
3. Material things do not matter, hence poor and rich can live equally good lives without any change in their material condition;
4. Poverty is a blessing, enabling one to learn humility or to turn away from material obsessions—hence the life of the poor is in fact equal, even superior, to the life of the better-off;
5. Poor people are "fitted" for a life of poverty—it is comfortable for them, and they would not enjoy a more luxurious life;
6. Poverty is necessary to keep poor people working, or to keep them away from drink—hence to their ability to have a good life;
7. The poor can only have a good life if they are taught manners and morals by the rich; or
8. The equal right of poor and rich to material goods, while real

enough, is overridden by other concerns, such as the importance of liberty.

Any of these premises, and several others, will block the move from metaphysical egalitarianism to political or social egalitarianism. And some or all such premises have been held by practically everyone in most societies, including all the societies of the West before about 1750.[7]

Another objector might complain that it is anachronistic, and an expression of Western bias, to require justice in general to have a secular foundation, as I do in premise 3—to require calls for distributions of goods, therefore, to be defended on secular grounds if they are to count as calls for *justice*. But in fact, not only in the Christian West, but in Jewish, Muslim, Buddhist, and many other traditions, a virtue much like what we call "justice" has been seen as the one thing that can be required of all human beings, whether or not they share the tradition's religious views. The jurisprudence of a wide variety of cultures regards it as largely inappropriate for religious views to be forced on people by government power while regarding it as perfectly appropriate, and independent of the promotion of religious views, to force individuals to refrain from murder, bodily assault, theft, and fraud.

Still, there are dissenters to this view even in the West. Plato identified justice as fundamental to all virtues, seeing it as consisting in the right order of the soul—in an order keeping our passions under the control of our reason—and arguing that only such an order will guarantee that people carry out such actions, normally understood to be required by justice, as keeping promises and paying debts. Aristotle, Plato's student, politely granted his teacher that this was *a* notion of justice—"universal justice"—but he separated off from it what he called "particular" justice, the virtue that governs political arrangements and judicial decisions.[8] It is clear that Aristotle regarded this latter meaning of "justice" as the common one, and in fact the term has been used for a political and judicial virtue, first and foremost, down to our own day. A few writers followed Plato in rejecting the distinction between a broadly ethical and a specifically political meaning for justice. If the universal kind of justice really is the foundation of all virtue, and if a virtuous citizenry is the best underpinning for a good state, then states should be concerned above all with fostering universal justice in their citizens. The great Christian Platonist, St. Augustine, used this position to argue that nobody can be truly just without being a faithful Christian. "[J]ustice is that virtue which gives to each his due," he says, but "what kind of justice is it, then, that takes a man away from the true God and subjects him to impure demons? Is this giving to each what is due?" Only a soul that submits to God will be able to exercise proper rule over its body; only such a soul, therefore, will be capable of justice.[9] There is, and can be, no justice in people who are not subject to God, Augustine maintains. There are and can be, therefore, just republics only where faithful Christians rule. This may mean that there never have been and never will be any truly just republics. Augustine is skeptical about the likelihood that truly faithful Christians will ever have much political power. His point is that faithful Christians should put their trust in God rather than in political rulers, that the City of God is radically different from, and more worthy of obedience than, the city of man.

Augustine is thus an apolitical, even an antipolitical, thinker, but there have also been figures who used this mode of argument to promote theocracy in practice. On the whole I will not be concerned with such views in this book. The main point of my digression into the argument for keeping "universal" and "particular" justice together is precisely to bring out why most thinkers in the Western tradition have rejected that argument. If society is to be possible among less than perfectly virtuous people, among people who may not grasp, let alone live out, virtue in its entirety, then it must be possible to separate a virtue for political purposes from the sphere of virtue as a whole. It must be possible to have a separate, political virtue by which citizens and state officials can be judged, independently of their commitment to the highest good, whether that good be faith in God or anything else.

And in fact the mainstream Western tradition of thinking about justice has always identified it as an especially secular virtue, as something one can fulfill even if one lacks the virtues that might take one into the presence of God. The very notion of natural law, of a law that all humans share, suggests that people can transcend differences in religion, culture, and philosophy for the purpose of political order. That implication is made more or less explicit by Thomas Aquinas and by orthodox Thomists after him. Faith is necessary to accept the divine law, say Aquinas and his followers, but all human beings, whether Christian or not, can and should grasp the natural law. Aquinas identifies natural law with "the light of natural reason" and sees it as the same in all people (ST I-II, Q 91, A2; Q 94, A4). He also says that human law aims properly at that *part* of natural law that has to do "chiefly [with the vices] which do harm to others and have to be stopped if human society is to be maintained, such as murder and theft, and so forth" (ST I-II, Q 96, A2). And he defines justice, in its literal sense at least, as the virtue governing human law and accordingly concerned solely with our relation to other human beings, not with our relation to ourselves or to God (ST II-II, Q 57, A1, Q 58, A1, A2). Similarly, Francesco de Vitoria separates sharply between violations of justice and violations of other virtues, admonishing the Spanish conquistadores that the Amerindians may be held responsible for failures to live up to justice but not for failing to be Christian.[10] Long after Aquinas and Vitoria, this view of justice as independent of other virtues shows up in Immanuel Kant's claim that duties of justice, unlike other moral duties, are not concerned with the intentions of those who must keep them, and in John Rawls's conception of justice and politics as abstracting from differences over religion, culture, or other comprehensive views about how to live.[11]

The mention of Rawls gives me an excuse to make two other preliminary points. First, while Rawls's secular understanding of justice and politics has ancient roots, what he includes in the content of justice does not. When Rawls tells us that retributive justice must be concerned with a person's character but distributive justice should not be so concerned (TJ 311–315), he almost *reverses* the view Aristotle had proposed of these two types of justice. He does not, however, seem aware of that. Rawls, as we shall see, has done more than anyone else to clarify the modern notion of distributive justice, but his work tends to obscure rather than to bring out the relative novelty of this idea. That is a small fault in the work of a systematic philosopher. It is rather more disturbing that people purporting to do intellectual history, in recent years, have tended to read the issues Rawls takes up back into works written at a time when "distributive justice" had a very different meaning. When Adam Smith writes, for instance, that distributive justice cannot be enforced (TMS 390, LJ 9), he is today widely understood to mean that distributive justice in its *modern* sense cannot be enforced. Attention to the history of the notion makes clear that he is actually talking about something quite different. The idea for this book in fact occurred to me while I was working on Smith, as I began to realize that the debates of contemporary scholars over Smith's attitudes toward distributive justice depend on giving that phrase a meaning that did not yet exist in Smith's day.

Second, it is tempting, but I think in the end unhelpful, to view the history I describe in this volume under the rubric of a distinction Rawls draws between "concepts" and "conceptions." Rawls suggests that a *concept* may be widely shared—his own example is the concept of justice—by people who differ significantly in the particular *conception* they bring under that concept (TJ 5–6, 9). Thus people may all agree that the concept of justice involves some sort of socioeconomic equality while some of them hold a conception by which the relevant equality is equality of opportunity while others think justice requires equality of outcome. With this distinction in mind, one might say that a *concept* of distributive justice has long been around even if *conceptions* of distributive justice have changed. Perhaps our differences with Aristotle are only differences in conception; perhaps the fact that we believe that distributions can be evaluated as fair and unfair is enough to show that we share the concept of distributive justice with Aristotle.

I think this understates the differences between Aristotle and ourselves. There are many differences between what Aristotle calls "distributive justice" and what we call by that name. Some of these can indeed be described as differences in conception rather than in concept. When Aristotle applies distributive justice to political goods rather than material goods, it is easy to say we differ only in conception: we apply the concept to different ranges of objects, but the same concept is at work in both applications. When Aristotle ties distributive justice to a notion of merit, however, that seems to me a deeper difference. Desert is *essentially* tied to merit for Aristotle; it makes no sense, in his framework, to think anyone could deserve something merely because she needs it. Even the *concept* of "distributive justice" with which Aristotle works seems best defined, not as the mere notion that "justice or fairness may apply to distributions," but as the notion that "justice or fairness applies to the distribution of goods *that one or more persons merit*." It is essential, that is, not accidental, to Aristotle's concept of distributive justice that a notion of merit is at work—a notion by which people deserve something because of excellent character traits they have or excellent actions they have performed. It is equally essential to the modern notion of distributive justice that people deserve certain goods *regardless* of their character traits or anything they have done.

There are various things one can do to try to bring the two notions together. One piece of the modern view is that laborers are undercompensated given the hard work they do, or the contribution of their labor to the common good, and this relies on a presumption that laboring is a merit, perhaps the only merit relevant to economic reward. Aristotle did not tend to look on laboring as particularly meritorious, as it happens. Still, this might mark a fairly small difference between us. More problematic is the fact that the modern view cannot rely primarily on this claim about the merits of labor. Those marching under the banner of distributive justice in modern times have regarded that notion as requiring a decent "starting position" for children and young adults before they ever enter the labor market, help for the disabled and structurally unemployed, and often, when they have used the notion as part of a socialist program, a distribution "to each in accordance with his needs" rather than "in accordance with his contribution."[12] None of these positions can be justified by saying that people deserve material goods as a reward for their labor.

Alternatively, one might say that need is a kind of merit. This would seem absurd to Aristotle, however. Aristotle allows the meaning of "merit" (axia) to vary quite widely—merit is for him often relative to a common project, such that a person who contributes more capital to a mercantile venture, for instance, deserves more of its profits (NE 1131b29–1131b30)—but it always describes something *good* about a person, something that that person, and others, can value about him- or herself. No one, including the needy person him- or herself, values neediness.[13]

A more promising approach would be to suggest that, after Kant, free will counts as a kind of merit and that insofar as the exercise of free will requires certain goods, all human beings merit these goods by virtue of their capacity for choice. Kant does make an argument along these lines, as I will show,[14] and a number of important modern theorists of distributive justice take their lead from Kant. Even with this help from Kant, however, it takes a good bit of pushing and shoving to bring modern and ancient distributive justice under the same concept. For Aristotle, the idea that the capacity for choice is itself meritorious would be strange, if not quite as bizarre as the idea that neediness is meritorious. Aristotle does not really have anything like our idea of "free will," but he does have an interesting discussion of choice in NE III.1–5, where he makes clear that excellence is expressed only in chosen acts. The capacity for choice itself is neither good nor bad, however; it is simply what makes possible both goodness and badness (1113b5–1113b14). So it is hard to imagine what sense Aristotle would make of Kant's claim that the absolute worth of human beings rests in their capacity for choice. And if we look in the other direction, despite the influence of Kant, modern distributivists usually do not say that free will is an excellence to which certain goods are fitting. They usually say instead that need, independent of excellence, is rightly the basis of a claim to certain goods. Again, this would make no sense to Aristotle. He would not find it intelligible that distributive justice, as he had defined it, could do without a notion of merit.

This seems enough to show that the modern and the ancient views make use of two different concepts, not merely two different conceptions, of distributive justice. But I am not inclined to press the point since it seems to me that the distinction between "concept" and "conception," while a useful rule of thumb, is not a hard and fast one. If we add up enough differences in conception, we can always make a plausible case that we have arrived at a difference in concept, while we can probably also always figure out some general framework under which to bring differences in conception if we feel a need to maintain that we are continuing to work with a single concept. How we draw these lines is to some extent arbitrary, or at least relative to our polemical purposes. Conceptions belong to the same concept if and only if they share certain family resemblances, but networks of family resemblances never make clear, on their own, where they ought to be broken up or kept together. As Wittgenstein says, "[W]e can draw a boundary [around a concept]— for a special purpose, [but it doesn't] take that to make the concept usable (except for that special purpose)."[15] I think there are a number of purposes for which it is useful to draw a boundary between the Aristotelian and the modern concepts of distributive justice, but I would not deny that the phrase is perfectly usable, for other purposes, without such a boundary.

Indeed, I do not want to draw too sharp a boundary between the concepts. I have talked in this introduction as though there is a certain set of premises that together constitute the modern concept of distributive justice and set it off from its Aristotelian ancestor. That way of talking is helpful for bringing out some crucial differences between what we and what Aristotle called by that name. But the history of ideas is a messy affair, and there is neither universal agreement today on what "distributive justice" means nor a neat time line in the past by which the premises I described as necessary for modern distributive justice came, one by one, into wide acceptance. Rather, occasionally some of the premises I have listed were held by premodern thinkers or political activists—Tiberius Gracchus saw poor soldiers, at least, as deserving a greater share of land than they had and thought the state should redistribute land accordingly, and Thomas More suggested that the hard work of the poor in general entitled them to greater wealth[16]—while even today there continues to be debate over exactly how these premises, or distributive justice as a whole, should be characterized. To make use again of a Wittgensteinian idea,[17] we might best say that modern distributive justice is constituted by a fiber of threads interwoven with one another, that some of these threads, but nothing strongly resembling the entire fiber, have appeared here and there in the past, and that ancient distributive justice, even if it shared some threads with the modern notion, as a whole constituted a clearly different fiber.

For some readers, this may not be enough to delineate a sharp distinction between two concepts of distributive justice. Such readers might characterize my project as demonstrating the many historical changes that led us from one conception of distributive justice to another—holding fixed, as the concept in question, the bare notion that there can be issues of fairness in distributing goods. I have no objection to this alternative characterization of my project. It doesn't matter terribly much if one sees the ancient and the modern as two conceptions rather than two concepts of justice, unless one is thereby led to underplay the relevant changes, to see Aristotle and Aquinas as essentially concerned with the same issues that trouble Rawls. That *would* be a great mistake, and it is against that kind of anachronism, surprisingly common even today, that I write.

1

From Aristotle to
Adam Smith

I have admonished the rich; now hear, ye poor. Ye rich, lay out
your money; ye poor, refrain from plundering. Ye rich, distribute your means; ye poor, bridle your desires. . . . [Y]e have not a
house in common with the rich, but ye have the heaven in
common, the light in common. Seek only for a sufficiency, seek
for what is enough, and do not wish for more.

— AUGUSTINE, *SERMONS ON THE NEW TESTAMENT*

I mentioned in the previous chapter that my interest in the history of
distributive justice was sparked by work on Adam Smith. As it happens,
Smith is an appropriate terminus ad quem for the first chapter of that
history. One reason for that is that Smith, one of the first philosophers
to include a history of philosophy in his writings, himself remarks interestingly on changes in the meaning of the phrase "distributive justice."[1]
Another reason is that Smith is about the last major thinker to use "distributive justice" in its premodern sense. As we shall see in the next
chapter, the modern notion that goes by that name was born at almost
exactly the moment when Smith died.

A third reason is that, perhaps because Smith marks the end of an
earlier way of thinking about distributive justice, what is wrong with
standard accounts of the history of that phrase comes out particularly
clearly when scholars address Smith. Practically all commentators on
Smith, including the best among them, describe him as rejecting the notion of distributive justice. Istvan Hont and Michael Ignatieff say that
Smith's views "effectively excluded 'distributive justice' from the appropriate functions of government in a market society," that he "insisted"
that only commutative justice could be enforced (NJ 24). Donald Winch
speaks of "the restriction of the application [of the notion of justice] in

[Smith's] *Theory of Moral Sentiments* to commutative as opposed to distributive justice."[2] Charles Griswold describes Smith as having made a "decision to focus on commutative justice and for the most part to assimilate distributive justice to [the private virtue of] beneficence."[3]

These commentators all write as though Smith did something new or controversial—"excluded" something from the notion of justice (Hont and Ignatieff), "restrict[ed]" the concept in some way (Winch), or made a "decision" to define the concept in an unusual way (Griswold). We are given the impression that, before Smith, there was a tradition that did include distributive justice among "the appropriate functions of government," that Smith is abandoning, to private beneficence, a task that government was traditionally obliged to carry out. This impression is quite mistaken. "Distributive justice" was already a private virtue, not a job for the state, at the point when Smith inherited the natural law tradition, and it had never, pace our commentators, had anything much to do with the distribution of property.

Hont and Ignatieff, especially, get this wrong. They see the natural law tradition as obsessed with the question of how "to ensure justice as between haves and have-nots" (NJ 35) and repeatedly frame the problem facing Thomas Aquinas, Hugo Grotius, Samuel Pufendorf, and John Locke as one of securing individual rights to property while simultaneously preserving "the poor's right of desert in the property of the rich" (31). Smith, they claim, starts from this same problem but has great difficulty addressing it because of his new, absolutist conception of property rights: "if property must be absolute, how then were those excluded from the partition of the world to be provided for?" (24). Smith's answer, according to Hont and Ignatieff, is that the market would supply most of the needs of the poor and that where it failed, beneficence, motivated by "pity and compassion towards the unfortunate" (24), would take the place that a true right of the poor had once occupied. One way to put the point of this book is to say that Hont and Ignatieff are reading the natural law tradition in exactly the wrong direction, that Aquinas and his followers do *not* recognize any right of the poor to material goods while Smith, although he does not use the word "right," is pivotal in bringing about this modern approach to poverty. Smith is of course not alone in this regard; above all, he looks back to Jean-Jacques Rousseau and forward to Immanuel Kant.

I will return to Rousseau and Kant in the next chapter. In this chapter,

I focus on their predecessors, on the degree to which a concern with "justice as between haves and have-nots" can be discerned in the natural law tradition as Smith found it, after it had been developed out of Aristotle by Aquinas, Grotius, Pufendorf, and Locke.

1. Two Kinds of Justice

The phrase "distributive justice" comes originally from Aristotle (NE V.2–4), who contrasts it with "corrective justice" (later called "commutative justice"), which concerns punishment. Aristotle draws two distinctions within the notion of justice. First, he distinguishes between a sense, later called "universal justice," in which the word covers all virtues—the sense in which Plato had used the word in the *Republic*[4]—and a more "particular justice" pertaining to political constitutions and judicial decisions. Second, within the latter sense of the term, he distinguishes between "distributive justice" and "corrective justice."[5] Distributive justice calls for honor or political office or money to be apportioned in accordance with merit—"all men agree that what is just in distribution must be according to merit" (NE 1131a25)—while corrective justice calls for wrongdoers to pay damages to their victims in accordance with the extent of the injury they have caused. Aristotle's discussion of this distinction is devoted to the different ways in which distributive and corrective justice represent a norm of equality: in the former case, the equality consists in the fact that everyone is rewarded in proportion to his or her merits, such that it is unjust for unequals in merit to be treated equally or equals in merit to be treated unequally (1131a23), while in the latter case, equality requires every victim of wrongdoing to be compensated equally, regardless of merit: "it makes no difference whether a good man has defrauded a bad man or a bad man a good one . . . ; the law looks only to the distinctive character of the injury" (1132a4–1132a5). The details of this formal point occupy more than two chapters (V.3 and V.4). Aristotle notes in passing that people may disagree about what counts as the appropriate kind of merit in distributive justice—oligarchs count wealth or noble birth as the appropriate merit for citizenship, aristocrats insist that only excellence entitles one to citizenship, and democrats say that simply being free rather than enslaved entitles one to citizenship—but he takes no stance on this dispute.

Aristotle is thus concerned to make a formal rather than a substantial point about distributive justice, and merit is essential to that point: the contrast between it and corrective justice turns on the relevance of merit.[6] We compensate even bad people who have been injured, paying attention only to the degree of harm done, but we distribute goods to people insofar as they deserve them. And the case of distributive justice that most concerns Aristotle is the case of how political participation (the ability to vote or hold office) should be distributed, to which he returns, later on, in the *Politics*.[7] He does mention occasionally that distributive justice can arise in connection with the distribution of material goods— when, for instance, partners in a business venture need to disburse common funds in proportion to each person's contribution to the venture (1131b29–1131b30). What he does not raise even as a possibility is that the state might be required by justice to organize the fundamental structure of material possession among its citizens. Even when he takes up Plato's proposals for communal ownership of material goods in *Politics* II.5, he does not so much as mention the possibility that *justice* might require (or forbid) a redistribution of goods by the state;[8] nor had Plato himself defended his proposals in such a way. What Plato had suggested, and what Aristotle denies, is that communal ownership of goods might help temper people's material desires, prevent political corruption, and create bonds of friendship. Plato did not suggest, and it does not occur to Aristotle to deny, that all human beings *deserve* an equal share of material goods—deserve, indeed, any share of material goods at all.[9]

The most important figure in the natural law tradition after Aristotle is Thomas Aquinas, but before we get to him, we should take a quick look at the Roman thinker Cicero. Cicero does not explicitly address Aristotle's discussion of justice, but he does introduce a distinction that was seen by later figures as paralleling the one between commutative and distributive justice. In his *De Officiis*, Cicero contrasts justice with beneficence, saying that justice can and should be legally required of us while beneficence should not be, that violations of justice inflict positive harm while failings of beneficence merely deprive people of a benefit and that duties of justice are owed to anyone, anywhere, while duties of beneficence are owed more to friends, relatives, and fellow citizens than to strangers.[10] As Martha Nussbaum has recently described in wonderful detail,[11] this account of the two virtues has been enormously influential, both on Christian writers such as Augustine and Aquinas and on later, more secular writers such as Grotius, Adam Smith, and Kant. Nussbaum offers a powerful critique of the distinction between doing "positive harm" and failing to provide benefits but notes also that this distinction is one of Cicero's most important legacies.[12] One reason for that may have to do with Christian theology. The notion that beneficence lies somehow outside the proper sphere of justice was welcome to a Christian world in which charity was a virtue that defined the special realm of Christ while justice characterized the world of Caesar (and Moses). And once the confusing terminology of Grotius, as we shall see, allowed "distributive justice" to be used as a synonym for charity or beneficence, one could easily come to regard distributive justice as by definition an unenforceable virtue, not part of justice proper at all.

But Cicero also said that beneficence is "connected with" justice *(iustitia . . . et huic coniuncta beneficentia).*[13] We might think that this allows us to defend exactly the opposite position—that beneficence, giving material aid to the needy, is a part of justice properly so-called. Cicero himself makes clear, however, that the connection between justice and beneficence he has in mind is one by which justice *constrains* beneficence. All forms of beneficence "ought to be referred" to justice *(De Officiis,* 1.42), he says, and his point here is precisely to rule *out* any kind of beneficence that would violate property rights: "the transference of money by Lucius Sulla and Gaius Caesar from its lawful owners to others ought not to be seen as liberal: nothing is liberal if it is not also just" (1.43). Cicero was fiercely opposed to all redistribution of property, including agrarian laws (II.73, 78). Beneficence complements justice for Cicero—only if beneficence accompanies justice can there be true human fellowship[14]—but it does not allow for any satisfaction of human needs that would be ruled out by justice.

Now Aquinas certainly agrees that justice takes priority over beneficence, but it is a little misleading to put his position that way since he returns far more to the account of justice in Aristotle than to the contrast between justice and beneficence in Cicero. Indeed, Aquinas takes over Aristotle's conception of distributive justice more or less intact. He contrasts commutative and distributive justice, says that the first rights wrongs while the second distributes goods, describes the first as following strict equality while the second proportions goods to merit, and gives the different ways that political offices are parceled out in aristocracies, oligarchies, and democracies as his example of the sort of issue to which distributive justice applies.[15] Again, distribution follows merit; again, the main kind of distribution in question has to do with political, not material, goods; and again, there is no suggestion that caring for the poor is a matter for distributive justice at all.

Aquinas dominated Western political thought until the beginning of the seventeenth century, when the natural law tradition was radically reconceived by Hugo Grotius. On distributive justice, as on many other things, Grotius both followed and revised the earlier tradition. Above all, he introduced a distinction between "expletive" and "attributive" justice that was meant to track Aristotle's and Aquinas's distinction between "commutative" and "distributive" justice but did not exactly do so. According to Grotius, "expletive" justice is legally enforceable while "attributive" justice is not (LWP I.i.vii–viii, 36–37). Expletive justice governs whatever human law does and should do, and the claims it seeks to satisfy are correspondingly called "legal rights" or "strict rights,"[16] while attributive justice embraces all "those virtues which have as their purpose to do good to others, as generosity, compassion, and foresight in matters of government" (LWP I.viii.1, 37). Grotius draws copiously on Cicero, and we may see Grotian "attributive justice" as a descendant of Ciceronian beneficence; he indeed cites Cicero as a source for the notion of an "aptitude," with which attributive justice is supposed to be concerned (36–37 and note on 36). Grotius also talks at times of "rules of love" that are broader than the rules of law (III.xiii.iv.1, 759; see also I.ii.viii.10, 75; III.i.iv.2, 601), and Jerome Schneewind has plausibly argued that for Grotius the law of love is closely connected to, perhaps identical with, the demands of attributive justice.[17] Grotius gives the bestowing of legacies as an example of an act expressing attributive justice and presenting full information to prospective business partners, sacrificing your life for your country, avoiding harm to innocent civilians in wartime, and being merciful to needy debtors as examples of acts demanded of us by "the law of love."[18] Note that only the last of these examples has anything to do with helping the needy; the others are expressions of familial love, honesty, patriotism, and sensitivity to the merits of innocence. Grotius's attributive justice is equivalent to social virtue in general, not merely to that element of social virtue in which we show generosity to the poor.

More precisely, Grotius's attributive justice, especially under the name "law of love," is equivalent to the *Christian* conception of social virtue. Grotius explicitly associates the law of love with the law of the Gospel, invoking, in this connection, the superiority of Gospel law to the law of

Moses.[19] This association sharply brings out the fact that the law of love cannot be compelled, else it would cease to be love, and that, like love, which is supposed to flow infinitely, beyond all limits, and unlike law in the strict sense, which must and always does have limits, the duties imposed on us by the "law of love" are potentially infinite—are, in principle, impossible to limit. Those who follow Grotius will call the rights corresponding to these duties "imperfect rights," as opposed to the "perfect rights" created by legal obligations, partly in order to suggest that the rights in question can never be completed (made "perfect"), that they impose demands on us that can never be fully satisfied. This sort of endless obligation cannot belong to justice in the strict sense, cannot be something we might enforce, because it is unjust to punish people for something they cannot do, and no one can fulfill an endless obligation. The law of love is thus something to be *set over against* all institutions of human law, not something that belongs to the legal domain. It denotes virtues that transcend human law. Christ demands of his followers that they go beyond the limits of all law, and Grotius's attributive justice gestures toward that super-nomian realm of virtue, not to a realm that might ever come under the proper dominion of human legislators and courts. So if generosity to the poor is a prime example of attributive justice, it is an example of something that goes beyond law, not of something that law ought to accomplish.

Grotius's views are unclear in a number of respects, and those who follow him devote considerable energy to interpreting the murkier passages in his writings. It is unclear why "attributive justice" should be considered a part of justice at all, for instance, or how one could possibly interpret Aristotle's two kinds of justice as dividing along the lines of what can and cannot be enforced. (Aristotle's "distributive justice" is supposed to characterize the constitution of a state—to characterize how rights to vote and hold office get distributed—so how could it possibly *not* be enforced?) Samuel Pufendorf, who was as lucid as Grotius was muddy, rightly noted that Grotius's attributive justice resembled Aristotle's "universal justice" more closely than it did his distributive justice (LNN I.vii.11, 122). Pufendorf also coined the phrase "imperfect right" to describe the object of attributive justice, making clear that an imperfect right is supposed to be something very similar to a legal or perfect right except that for the most part only the latter, not the former, should be politically enforced. "It is less necessary that [imperfect rights] be observed towards another than [perfect rights]," he says, and "it is, therefore, reasonable that [perfect rights] can be exacted more rigorously than [imperfect ones], for it is foolish to prescribe a medicine far more troublesome and dangerous than the disease" (LNN I.vii.7, 118). In addition, imperfect rights are usually "left to a man's sense of decency and conscience" (119), so it would be "inconsistent" to enforce them. The point of fulfilling imperfect rights is at least in part to display one's decency and conscience, but if such rights are enforced, those who fulfill them will display fear of the law, not decency or conscience.

It is important to note that on the first of Pufendorf's lines of reasoning, perfect and imperfect rights are of the same kind, even if they differ in degree. Pufendorf implicitly compares the two: "some things are due us by a perfect, some by an imperfect right," he says, and goes on to line up the first with particular justice and the second with universal justice (LNN I.vii.7–8, 118–119). Moreover, universal justice for Pufendorf has a quasi-legal structure: it is a structure for ordering our lives, which is both decreed and enforced by God's Will.[20] The rights that correspond to universal justice are therefore just like the rights that correspond to particular justice, except that God establishes and enforces the former while human beings establish and enforce the latter. That this is what Grotius meant is unclear, but Pufendorf's way of construing the distinction became standard. Even moral philosophers such as Frances Hutcheson and Adam Smith, who did not take morality in general to be like law, maintained the phrase "imperfect rights" for claims a person might make by way of morality alone. For Hutcheson and especially Smith, these "imperfect rights" did not much resemble their perfect cousins, did not, in particular, lend themselves well to legal formulation.

However, both the language and the argumentation Pufendorf introduced made it hard to see why there should be any objection in *principle* to incorporating imperfect rights into law. On Pufendorf's own account, imperfect rights are less necessary than perfect ones, but they may still be necessary; perfect rights can be exacted more rigorously than imperfect ones, but imperfect ones can in principle also be exacted. What stands in the way of exacting them is that trying to do so will be a "medicine" that is worse than the disease—people will be worse off if the imperfect rights are enforced than if they go unfulfilled. But it is hard to see why the imperfect rights should not be enforced if the medicine of enforcing them ever happens to be better than allowing the disease to run its course.

Pufendorf himself says that they can be enforced when "a grave necessity happens to arise" (LNN I.vii.7, 119)[21] and allows for the possibility that states may build a greater or lesser enforcement of imperfect rights into their civil laws. He thereby paves the way for the utilitarians who would worry simply about whether state aid to the poor served the common good, not whether it belonged to the sphere of beneficence or the sphere of justice. It is not implausible to find the seed of the modern notion of distributive justice already in Pufendorf. Yet Pufendorf himself says nothing to suggest either that private property ought to be redistributed—he is a harsh critic of communal schemes such as Thomas More's *Utopia*—or that the existence of poverty constitutes any kind of injustice. He also appears to have no doubt that there is a definite distinction between justice and beneficence, however much the lines between the two might blur at the margin.

It was this somewhat unsettled account of justice, and perfect and imperfect rights, that the eighteenth century inherited. Pufendorf was a direct, important influence on the political philosophy of eighteenth-century Scotland—via Gershom Carmichael, who taught Pufendorf's work in his capacity as the first holder of a chair at the University of Glasgow, later held by Hutcheson and Smith—and in any case, no one, including his contemporary Locke, took the discussion of distributive justice any further. Locke did contribute something that would become important to modern distributive justice—a powerful formulation of the intuition that labor constitutes the primary source of the "merit" by which anyone can rightly claim to deserve material goods[22]—but he followed the natural law tradition precisely in distinguishing between the rights protected by justice and the rights protected by charity: "As justice gives every man a title to the product of his honest industry and the fair acquisitions of his ancestors . . . , so charity gives every man a title to so much out of another's plenty as will keep him from extreme want where he has no means to subsist otherwise" (Tr I 4.42).[23] Similarly, in the late 1690s, the Quaker John Bellers recommended his remarkably forward-looking programs for eliminating poverty as an exercise of "Charity," or "Mercy and Virtue," not an expression of justice. He was indeed very ready to grant that the poor are filled with "evil Qualities," that they are undeserving of help, and that only the love that comes of faithful Christianity can motivate such help.[24]

So we should not be surprised to find that justice does not include aid

for the poor in Hutcheson's and Smith's writings. Hutcheson, like Pufendorf, distinguishes between perfect and imperfect rights and characterizes
the latter as a matter of those claims we make on "the charitable aids of
others."[25] Perfect rights include our right to life, bodily integrity, chastity,
liberty, property, and reputation. Imperfect rights consist in the claims
we make to positions and honors we have earned by our merits and to
the aid of our friends, neighbors, and relatives. Hutcheson says that the
obligations corresponding to imperfect rights "are of such a nature that
greater evils would ensue in society from making them matters of com-
pulsion, than from leaving them free to each one's honour and conscience
to comply with them or not."[26] Imperfect rights come in "a sort of scale
or gradual ascent through . . . insensible steps," however, gaining in
strength in accordance with both the merits or needs of the person claiming help and the closeness of the bond between that person and the one
from whom she asks help, until at last we reach some imperfect rights
"so strong that they can scarce be distinguished from the perfect."[27] The
notion of imperfect rights rising, at some point, to the level of perfect
ones seems to be new with Hutcheson, a contribution to the tradition
that begins to blur the distinction between Grotius's two kinds of justice
and to suggest that the distributive or attributive kind may not always be
a matter of love alone.

On each of these points, including the last one, Smith is Hutcheson's
faithful student. Quoting Hutcheson and Pufendorf, he distinguishes between perfect and imperfect rights, connecting the first to commutative
justice and the second to distributive justice (LJ 9). He includes in the
first rights to life, bodily integrity, chastity, liberty, property, and reputation and sees distributive justice as responding to the claims made on
us by the needs and merits of others. Perfect rights may be enforced;
imperfect ones generally should not be and to try to do so can be "de-
structive of liberty, security, and justice" (TMS 81). But duties of beneficence vary in their strength in accordance with the claimant's "character,
. . . situation, and . . . connexion with ourselves" (TMS 269), and at their
strongest, some of them "approach . . . what is called a perfect and complete obligation" (TMS 79). Once civil government has been established,
the strongest of these may be underwritten with force, and "all civilized
nations" rightly enforce the obligations on parents and children to take
care of each other along with "many other duties of beneficence" (TMS
81). More explicitly than Hutcheson, Smith avows the legitimacy of using

state power to "impose . . . duties of beneficence" (loc. cit.). So Smith moves the jurisprudential tradition closer to, not farther away from, a recognition that people in certain circumstances have a strict, enforceable right to beneficence. When he associates distributive justice with beneficence, or says that a beggar's "right" to demand charity from us is so-called only "in a metaphoricall sense" (LJ 9), he is reporting the common sense of his moral and legal tradition. When he says that governments do and should enforce certain duties of beneficence, he steps a little beyond that tradition.

But for Smith, distributive justice still is not primarily directed toward relieving the misery of the poor. Like the tradition before him, Smith takes distributive justice to include duties of parents to children, of beneficiaries to benefactors, of friends and neighbors to one another, and of everyone to people "of merit." To illustrate distributive justice in the *Theory of Moral Sentiments*, he remarks that "we are said to do injustice to a man of merit who is connected with us . . . if we do not exert ourselves to serve him" (TMS 269). His first example of a duty of beneficence in the *Lectures on Jurisprudence* is the praise due to "a man of bright parts or remarkable learning" (LJ 9). So "distributive justice" is connected for him, as for Grotius, with "all the social virtues" (TMS 270), not merely with charity to the poor, and it retains the connotation it had for Aristotle of matching goods to merit rather than calling for goods to be handed out, as a modern distributivist would, independently of merit.

Which is to say that when Smith remarks that distributive justice in its post-Grotian sense cannot be enforced, he is not, as Griswold, Winch, and Hont and Ignatieff would have it, rejecting an earlier conception of distributive justice by which the state had a duty to direct or supervise the distribution of property. Rather, he is accepting, as a matter of terminology, a historical distinction by which "commutative justice" means protection from injury and "distributive justice" is a catch-all term for the social virtues. And according to the tradition that had drawn this distinction, distributive justice had little or nothing to do with property arrangements. Not a single jurisprudential thinker before Smith—not Aristotle, not Aquinas, not Grotius, not Pufendorf, not Hutcheson, not William Blackstone or David Hume—put the justification of property rights under the heading of distributive justice. Claims to property, like violations of property, were matters for commutative justice; no one was given a right to claim property by distributive justice. As I will show later, even the famous right of necessity, by which those in extreme need might make use of others' goods without permission, falls under the heading of commutative justice for Aquinas and his followers, not, as Hont and Ignatieff have claimed, under that of distributive justice.[28]

So much for the phrase "distributive justice" before the late eighteenth century. It remains of course possible that the modern notion that goes by that name existed in premodern times under some other name or was implicit in political or legal practice. Hont and Ignatieff find modern distributive justice in many aspects of the natural law tradition, and others have found it implicit in Platonic and Christian utopianism and in the practice of premodern poor laws. The remainder of this chapter is devoted to these alternative sources for the modern notion of distributive justice. Properly understood, I believe they do not support anything like the claims that have been made for them.

2. The Right of Necessity

Hont and Ignatieff rely particularly heavily on the right of necessity to make their case that Aquinas and other premodern thinkers constrained property by way of legal obligations to sustain the poor. But that principle is badly misunderstood when regarded as an ancestor of modern welfare rights.

In the question of the *Summa* concerned with property ownership and theft (ST II-II, Q 66) Aquinas devotes one article (A7) to the notion that people may claim as their property anything they need if they are in imminent danger of dying without that thing. When an individual is in danger of starvation, she may pull fruit from a nearby tree or drink from a well she comes across, regardless of who owns the tree or well, and the food and drink she needs *belong* to her during the time she needs it, not to the person who ordinarily has title to it. Similarly, one may make use of medicine if one is about to die without it, or shelter if one is caught in a terrible storm, or anything else one needs for immediate survival. Private property, says Aquinas, is permitted to human beings by divine law because it is normally a good way by which everyone can both satisfy his own needs and help succor the poor, but when a need is "so urgent and blatant . . . that the immediate needs must be met out of whatever is available," then the fundamental purpose of property takes precedence over the normal rules governing property, and "a person may legitimately supply his own needs out of another's property . . . [I]n such a case there is strictly speaking no theft or robbery." Taking what one needs in a desperate situation like this is thus for Aquinas not even justified theft, a property violation legitimized by a need that overrides property rights, but a legitimate act within the system of property itself, an aberrant but legitimate case of property rights. Extreme need, the need for survival, can create a rightful claim to property, even though such claims are not ordinarily determined by need. It is worth noting that by giving people property in what they need to survive an emergency, Aquinas brings the right of necessity under the rubric of commutative, not distributive, justice, and there it would remain in its subsequent treatments by Grotius and his followers.[29]

It is also worth noting how very limited this right of necessity is, for Aquinas and for all who followed him on this. Aquinas places the seventh article of Q 66, which justifies taking property in need, right after two articles making clear that theft is always a mortal sin, even when one merely keeps a lost item one happens to find or secretly takes back what is one's own from a depositary. Having affirmed a strong view of the centrality of property rights to the normal order of justice in articles 5 and 6, Aquinas uses article 7 to carve out a license for the desperately needy to rely on in cases that by definition lie far outside the normal order of social life.[30] That license is very tightly circumscribed, moreover, as the first objection and its reply make clear. The first objection quotes the *Decretals* of Gregory IX: "Any person who steals food, clothes or cattle when he is [hungry] or naked must do three weeks' penance."[31] The reply declares that this stricture "is not dealing with case of urgent necessity." So being "hungry or naked" does not constitute "urgent necessity"! Only where a need is "so urgent and blatant" that there is *no* other way of satisfying it—only where, as Aquinas explicitly says in a parenthetical remark, "a person is in imminent danger, and he cannot be helped in any other way"—does the right of necessity come into play.

As Aquinas has conceived it, this right can hardly be enforced, much less institutionalized. In most cases, it will be very difficult to determine whether a person who takes food was truly starving or merely "hungry" at the point when he took the food, and while a judge might commendably believe the poor person in all cases, it would also be understandable if he regularly took the prosecution's side. Aquinas provides no guidance to a human court for distinguishing between "urgent necessity" and mere "hunger or nakedness," and his placement of this article right after an article on the mortal sin of theft, and right before two articles on the degrees of sinfulness in different types of theft, suggests strongly that he is primarily concerned with the judgments of the heavenly court, not the earthly one. God knows when needs are urgent, and the person who takes property because of urgent need presumably knows herself that her need was urgent. That person can be assured that in such cases he or she has not committed a sin and does not owe a penance. What human law and human courts are to do about these cases does not seem to concern Aquinas much, and he certainly does not translate this marginal kind of case into a general call for human law to distribute property in accordance with the needs of the poor.

Grotius, who was a jurist rather than a theologian, discusses the right of necessity with more of an eye toward its application in human legal systems, but otherwise he follows Aquinas closely. The right to use someone else's property in times of dire need is not a mere extension of the law of love, he says, but a true right, originating in the principles that ground the order of property (LWP II.vi.1–4, 193).[32] Once again, however, this right is severely constrained. "Every effort should be made to see whether the necessity can be avoided in any other way, as for example, by appealing to a magistrate, or even by trying through entreaties to obtain the use of the thing from the owner" (194). One is not allowed to make use of the right "if the owner himself is under an equal necessity," and one should, if at all possible, make restitution of whatever one uses after the period of necessity is over (194–195).[33] Grotius is very concerned that "this permission to use property belonging to another . . . not be carried beyond its proper limits" (194), and he makes clear elsewhere that these proper limits are narrow ones:

> He who is rich will be guilty of heartlessness if, in order that he himself may exact the last penny, he deprives a needy debtor of all his small possessions; . . . Nevertheless so hard a creditor does nothing contrary to his right according to a strict interpretation. (759)

The law of love asks that the rich not impoverish poor debtors, but the strict law, the enforceable law, does not. So the poor have no right not to be poor, no right even against rich people who would claim "all [their] small possessions"; they just have a right, in the direst of cases, to use what they need to stay alive.

Once we keep in mind that, for both Aquinas and Grotius, the right of necessity is distinct from the demands of benevolence, and that it is the unenforceable latter and not the enforceable former to which the poor normally appeal when they need help, it becomes clear that Hume maintains the natural law tradition intact on these matters, rather than altering it in favor of a more absolutist view of property rights. Alasdair MacIntyre has suggested otherwise:

> [W]hat the rules of justice are taken to enforce[, according to Hume,] is a right to property unmodified by the necessities of human need. The rules of justice are to be enforced in every particular instance . . . , [even] in the face of that traditional figure, the person who can only succor his family . . . by doing what would otherwise be an act of theft. The tradition of moral thinking . . . shared . . . by Aquinas . . . saw in such an act no violation of justice, but Hume, asking the rhetorical question "What if I be in necessity, and have urgent motives to acquire something to my family?" sees such a person as one who may look [only] to the generosity of "a rich man."[34]

But MacIntyre misrepresents Hume. The rhetorical question he quotes comes from a passage in the *Treatise* where Hume is talking about the *normal* course of justice, not the circumstances that might give rise to a right of necessity (T 482). Despite Hume's use of the word "necessity," he is talking about the kinds of cases in which Aquinas and Grotius also thought that the poor must rely on rich people's generosity. Hume does take up the Thomist right of necessity, but only in the second *Enquiry*, where what he says could easily have been said by Grotius:

> Where the society is ready to perish from extreme necessity, no greater evil can be dreaded from violence and injustice; and every man may provide for himself by all the means which prudence can dictate, or humanity permit. The public, even in less urgent necessities, opens granaries, without the consent of the proprietors; as justly supposing, that the authority of magistracy may, consistent with equity, extend so far. (E 186)

It is important to note that for Hume the point is more that justice falls away altogether in the face of necessity—such that opening granaries is, strictly speaking, neither "wrong" nor "right"—than that a special *kind* of justice applies to cases of necessity, but he is clearly trying to accommodate what the earlier jurisprudential tradition had called "the right of necessity" within his own theory. Before and after this passage, he gives examples of other cases where necessity overrules the usual laws of justice—after a shipwreck, in a siege, in a famine—all of which closely resemble the cases that Grotius gave to illustrate the right of necessity (cf. LWP 193–195).[35]

Like Aquinas and Grotius, therefore, Hume distinguishes the right of necessity from the normal course of justice, in which the poor may appeal only to the beneficence of the rich. For Aquinas, even a person faced by hunger and nakedness has no right to steal to meet those needs as long as the hunger and nakedness are not life-threatening, yet the rich should see themselves as morally obliged to "communicate [their external goods] to others in their need" (ST II-II, Q 66 A2).[36] For Grotius, only the law of love, not law in the strict sense, demands that a rich person refrain from taking all of a poor debtor's "small possessions"; a fortiori, only the law of love could give us an obligation actively to help needy people. Hume is no less insistent than Aquinas and Grotius that morality demands that we help the needy: "A rich man lies under a moral obligation to communicate to those in necessity a share of his superfluities" (T 482). (The language indeed suggests that Hume had recently been reading the passage in Aquinas just cited; more probably, they both have in mind the same New Testament verse—1 Tim. 6:18.) But the rich man does not violate *justice* if he fails to live up to this obligation. Thus Hume, despite his famously original defense for justice and property rights, does not introduce any new notion of how strictly, vis-à-vis human needs, they are to be enforced. Rather, he holds the same two-sided view that we have seen in his predecessors. In ordinary cases, the poor must rely on beneficence for their claims on the property of the rich, but they may justly take property without permission in cases of extraordinarily urgent need.

And Smith? Where does he fit into this tradition? Hont and Ignatieff, who rightly place Hume within the tradition, wrongly imply that Smith gave more limited scope to the right of necessity. Smith invokes the right of necessity three times in his *Lectures on Jurisprudence* (115, 197, 547), endorsing it as a proper part of justice implicitly in the first two cases and explicitly in the third: "necessity . . . indeed in this case is part of justice."[37] About the opening of granaries, he writes:

It is a rule generally observed that no one can be obliged to sell his goods when he is not willing. Bu[t] in time of necessity the people will break thro all laws. In a famine it often happens that they will break open granaries and force the owners to sell at what they think a reasonable price. (LJ 197)

Smith may be quoting Hume in this passage, as the editors of the *Lectures in Jurisprudence* suggest; at any rate, he seems to find the opening of granaries just as acceptable as Hume does. Hont and Ignatieff overlook the passage entirely, and its resemblance to Hume. Instead they compare Hume's remark on opening granaries with a passage in the *Wealth of Nations* in which Smith says that "the ordinary laws of justice" may be sacrificed to public utility "only in cases of the most urgent necessity" (WN 539). Since Hume says that granaries may be opened "even in *less* urgent necessities" while Smith declares that the laws of justice can be suspended only under "the *most* urgent necessity," they reason that Smith has a stricter notion of when human survival might trump laws of justice than Hume does (NJ 20–21). The problem with this reasoning is that the remark in the *Wealth of Nations* occurs in the course of a discussion that has nothing to do with opening granaries. Where Smith does address the subject, in the passage from the *Lectures on Jurisprudence* above, he seems to agree with Hume.

Hont and Ignatieff make a similar error when they quote the *Lectures on Jurisprudence* to the effect that beggars have a right to our charity "not in a proper but in a metaphoricall sense" and see this as implying that Smith (here together with Hume) wants to replace the ancient right of necessity with an unenforceable duty of benevolence: "It was to this discretionary sentiment that [Hume and Smith] looked to the relief of the necessities of the poor in any emergency" (NJ 24). But Smith is once again simply following the traditional jurisprudential view. Every thinker who recognized a right of necessity before Smith and Hume, including Aquinas, took the "discretionary sentiment" of benevolence to be the proper source of aid to the poor in all but life-threatening cases. Smith would differ from the tradition he inherited only if he held, as he does not, that the poor must rely on the benevolence of the rich *even* in life-threatening cases.

What leads Hont and Ignatieff astray is that they assimilate certain positions in the eighteenth-century debate over famine policy to the right of necessity. Not only the opening of granaries, but laws imposing a maximum price on grain or against exporting or "engrossing" it (buying it up early in the season to sell it at a higher price when supplies grow short), all derive, they suggest, from the logic behind the ancient right of necessity (NJ 18–20). But this is a questionable assimilation. Even the opening of granaries, as Hume points out, is only dubiously justified by the right of necessity, and any set of *laws* to protect the grain trade cannot possibly fit into the exception to all law that Aquinas and Grotius carved out for cases of extreme and urgent need.[38] The right of necessity is, by definition, an exception to the ordinary course of justice and not a part of that course. It is designed precisely for emergencies, precisely for circumstances where the ordinary legal and political framework—which, it is hoped, is generally a good way of meeting human needs—fails miserably. Law and policy are general tools meant to cover the usual, more or less predictable run of affairs; to the extent that certain disastrous circumstances fall outside of that usual run of affairs, a right of necessity is proclaimed as a *supplement* to law and policy, justifying extraordinary measures until the ordinary framework can take over again.

It follows that no law or general policy could possibly be an extension of the right of necessity. If law and general policy can handle a set of circumstances, those circumstances cannot constitute the sort of unmanageable and unpredictable exception to which "necessity," in this sense, applies. Thus the opening of granaries is quite far from the sort of situation that Aquinas and Grotius had in mind (a mob opening a granary has time to bake bread and therefore time to "appeal to a magistrate" for help), and all laws, like those policing the grain market, are by definition not an exercise of the right of necessity. If famine or dearth is predictable enough that laws can prevent or limit it, then it is something that can and should be dealt with by the ordinary course of justice and not by an extralegal device designed for circumstances that law cannot handle. So Smith's endorsement of the right of necessity was as full as that of all his predecessors—and for him, as for his predecessors, it made very little difference to ordinary law and politics.[39]

3. Property Rights

Hont and Ignatieff see the problem of securing "justice as between haves and have-nots" (NJ 35) as haunting the natural law tradition's approach to the justification of property rights. They argue that Aquinas begins from the assumption that the world belongs properly to all human beings in common—that God originally gave the world "to the collective stewardship of the human species as a community of goods" (NJ 27)—and then allows for individual property rights under the strict condition that such rights be used to meet the needs of the poor. But this badly distorts Aquinas's view. Aquinas does not suppose an original "collective stewardship of the human species" over material goods; he explicitly *denies* that natural law recommends collective ownership.[40] Rather, for Aquinas, people participated in a sort of negative common before private property was instituted, in which it was legitimate for anyone to use any good. This is a far cry from "collective stewardship," which implies a communal organization of production and distribution, and which Aquinas actually considers to be a violation of the natural order: he says that individual ownership of goods, as opposed to common ownership, is not merely legitimate but "necessary for human life" (ST II-II, Q66 A2).

Nor is the main problem about property rights, for Aquinas, the possibility that the poor might thereby be kept from the means for their subsistence. He does mention that possibility, but only in a digression from his main theme. His overarching concern is to refute a type of extreme religious asceticism, according to which the individual ownership of material goods gets in the way of true communion with Christ. In particular, he wants to refute a pair of linked theological propositions: (1) that all material things belong to God alone, and (2) that God licenses the use of His things, at most, to the species of human beings as a corporate body, not to individual people. Drawing on both biblical texts and secular arguments in Aristotle, Aquinas maintains that God grants us a "natural dominion over external things" (ST II-II, Q 66, A1) and that the most peaceful and efficient way of exercising that dominion takes the form of individual property rights. He then condemns as heretics those in the early church who regarded individual ownership of things (along with marriage) as blocking salvation. The heretics who get thus condemned are probably standing in for more contemporary theological opponents. As Richard Tuck has pointed out, one of Aquinas's main purposes here is to challenge "the life of apostolic poverty as practised . . . by the great rivals of his Dominican order, the Franciscans."[41] But that is to say that the opponents with whom Aquinas is wrestling are people who feel that property rights constitute a religiously impermissible attachment to material things, an immersion in the world that will distract irredeemably from one's worship of God, not people concerned with the injustice of a division between rich and poor. That communal ownership of goods also maintained the poor was incidental to their religious vision: it was, after all, not uncommon for an entire community constituted in this way to be poor, and such poverty was a badge of honor, not something to regret or solve. Aquinas rejects the otherworldliness of these communities. He understands the natural order of human relations as requiring property rights and regards his religious adversaries as placing God's way, wrongly, in opposition to the natural order. Here, as throughout his theology, Aquinas integrates God more fully with His creation, and the worship of God more fully with a delight in that creation, than do his more mystical, and perhaps more dualistic, predecessors and peers. But both he and his opponents are concerned about the place of material goods in a Christian life; they are not concerned, except incidentally, about the relationship between property ownership and the poor.

Grotius does not share Aquinas's theological concerns, but his defense of property rights is similarly unprovoked by a worry about "justice as between haves and have-nots." Instead, he takes up property rights as a part of his investigation into the law of war and peace. Accordingly, he is concerned about such issues as how property rights can give rise to a just cause of war and what kinds of property can legitimately be claimed in the course of war to secure provisions for an invading army. The origin of property rights comes up largely as a basis for considering the extent to which the sea and other large waterways properly belong in common to all human beings and should not be controlled by one country to the prejudice of others. And the justification Grotius gives for property rights turns essentially on the fact that without such rights, people get into constant conflicts.

Thus when Hont and Ignatieff say that concern for the poor was integral to the justification of property until Locke and only becomes "a side-constraint, rather than a structuring condition" on property from Locke on (NJ 37), they get the history of the natural law tradition exactly backward.[42] For Grotius, as for Aquinas, the question of how the poor may get their needs met is very much an incidental one, leading to a side constraint on the system of property but emphatically not a structuring feature of that system. By contrast, when Locke offers his famous justification of property rights as a way of increasing the "conveniences of life" (Tr II, V.34), as dependent, ultimately, on labor and as resulting, when carried out most fully, in a world in which poor people can live well, he makes the effectiveness of property rights in helping the poor much more central to the function of property than do Aquinas and Grotius.

The issue still lurks a bit behind Locke's main concerns, however. The claim that property depends on labor served Locke's political purposes as part of an argument that taxation requires the consent of the people. Kings had no right to collect taxes without the consent of Parliament, Locke maintained, since taxes come out of people's property, and property, however much it might be shifted around by systems of positive law, is rooted in a prepolitical right to own the fruits of one's labor. In the course of defending this claim, Locke points to the overwhelming utility of labor, and part of his demonstration of that point involves the claim, later picked up by Smith, that an Amerindian king, ruling over people who fail to improve their land by labor, "feeds, lodges, and is clad worse than a day-labourer in England" (Tr II, V.41). So Locke makes this point to bring out the tremendous productive power of labor, not to show that a system of property rights deals justice to the poor.[43]

It is Hume who first does the latter, and Smith develops the argument more fully. Hume begins his discussions of justice and property, in both the *Treatise* and the second *Enquiry*, by stressing the way in which particular acts of justice may seem silly or cruel taken on their own. In the *Treatise* this leads him to ask why I have no right to take a rich man's property even "if I be in necessity, and have urgent motives to acquire something to my family?" In the *Enquiry*, he defends the inequalities of property after first conceding that

> nature is so liberal to mankind, that, were all her presents equally divided among the species, and improved by art and industry, every individual would enjoy all the necessaries, and even most of the comforts of life . . . [,] that, wherever we depart from this equality, we rob the poor of more satisfaction than we add to the rich, and that the slight gratification of a frivolous vanity, in one individual, frequently costs more than bread to many families. (E 155)[44]

Having made this concession, Hume goes on to argue that any attempt to establish complete equality will (1) reduce the entire society to poverty, (2) require extreme restrictions on liberty, and (3) undermine the political structure that is supposed to ensure the equality. It is therefore better for everyone, including the poor who suffer from inequality, to live under the relatively unsupervised principles of private property than to try to replace them with an equal distribution of goods. Property has bad effects in many cases but provides, as an entire scheme, far more good than harm to everyone.

Smith takes over much of this view but sets it up with an even greater emphasis on the ways in which systems of private property burden the poor. In his lectures on jurisprudence, Smith began discussing political economy with a vivid dramatization of the injustice that seems to be involved in the division between rich and poor:

> Of 10,000 families which are supported by each other, 100 perhaps labour not at all and do nothing to the common support. The others have them to maintain beside themselves, and . . . have a far less share of ease, convenience, and abundance than those who work not at all. The rich and opulent merchant who does nothing but give a few directions, lives in far greater state and luxury and ease . . . than his clerks, who do all the business. They, too, excepting their confinement, are in a state of ease and plenty far superior to that of the artizan by whose labour these commodities were furnished. The labour of this man too is pretty tollerable; he works under cover protected from the inclemency in the weather, and has his livelihood in no uncomfortable way if we compare him with the poor labourer. He has all the inconveniencies of the soil and the season to struggle with, is continually exposed to the inclemency of the weather and the most severe labour at the same time. Thus he who as it were supports the whole frame of society and furnishes the means of the convenience and ease of all the rest is himself possessed of a very small share and is buried in obscurity. He bears on his shoulders the whole of mankind, and unable to sustain the load is buried by the weight of it and thrust down into the lowest parts of the earth. (LJ 341)

The poor worker is Atlas, holding up the human universe. Smith calls up a picture here that might have served, literally, as a program for the heroic "worker monuments" that were put up under socialist regimes in the 1930s and '40s. He is presumably influenced by Rousseau, yet Rousseau himself wrote nothing that dramatizes the unfairness of capitalist systems to the poor quite so strikingly.[45] Smith goes on to say, as did Hume, that the apparently unfair division of goods he describes still leaves poor workers much better off than the richest people in more egalitarian societies. It is at this point that we get Locke's Amerindian king,[46] who is materially worse off than the poorest day laborer in England. Smith thus gives us essentially the same justification for inequalities that John Rawls was to propose two centuries later: they are acceptable if and only if the worst-off people under a system of inequality are better off than they would be under an egalitarian distribution of goods.

Now in its final, published form, the *Wealth of Nations* does not include the detailed breakdown of employments in society, rubbing our noses in the inverse relationship between hard work and comfort, that appears in the *Lectures on Jurisprudence*. Nonetheless, the point about the poorest people in commercial societies being better off than the wealthiest members of egalitarian tribes provides the famous, dramatic ending of the opening chapter—and the placement of the point makes it more effective, rhetorically, than it was in Locke—and Smith continues to note that systems of private property protect the rich against the poor, in the first instance, and only indirectly benefit the poor themselves (WN 710, 715). Moreover, the bitter tone that so marks the passage in the *Lectures on Jurisprudence* reappears in Smith's many comments on the way "masters" oppress their workers.

So it is David Hume and especially Adam Smith—prodded, surely, by Rousseau, but, as we shall see in the next chapter, not precisely anticipated by him—who first starkly present the system of private property as standing under a presumption of unfairness because of the way the poor suffer to provide luxury for the rich. They have what they think is an excellent *answer* to that presumption, but they contribute something new to the discourse on property simply by making the problem central to their accounts. It seems absurd, even immoral, to Smith and Hume that misers and scoundrels should be able to claim large amounts of property while hardworking people make do with virtually nothing. Only once we understand that a system of strict property rights on the whole protects the liberty of everyone in society, and in the long run leads everyone to be better off than they would be under an egalitarian distribution of goods, should we accept such rights as justified. That the poor should suffer while the wealthy have their goods protected constitutes, for both Hume and Smith, what we might call a paradox of justice (cf. NJ 42), and, far from hiding that paradox or ignoring it, they frame their defense of property rights by exposing it as starkly as possible. In this mode of presentation, they differ from Aquinas and Grotius, for whom the paradox of justice at most lurks dimly behind concerns about God or war. Hume and Smith are thus the first to make the suffering of the poor *the* problem for the justification of property.

After Hume and Smith, some radicals came to deny that property is justified at all, to maintain that justice requires the abolition of private property or that justice itself is but a construct of bourgeois interests. But the radicals who made these moves were piggybacking on Hume's and Smith's question: "How can property rights be justified if they protect the rich while making the poor miserable?" They *answer* that question differently, rejecting the story Hume and Smith tell by which property rights, in the long run, actually help the poor. But it is Hume and Smith, more than anyone earlier in the natural law tradition, who taught them to ask this question in the first place.

4. Communal Experiments and Utopian Writings

Can we not find a source for what today we call distributive justice in premodern experiments with or proposals for the equalization of property? Plato famously proposed communal property arrangements for his Guardians in the *Republic;* Thomas More, Thomas Campanella, and others described utopias in which everyone participated in a community of property; the apostles in the *New Testament* had a community in which "distribution was made unto every man according as he had need" (Acts 4:35); and the apostles' community was a model for the way of life many later Christian groups practiced. Can these ideas and experiments be seen as instantiations of distributive justice?

I think not. Premodern egalitarian communities and political writings gave a variety of interesting reasons for socioeconomic equality. But these reasons had little or nothing to do with justice.

Hebrew prophets such as Amos and Isaiah angrily condemn those who "oppress the poor [and] crush the needy" (Amos 4:1) and call on the wealthy to "deal thy bread to the hungry" and to "bring the poor that are cast out to thy house" (Isa. 58:7). The Mosaic Code demands that people leave the corners of their fields for the poor to glean and requires everyone not to "harden thy heart, nor shut thy hand from thy needy brother" but instead to "lend him sufficient for his need" (Deut. 15:7–8). But the Mosaic Code also says that "the poor shall never cease out of the land" (Deut. 15:11), giving this as the reason why people need to be ever ready to help their poor neighbors with loans. The right it grants to the poor in the corner of the field, moreover, is clearly a means merely to subsistence, not a step toward the eradication of poverty. And while both the Mosaic Code and the Hebrew prophetic writings do talk of a certain "justice" due the poor, by this they mean only that courts need jealously to guard the *legal* rights of the poor (see, for instance, Exod. 23: 6). The poor have equal rights with everyone else before the law—the Mosaic Code is particularly good about insisting on equality before the law—and they have a right to subsistence. But they do not have a right to be raised out of poverty.

Some have found more radical notions in Jesus's teachings.[47] Jesus surrounded himself with poor people, and some of his apostles, like other Jewish groups at the time, lived in communities that did without private property. But Jesus's and his early followers' overwhelming concern, in this regard, seems to be with the way in which covetousness takes one away from spiritual things.[48] Why is it harder for a rich man to enter heaven than for a camel to go through the eye of a needle? Not because the rich man fails to care for the poor, but because wealth is a false god, and its pursuit is in direct competition with devotion to God's ways; one cannot serve both God and mammon. "What shall it profit a man," Jesus asks, "if he shall gain the whole world, and lose his own soul?" (Mark 8: 36). Gaining the world here competes with saving one's soul, whether or not one gives large parts of one's gain to the needy. In this context, to say that the meek shall inherit the earth is certainly not to say that they shall "gain the whole world." Rather, their souls will be saved, in the eschatological time in which God's followers survive and the forces of evil fall away. In this context, the protocommunism described in Acts 4:35 is, like the similar arrangements among the Essenes, a spiritual discipline that helps prepare the group for salvation when the Messiah returns. Communal ownership is here a priestly practice—shared property and labor are characteristic of priestly orders in many cultures—rather than a solution to political and social problems. The early Christians treat material goods as a distraction from spiritual devotion: an unavoidable distraction, perhaps, insofar as they are needed for survival, but in that case a necessary evil, not something one wants to bestow lavishly on everyone. Nothing except wishful latter-day thinking can turn the Gospels into a call for the abolition of distinctions between rich and poor *within the ongoing political and economic order* on earth.[49]

Similarly, Christian monks were not concerned with changing the earthly political or economic structure under which most people lived. The monastic movement grew out of earlier eremitical traditions in which individuals would renounce sexual activity and some material comforts (meat and alcoholic drink, especially), and sometimes they pursued this ascetic life in one another's company. Both the earlier hermits and the later monks separated themselves from material attachments as a spiritual discipline, not to promote the cause of the poor. Monastic communities were not formed as even a first small step in the *solution* to poverty; they were formed to *participate* in poverty, to celebrate it as the ideal condition in which to worship God.[50] Perhaps the Franciscans saw their commitment as in part a way of showing solidarity with poor people; certainly St. Francis himself devoted his efforts particularly to the service of the poor. But even he never indicated that poverty, on earth, ought to be abolished.

A more reasonable ancestor of modern calls for "social and economic justice" is to be found in Plato. In the *Republic,* Plato establishes communal property for his ruling class, saying that private property breeds dissension and a focus on one's selfish desires as opposed to the desires one shares with one's community. He also makes the eradication of great economic inequality, across all classes, a condition for the existence of a good society. Any city that contains wealth and poverty is really two cities "opposed to one another," says Socrates: "A city of the poor, and a city of the rich" (*Republic* 422e–423a). Note, however, that private property gets abolished only among the rulers; property, and some inequalities of wealth, will continue to exist in the lower, worker class. Furthermore, Plato does not call his ideal society "just" in virtue of its softening of the distinction between rich and poor. Diminishing inequalities of wealth is a way of bringing about social *harmony* for Plato, not justice. The ideal city is *just,* it "gives each his due," insofar as it slots people into their proper caste in a social hierarchy.

So neither in the Jewish and Christian Bibles nor in Plato do we find the idea that governments are obliged, in virtue of the justice that is due the poor, to try to eradicate poverty. Rather, we see (1) religious reasons for suspicion of wealth, (2) a notion that significant inequalities in wealth breed disharmony in society, are a source of crime and rebellion, and (3) a belief that great gaps between rich and poor citizens make it more likely that political power and economic power will become identical, that law will be used to serve the interests of the wealthy rather than to further the common good. All three of these convictions, but not the belief that justice demands redistribution of wealth, were to have great impact on proposals for redistributing wealth in the medieval and early modern periods. They gave rise to three fairly distinct traditions of egalitarianism: (1) Christian experiments in communal living, designed to express a religiously-based indifference to material goods and thereby prepare the faithful for the second coming of Christ; (2) Platonic proposals for reducing violence and increasing communal fellow-feeling by minimizing differences between rich and poor; and (3) civic republican proposals for redistributing wealth so as to minimize the corruption of the political realm and increase the ability of the polis to express the will of all its citizens.

The first was expressed in a series of utopian experiments, modeled on the apostles' community in Acts, in which devout Christians shared property and shunned wealth to bring themselves closer to God: examples include the Franciscan order, the Anabaptist rule in Münster in 1534–35,[51] the community of the Diggers in 1649,[52] and many later communal movements such as the Shakers or the inhabitants of Oneida, New York, in the nineteenth and twentieth centuries.[53] The second tradition shows up in a series of utopian writings, most famously Thomas More's *Utopia*, that preached the abolition of private property, now for the whole community and not just for the rulers, so as to bring about the "true city," the truly shared community of which Plato had spoken. The third is concerned primarily with the equal distribution of political rights, not of material goods. Civic republicans propose some equalization of property only as a means to achieve greater effective equality in citizens' ability to shape their governments. James Harrington's *Oceana* (1656) is the paradigm example of this third tradition, although according to John Pocock, its preeminent historian, it dates back at least to Machiavelli. Pocock's brilliant study of this tradition demonstrates how it shows up in the ideology of the seventeenth-century Levellers, permeates English and American political discourse in the eighteenth century, and strongly influences Rousseau.[54]

Political thinkers or movements that fit into one of these three categories will often be influenced by the others as well. Rousseau, for instance, is primarily a civic republican, but he is also a descendant of Plato and More, attacking private property as a fount of violence and social disharmony, while the Levellers show the influence of Christian egalitarianism, if not millenarianism, alongside their civic republican commitments. Many a utopian proposal will argue simultaneously that distinctions between rich and poor breed dissension and violence, that wealth is morally and spiritually a bad thing, and that great differences in wealth corrupt the political realm. Rousseau carries into his very secular language some of the Christian suspicion of wealth as a distraction from the true value and meaning of life: the accumulation of wealth, in his *Second Discourse,* replaces such more innocent pleasures as the appreciation of nature. So Christian concerns about the evils of wealth, Platonic concerns about social harmony, and civic republican worries about political corruption interweave with one another, to some extent, to produce a variety of arguments for mitigating the differences between rich and poor.

But *none* of these traditions says that a certain level of material comfort is owed to the poor by virtue of their being human beings, that *justice* demands some distribution of goods to all. The Christian egalitarians appeal to a virtue that is supposed to transcend justice and ground their arguments on faith-based premises that are incompatible with claims of justice. Civic republicans often believe that the poor have equal rights with the rich to *political* participation—the Levellers' spokesman Colonel Thomas Rainborough famously defends universal franchise with the words, "For really I think that the poorest he that is in England hath a life to live, as the greatest he"[55]—but they are not interested in socioeconomic equality (except as a means to political equality).[56] And the Platonic tradition almost never couches its call for socioeconomic equality in terms of justice. Over and over again, in Thomas Campanella, in John Bellers, in Rousseau, in Morelly and Mably, the call for eradicating poverty is predicated, not on any claim that the poor deserve to be raised out of poverty, but on the argument that poverty breeds crime and discontent and that it is therefore in everyone's interest to have as little poverty as possible. More's *Utopia* is a partial exception to this claim. In a remarkably forward-looking passage, More argues that it is unjust for idle people to be rich and hard-working people to be poor.[57] Yet he also argues for the abolition of private property primarily on the grounds that that would "eliminate . . . the root-causes of ambition [and] political conflict" and that it would enable people to turn from foolish material pleasures toward social, spiritual, and intellectual activities.[58] And Campanella, who greatly admired More, did not take up the argument for shared wealth on grounds of justice at all, rejecting private property instead on strictly Platonic grounds: because it fosters self-love, and self-love conflicts with love for one's community. If one removes private property, and thereby self-love, Campanella says, "there remains only love for the state."[59] Similarly, Bellers offers his proposals for employing the poor as a way of reducing violence and increasing social harmony rather than on grounds of justice. Lack of education and employment, he says, "fills the Gaols with Malefactors,"[60] and he repeatedly compares managing the restless poor with fighting foreign wars.[61]

When we come to the eighteenth century, we find Morelly offering us an imagined continent where ignorance of property leads everyone to feel "obligated to participate in making [the land] fertile," to work joyously together and to engage only in "friendly rivalry."[62] People in this world also fill their lives with the "natural" pleasures of homegrown food and promiscuous sex.[63] Again, social harmony and the promotion of a simple mode of life, not justice, is the ground for abolishing property and the distinction between rich and poor. Rousseau's *Discourse on Inequality,* which appeared one year after Morelly's *Basiliade,* also belongs in the utopian tradition for its description of an idyllic, presocial human world in the remote past, and it is also concerned with violence, disharmony, and the unnecessary luxury of civilized life rather than with justice. Rousseau calls private property the source of "crimes, wars, murders, . . . miseries and horrors," of disputes between people and the bloodshed and vengeance to which such disputes lead (FSD 141, 149–150). But he does not call private property, or the distinctions in wealth to which it leads, unjust.

All of these utopians, moreover, tend to avoid presenting their visions as a practicable goal for their own societies to adopt. If justice is a virtue concerned with the practicable, then it is unclear whether utopias have any real contribution to make to justice. "Utopia" literally means "Noplace," and many utopian writers after More couch their proposals, as he had done, in the form of a fictional description of a distant society, in the South Seas or even on the moon.[64] One feature of these descriptions, which comes with their being fictional, is that their authors feel free to solve the potential economic problems that might arise from dispensing with private property by stipulating that the geographical circumstances of their favored paradise make it unnecessary to worry about running short of goods. The anonymous *Island of Content* (1720) is typical:

We are happily seated in a very moderate Climate . . . [W]e are such absolute Stranger to all manner of Extreams, that we never need Fire, in Winter, to warm our Fingers, or Water, in Summer, to cool our Wines, but enjoy, thro' the Circle of the whole Year, such a peaceful Serenity in all the Elements, that the Distillations of the Clouds are but gentle Dews, that give a lasting Fertility to the fragrant Earth, and only keep the Dust from rising, to the Injury of our Eyes.[65]

Compare the setting for Morelly's ideal community:

> In the bosom of a vast sea, . . . there lies a rich and fertile continent. There, under a pure and serene sky, nature spreads out her most precious treasures. There she has not, as in our sad parts, locked them away in the bowels of the earth, from which insatiable greed tries to wrest them without ever having a chance to enjoy them. There lie fertile and broad fields which, with the help of light cultivation, bring forth from their bosom all that can render this life delightful.[66]

But under these conditions, one can dispense with justice. As Hume pointed out, where there is no scarcity, there is no need for justice; justice is a virtue that comes into play to determine ownership precisely where there is not enough to satisfy everybody. So, while poetic license allows authors to stipulate a lack of scarcity in their fantasy worlds, relying on poetic license ensures that the fantasies remain just that—fantasies, rather than something at which justice might aim.

There is a similar problem with the way utopian writers tend to treat the facts of human nature. The author of a utopia will often simply stipulate that the inhabitants of his wonderful country are born with equally wonderful characters, free of the unpleasant emotions and desires that plague the rest of us. Morelly's people spontaneously love one another and work joyously, and all Morelly has to say in explanation of this wondrous fact is that his continent happened, fortunately, to be "the habitation of a people whose innocent ways made them worthy of their rich possession."[67] More, Campanella, and Rousseau, like Plato, do more to argue for a link between the absence of private property and the civic virtue of their imagined people, but they too allow poetic license to relieve them of the responsibility of giving empirical evidence for this link. In Campanella's *City of the Sun*, a sea captain describes the utopia to a somewhat skeptical listener. At one point, the listener remarks that in the absence of private property, "no one will be willing to labor, while he expects others to work." To which the captain replies, "I do not know how to deal with that argument, but I declare to you that [the inhabitants of this city] burn with so great a love for their fatherland, as I could scarcely have believed possible."[68] One reader who found this insouciant dismissal of argument frustrating was Pufendorf. After giving the standard Aristotelian arguments for private property—that it prevents quarrels, provides incentives for work, and allows for generosity—Pufendorf notes that these arguments "have not prevented Thomas More and Thomas Campanella from introducing community of property." He then adds acidly, "I suppose . . . perfect men are more easily imagined than found" (LNN IV.iv.7, 541). Several pages follow on the distinction between poetic and "sensible" political writings; fiction, it seems, is a dangerous mode for political speculation precisely because it encourages the irresponsible ignoring of relevant facts.

Pufendorf's insight here is a profound one, and indeed he may not have taken it quite far enough. For the utopians' reliance on fantasy goes hand in hand with a quiet streak of authoritarianism. Fantasy enables utopians to hide the more disturbing implications of the visions they describe, to avoid, by escaping from reality, the possibility that their visions can be reached only by way of great force. On occasion, they come close to recognizing this dark possibility. To the extent that they recognize that their ideal communities depend on virtues that real people do not possess, they propose structures of authority to monitor and control daily life to a chilling extent. Campanella has his citizens punished for indolence, sadness, and anger, as well as slander and dishonesty.[69] Everybody wears the same clothes in More's Utopia; everyone is made to work and forbidden to "waste their time" when they are not working; and people need a license, with a time for their return, if they want to travel.[70] Morelly supplemented his utopia with a "Code of Nature" that prescribed strict sumptuary laws and a sort of army hierarchy to organize work and make sure that it gets done.[71] The fact that a society without private property would have to force people to contribute to the community, and especially to work, is thus tacitly recognized even by the utopians. It was to be explicitly recognized by state socialists, from "Gracchus" Babeuf to Karl Marx and his followers.[72]

This enforcement of labor, let alone the array of other ways in which utopias control people's daily lives, would for most political thinkers be a terrible *violation* of justice, not a realization of it. That brings out the error involved in thinking of the utopian tradition as particularly concerned with justice. The respect for the individual that is essential to all varieties of justice, whether commutative or distributive or any other kind, does not sit easily with the political vision of most utopians. Radical Christians who participated in communities of shared wealth thought that they were expressing a virtue far higher than that of justice, that justice was a virtue too focused on the importance of the individual and that human beings should properly submerge their individual goals in a higher Good. Civic republicans were concerned with political justice but not with economic justice. And not only do the Platonic writings of More and his followers fail to justify their proposals about property in terms of justice, but the whole genre in which they work, the genre of fantasy, is ill-suited to the proper domain of justice. Justice is a practical virtue, a virtue that pertains to the concerns of this life rather than to the concerns we might have as denizens of any kind of imaginary or otherworldly realm. Fantasies about how we might all have kinder and wiser natures or love each other more deeply or attend more to spiritual and intellectual things than to material vanities have no direct relevance to a theory of justice. But that suggests that utopian writings before the late eighteenth century had little to do with justice. They were, certainly, not intended to offer a blueprint for a community that might actually come into existence, nor even to offer much in the way of concrete suggestions about how communities should be governed. Rather, they described an ideal world, perhaps thereby trying to expand our moral imaginations—to contribute *indirectly* to the practical realm with which justice is concerned. As François Furet writes, about "Gracchus" Babeuf's proposals for an egalitarian community of land in the 1780s and '90s, "Such sharing agrarian communism was not unknown in the store-house of eighteenth-century literary utopias, but in Babouvism it presented the new characteristic of constituting a revolutionary programme. It . . . marked the entry of communism into public life."[73] With Babeuf, utopia became something one might try to achieve. Before him, that was not the purpose of utopian visions.

5. Poor Laws

Finally, we might suppose that the modern notion of distributive justice is implicit in premodern poor laws. Walter Trattner writes that early Christian social welfare policy "assumed that need arose as a result of misfortune for which society, in an act of justice, not charity or mercy, had to assume responsibility. In short, the needy had a right to assistance, and those who were better off had a duty to provide it."[74] But Trattner inverts the history of premodern legal practice in exactly the way that Hont and Ignatieff invert the history of premodern political theory. It would be closer to the truth to say that the premodern church saw assistance to the poor as an obligation of charity or mercy and not as an act of justice, not as something to which the needy had a right. This goes a bit too far in the opposite direction since the urgently needy—those in immediate danger of perishing—were understood to have a right to whatever would enable them to survive, and since the rich were sometimes said to have a duty to give of their superfluities to the poor. But this latter duty was a moral, not a legal one, at most something required by justice in its "universal," Platonic sense rather than its strict, legal sense. Certainly, there was no thought that the duty thus incumbent on the rich corresponded to any legal right of the poor to assistance.

On the other hand, private charity was not the only sort of aid to the poor in premodern times. I have noted already that the Mosaic Code contained provisions for alleviating the condition of the poor; some sort of relief for the poor was mandated, similarly, either by government or by religious tradition in many countries long before the modern era. But such aid did not follow the procedures we would expect to see in a system dedicated to justice. In pre-Reformation Europe, poor relief was primarily in the hands of the church[75] and was administered in ways that reflected Christian teachings and practice. Charity was disbursed on occasions of significance to the particular church or order and the "souls of the givers," as Jan de Vries and Ad van der Woude say, "had a more prominent place in these arrangements than did the needs of the recipients."[76] Canon lawyers worried also about the proper soul-state of the beneficiaries of charity. Acts of charity were opportunities for the display of two virtues: generosity on the part of the giver and humility on the part of the receiver.[77] Unsurprisingly, the poor person's relationship with the church, in this context, made a difference to his or her ability to obtain relief. Those who were poor by reason of sin or who committed the sin of refusing to work for their living were not to be helped.[78]

This attitude continued into systems of poor relief long after they were run by the state rather than by the church, so one may regard it as not particularly tied to religious precepts[79]—but the church also tied its generosity to its teachings in more explicit ways. St. John Chrysostom said that if a poor person asked for food because he was in need, "he was to be helped without any inquisition"; others, however, held not only that one should first check carefully into whether the person was truly needy, but that faithful Christians should receive priority over infidels and ex-communicates.[80] Scholars have tended to miss the significance of this fact: de Vries and van der Woude say that in seventeenth-century Amsterdam "any baptized resident in need could apply" for poor relief, without marking the importance of the word "baptized" (in a city with a particularly large Jewish population, no less). Churches also used the giving of aid as a means to attract converts to their particular brand of Christianity. This practice was controversial,[81] but it was in any case an effect of the way relief was organized that churches dispensing charity tended to attract members and that those, such as Jews and Protestants, who wanted to remain outside the Catholic church, developed their own institutions to help their poor.[82]

It should be obvious that a system of this kind treats relief as a work of mercy rather than justice. The recipient of relief is regarded as primarily a member of a religious community rather than a citizen or a human being, and religious strings are attached to the help given, in subtle and not-so-subtle ways. The system thus both symbolically represents a notion that aid to the poor should be motivated by religious, not secular, commitments and in practice treats poor people as deserving aid only on certain conditions, as not being entitled to such aid by virtue of their membership in a polis, much less their membership in the human race. The presuppositions of the system are very far from those that we have identified as characteristic of justice.

By the middle of the sixteenth century, however, states were at least nominally wresting control over poor relief from the church. Charles V tried to regularize relief throughout the Netherlands in 1531, decreeing that it should be centralized and laying down certain general conditions for the poor to receive support; his decree met, however, "with the determined and effective resistance of the Church and was fully implemented nowhere in the Northern Netherlands."[83] Hamburg mandated employment and easy loans for the able-bodied poor and aid to the disabled in 1529, Sweden set up a system of poor relief in 1571, and the German Empire demanded that all parishes "support their own poor, send away strangers, and provide accommodation for the sick" in 1577.[84]

The English Poor Law of 1601 formalized a similar requirement, which had existed in English practice for several centuries.[85] Not unimportantly, the requirement to aid the poor went along with severe penalties for able-bodied people who sought help instead of working; poor laws were at least as much an attempt to control the poor as to help them.[86] They were also attempts to control the church. It is no accident that these steps occurred at the height of the struggles surrounding the Reformation: as the resistance of the Netherlandish church to Charles V demonstrates, they are all in part efforts by the state to bring the church under its sway. For that reason, they are an important step in the transformation of poor relief from a religious to a civil right.

But only a small step. To a great extent, the state continued to work *through* the church. In England—long regarded as having one of the first secular poverty programs—for centuries after the 1601 Poor Law, the parish was the unit of administration; monies were collected by church-wardens; and churchwardens were empowered to set children and able-bodied adults to work.[87] The laws, in England and elsewhere, continued the earlier church policies of distinguishing between "deserving" and "un-deserving" poor and imposing severe penalties on those who sinned by begging instead of working. The state also continued to justify its policies by appealing to the virtue of charity rather than the virtue of justice.[88] As late as 1859, the state constitution of Kansas obliged all its counties to care for those among its inhabitants "who, by reason of old age, infirmity, or other misfortune, may have claims upon the *sympathy and aid* of society," and in 1875 Judge David Brewer (later a Justice on the U.S. Supreme Court) declared that the obligation to care for the poor is rooted in "the impulses of common humanity."[89] So the state's obligation to care for the needy was traced to "humanity" and "sympathy," not justice, and there was no suggestion that the needy had a *right* to care. T. H. Marshall quotes a 1953 survey of northern European countries to the effect that "[a]ssistance from the community as a legal right of the citizen in need is barely a century old." And in England, as Marshall says, the "pauper" was understood to be "a person deprived of rights, not invested with them." That was crystal clear when the Poor Law Amendment of 1834 made the renunciation of liberties the price of poor relief, but even the 1930 Poor Law treated the duty to relieve the poor as something "owed to the public and not to the poor person himself." Accordingly, if a government agency failed in this duty, the poor person to whom relief was denied could bring no legal action him- or herself—nor has that been possible anywhere until very recently.[90] (Even today, it is difficult except in very limited circumstances.)

So it is mercy, a virtue in which the agent, out of humane feelings, does good to a recipient who has no right to that good, and not justice, in which agents are obliged, regardless of their feelings, to accord recipients their rightful due, that provides the moral background to British welfare practices even in the early twentieth century. But that suggests that we will hunt in vain for a robust notion of justice behind the practice of poor relief in earlier centuries and less liberal nations than Britain. I have given, of course, a very brief treatment of a set of institutions that existed in many different places across a long span of time, but I think even this brief sketch is enough to show that the history of poor relief is an unpromising resource for premodern intimations of the idea that justice calls on societies to alleviate or eliminate poverty.

Of course, if my argument thus far is correct, there are few intimations of that idea in any premodern practice or writing. The dominant—and almost entirely unquestioned—view was that poor people deserved to remain poor. To find the idea that people have a right to rise out of poverty, we need to turn to the eighteenth century.

2

The Eighteenth Century

FIGARO: Nobility, fortune, rank, position! How proud they
make a man feel! What have *you* done to deserve such advantages? Put yourself to the trouble of being born—nothing more!
For the rest—a very ordinary man! Whereas I, lost among the
obscure crowd, have had to deploy more knowledge, more cal-
culation and skill, merely to survive than has sufficed to rule all
the provinces of Spain for a century!

— BEAUMARCHAIS, *THE MARRIAGE OF FIGARO* (1784)

The eighteenth century witnessed a sea change in attitudes toward the
poor. At the beginning and even in the middle of the century, the traditional Christian notion of a social hierarchy, with poor people forever
at the bottom, still prevailed. By century's end, Immanuel Kant could say
that everyone should be able to achieve social position by "talent, industry, and luck," and people all over France and America were celebrating
social mobility as a positive good. In the middle of the century, many
English writers warned darkly that "the very Dregs of the People" were
aspiring to "a degree beyond that which belongs to them," that "the
different ranks of people" were in danger of blurring into one another.
By the end of the century, many of the marks that distinguished these
ranks had in fact disappeared.[1] In the mid-1740s, it was uncontroversial
even in the relatively unaristocratic American colonies to say that God
was "pleas'd to constitute a Difference in Families" and to dismiss large
numbers of people as of "low extraction." By the end of the century, it
was equally common in America to sneer at those who were proud of
their family backgrounds. The very phrase "the better sort of people,"
which had been used without irony through the middle of the century,
became "thoroughly contemptible and odious" by the end of it.[2] Novels
and other forms of narrative that emphasized the lives of ordinary people
became widespread.[3] And in France, even before the 1789 revolution, a

play by Beaumarchais that attacked the pretensions of rank became the greatest theatrical success of the century.[4]

The Marriage of Figaro marks the cultural shift extremely well. Clever servants had been a stock element of comedy since the days of ancient Greece, but they had always been *servile*, characters who knew their place and betrayed in their accents, vocabulary, and deportment that they were inferior in dignity to their masters. Figaro himself had more or less fit that mode in *The Barber of Seville*, a decade before the *Marriage*, but now he and his bride-to-be were transformed into characters with every bit as much dignity and self-possession as the people they served. The play is, even today, a very funny one, but there is nothing funny about Figaro's description of his aristocratic master as "a very ordinary man" and claim that he, Figaro, is rather more interesting. The crowds did not flock to the Paris theaters to laugh at this outrageous suggestion on the part of a servant. They came, rather, to laugh *with* Figaro at the social hierarchy under which they all lived.

It is this change in attitudes, accompanied by a series of scientific and political developments that made the eradication of poverty begin to look possible, out of which the modern notion of distributive justice was born. By the end of the century, we begin clearly to see a belief that the state both can and should raise people out of poverty, that nobody deserves to be poor and nobody need be poor, and that it is, therefore, at least partly the state's job to distribute or redistribute goods. The belief was not widespread, however, and came to the fore only in the abortive revolt led by "Gracchus" Babeuf at the end of the French Revolution. It was to become more common in the nineteenth century, although even then it had to struggle with a strong opposing belief—also a product of the eighteenth century—that no redistribution of goods can ever be just and that it is good that the poor live at the verge of starvation.

Both of these beliefs—full-scale redistributivism and the extreme libertarian rejection of redistributivism—express philosophical views and not mere dogmas. I say that they were born out of a change in cultural attitudes, but I do not take cultural attitudes, in general, to arise merely from arbitrary shifts in the historical winds, and views on poverty, in particular, were often defended by philosophical argument. As regards distributive justice, Rousseau, Adam Smith, and Kant at least helped to clarify and probably also helped change many nonphilosophers' views of property, of human nature, and of human equality—and, consequently, of what the poor deserve. Whether these or any other philosophers invented the notion of distributive justice or whether they merely reflected a broader change in the culture around them is a question I shall not try to settle. To some extent, they were surely doing both: following their peers in moral attitudes; leading their peers in the rigor and clarity with which they explored those attitudes. I use their work, in this chapter, to bring out the system of beliefs that made possible the notion of distributive justice, then turn to the first definite expression of that notion in Babeuf's radical declaration that all human beings have an equal right to all wealth.

1. Citizen Equality: Rousseau

Jean-Jacques Rousseau was an emotionally unstable misanthrope, cold or irresponsible enough to send off each of his five children, at birth, to an orphanage; passionately concerned with his own fame and increasingly obsessed, as he grew older, with fears of persecution; an unpleasant person who contributed little to actual political struggles in his lifetime and who violated his own praise of compassion, friendship, and courage throughout his personal relationships. At the same time, he did more than anyone before him to inspire political programs on behalf of the poor, in part because of some profound insights he had into the nature of both society and the state and in part because he was the greatest writer, with the possible exception of Plato, in the history of political thought.

It is from Rousseau that the French revolutionaries were to claim they learned the need for the state to rectify inequality, and it is from Rousseau that Kant, according to a famous self-description, learned the true equality of human beings:

> I am an inquirer by inclination. I feel a consuming thirst for knowledge, the unrest which goes with the desire to progress in it, and satisfaction at every advance in it. There was a time when I believed this constituted the honor of humanity, and I despised the people, who know nothing. Rousseau set me right about this. . . . I learned to honor humanity, and I would find myself more useless than the common laborer if I did not believe that this attitude of mine can give worth to all others in establishing the rights of humanity.[5]

Kant was not the only one to learn from Rousseau a lesson of this sort. Rousseau has been a hero to the egalitarian left throughout the past two centuries. But his major contribution to distributivist political economy was quite different from what it is generally taken to be.

What Rousseau is *thought* to have contributed to distributivism is the notion that private property is questionable or even unjust, that capitalist or commercial society cruelly oppresses the poor, and that a proper solution to both of these problems is a radically democratic government that would control the economy along with all other aspects of society. The first of these attributions is false, and the other two are badly misleading. What Rousseau *actually* contributed to distributivism was something more general: an attitude of suspicion toward commercial society; an attention to its costs, particularly for the worse off; and a suggestion that the solution to its problems lies in politics rather than in religious or philosophical attitudes that might enable the sufferers to bear their troubles.

To take the positive part first: In both Rousseau's first *Discourse,* on the sciences and arts, and his second *Discourse,* on inequality, the progress of society is made to look suspect. Rousseau confronted the Enlightenment, which believed strongly both in freedom from prejudice and in historical progress, with the possibility that its belief in progress was itself a prejudice. When Rousseau said that cultivating the sciences "adorns our mind and corrupts our [moral] judgment" (FSD 56); when he described reason and philosophy as "engender[ing] vanity" and "turn[ing] man back upon himself" (FSD 132), as isolating us and switching off our natural compassion for other people; when he contrasted all of this with a supremely beautiful description of a state of nature in which everyone is satisfied, honest, and free, he made his public confront the question of whether the much vaunted achievements of human "progress" were really all that worthwhile. From Rousseau on, the story of historical progress would have to be more complicated. Hegelians—and, later, Marxists— still believed in progress, but they saw society as taking one step back for every two steps forward, as paying a price for every advantage it gained, often a price somehow embedded within the advantage itself. Thus politeness brings with it insincerity, liberty increases vice, and commerce can both enlarge a society's wealth and make the condition of the poor more miserable. After Rousseau, one could still justify a belief in progress, but one had to work a lot harder at it.

Rousseau himself declared that he had no interest in leading people "back to live with the bears" (FSD 201), and his attention to the costs of society must be understood as a way to get us to rethink society, not to abandon it. His contrast between our bad faith and the noble simplicity of the presocial human leads one to ask what society is *for*, exactly *why* we should pay its costs. And simply asking that question makes society look like a choice rather than an inevitability, like something over which we might have control, and something we should therefore seek to direct to certain ends. It is in this way that Rousseau inspired movements for radical reform. His own intention seems clearly to have been, not to provoke radical political change (which seems alien to both his temperament and the content of his writings), but to inspire people with the feeling that they all ought to take responsibility for their society, that they have a responsibility to be active citizens. We may see him as contributing to theodicy, to the old philosophical debate about why there is evil in the world. His answer is that human beings are directly responsible for almost all human misery. In the second *Discourse*, Rousseau denounces society in furious detail for every evil from erotic jealousy to deaths in earthquakes: if people didn't live packed so closely together in cities, earthquakes would cause many fewer deaths (FSD 196).[6]

But if society causes most human suffering, we can infer that society should also be able to *cure* most human evils. If society causes evil, society should be able to get rid of it; only if evil is inflicted on us by nature or God do we have to fear that we can do nothing about it. Thus if the institution of property is responsible for hatred, conflict, and poverty, as Rousseau suggests, then limiting or abolishing that institution may also be the path to eliminating hatred, conflict, and poverty. More generally, the condemnation of social evils in the two *Discourses* is followed by recommendations, in the "Discourse on Political Economy" and the *Social Contract*, urging states to teach virtue, to "make men, . . . if you would command men" (DPE 139)—to empower their citizens to solve their own problems via good laws. Society's problems, for Rousseau, can be solved by society; the ills we bring on ourselves have a homeopathic cure. A good state, a democratic state of committed citizens, can overcome practically all evils. This very broad conception of what the state can and should do was to have a powerful impact on later reformers and radicals. Recall that one premise we need to arrive at the modern concept of distributive justice is the belief that redistributing property so as to minimize or eradicate poverty is *possible*. Rousseau greatly helped to inspire people with that belief, with the belief that all social evils can be overcome—and with the belief that it is political entities, above all, that must do the overcoming.

So much for Rousseau's positive contribution to the history of distributive justice. It is far less clear that he offered the critique of property rights or economic inequality that socialists later wanted to see in his work.

In his 1755 *Discourse on Political Economy,* Rousseau says that "the right of property is the most sacred of all the rights of citizenship, and even more important in some respects than liberty itself" (DPE 151). He goes on to worry about the legitimacy of taxation and speaks of the "cruel alternative of letting the State perish, or of violating the sacred right of property" (DPE 155). Reading this passage, it is hard to understand how Rousseau ever got a reputation for being opposed to property rights; his views are more libertarian than those of David Hume or Adam Smith.[7] On the other hand, one year earlier, in his *Discourse on Inequality* (the so-called "Second Discourse"), he had presented the establishment of property as the source of poverty, oppression, crime, and war. How do we reconcile this apparent contradiction, the emphasis on the sacredness of property in one work with the attribution of all human evils to property in another?

Well, first we should note that even in the *Discourse on Inequality* Rousseau does not say that the establishment of property, or the inequality that comes with it, is *unjust*. Rather, he accepts the view that "justice" is a term for offenses against property, so that it makes no sense to describe the institution of property itself as either just or unjust. "[A]ccording to the axiom of the wise Locke," he says, "where there is no property, there is no injury" (FSD 150). The paradise Rousseau imagines is one that lies beyond both property and justice.

Second, the state of nature Rousseau describes, before and beyond property and justice, *is* clearly meant to be a paradise, not a society to which we can realistically aspire. In a footnote to the *Discourse on Inequality* he asks, "What! must we destroy societies, annihilate thine and mine, and go back to live in forests with bears?" (FSD 201). This is the sort of question with which his adversaries mock his views, he says, and while proclaiming his admiration for people who might in fact be willing to live in the woods, he describes himself as one of the many "whose passions can no longer nourish themselves on grass and nuts, nor do without laws and chiefs" and who, in part for religious reasons, "will respect the sacred bonds of the societies of which they are members" and "scrupulously obey the laws, and the men who are their authors and ministers" (FSD 202). Rousseau's ambitions for social change were restricted to the educational proposals of *Émile* and the republican constitution of *The Social Contract.* Nowhere did he propose the abolition of property or of inequality in wealth. He did propose redistributive measures to avoid *gross* inequalities, but this was just an endorsement of the standard civic republican view that great inequality in wealth corrupts politics. Rousseau separated his dream of presocial humanity from the practical proposals he made to human beings in society.[8] He wanted society to recapture some of the virtues of his imagined presocial condition, but he did not propose, as a radical revolutionary might, that the social world be transformed into the presocial one. And he certainly never said that *justice* demanded such a revolution.

Finally, while Rousseau did worry obsessively about inequality in society, and did diagnose that inequality as arising from the institution of property, he rarely worried about it *out of concern for the plight of the poor.* Rather, he is an heir to the civic republican tradition I mentioned in Chapter 1 (Section 4), which saw wealth as corrupting morals and inequality as corrupting politics. For Rousseau, wealth breeds vanity, and inequality breeds jealousy and hatred. The establishment of property, he says, makes possible a world in which *amour propre,* an unhealthy comparing of oneself with others, replaces *amour-de-soi-meme,* the natural instinct of self-preservation.[9] *Amour propre* breeds an endless competition between people. Such competition in turn leads to conflict and to relationships of dominance and dependency. Rousseau is a true Enlightenment modern in that he sees the ideal human relationship as one of equality rather than hierarchy and looks to conversation among equals, rather than the wisdom of an elite, as the ideal mode of political decision making. But this should not distract us from the fact that his concerns about inequality are very much of the same type as those of Plato and Aristotle: he worries about inequality and poverty insofar as they affect *politics,*[10] not insofar as they reflect a condition that constricts an individual's *private* life.

Consider the following passage, the one extended place in Rousseau's writings, as far as I have found, that dwells on the suffering of the poor:

[T]he social confederacy ... provides a powerful protection for the immense possessions of the rich, and hardly leaves the poor man in quiet
possession of the cottage he builds with his own hands. Are not all the
advantages of society for the rich and powerful? Are not all lucrative
posts in their hands? Are not all privileges and exemptions reserved for
them alone? Is not the public authority always on their side? Are not
the assaults, acts of violence, assassinations, and even murders committed by the great, matters that are hushed up in a few months, and
of which nothing more is thought? But if a great man himself is robbed
or insulted, the whole police force is immediately in motion, and woe
even to innocent persons who chance to be suspected. If he has to pass
through any dangerous road, the country is up in arms to escort him.
If the axle-tree of his chaise breaks, everybody flies to his assistance. If
there is a noise at his door, he speaks but a word, and all is silent. . . .
Yet all this respect costs him not a farthing: it is the rich man's right,
and not what he buys with his wealth. How different is the case of the
poor man! the more humanity owes him the more society denies him.
Every door is shut against him, even when he has a right to its being
opened: and if ever he obtains justice, it is with much more difficulty
than others obtain favours. . . . I look upon any poor man as totally
undone, if he has the misfortune to have an honest heart, a fine daugh-
ter, and a powerful neighbour. (DPE 161)

Rousseau is a superb rhetorician, and one can hardly read through the
rhythmic waves of questions in the beginning of this passage, much less
the dramatic contrast between the arrogant rich man "who speaks but a
word, and all is silent" and the decent poor man standing before a closed
door, without anger welling up inside one, impelling one out to the bar-
ricades. It is easy to see why revolutionaries have so often been inspired
by Rousseau. But if we strip away the rhetoric and look at the argument
alone, it is remarkable what a modest, uncontroversial point this passage
makes. Rich people tend to get away with crimes while simultaneously
being protected against criminals; poor people are disproportionately tar-
geted by the police while simultaneously finding it difficult to mobilize
the legal system on behalf of their own rights. One can find this worry
as far back as the Hebrew Bible, with its warning not to pervert the justice
due to the poor (Exod. 23:6).

Rousseau does differ from the Bible and go beyond many of his predecessors by seeing the solution to the straightforward injustices suffered by the poor in substantial reform of the political realm, rather than in moral or religious admonitions addressed to the powerful or in a mere call for a fairer administration of existing laws. For Rousseau, a fair system of justice can only arise out of a democratic polity, one in which the very process of making laws expresses the equality of all citizens. Indeed, Rousseau's central and most important thought is probably his insight into the relationship between freedom and citizenship. "If I had to choose my birthplace," he says in the introduction to his *Discourse on Inequality,* "I would have wished to live and die free: that is to say so subject to the laws that neither I nor anyone else could shake off their honorable yoke" (FSD 78–79). Freedom consists in being subject to laws that one has also authored, and one "authors" a law by being part of a democratic polity in which laws express the general will.[11] Socioeconomic inequality gives some in the community disproportionate influence over lawmaking and divides the community into hostile groups unwilling to submit their separate interests to the interest of all. Great wealth and poverty will cause "mutual hatred among citizens" and "indifference to the common cause."[12] Economic inequality is thus an obstacle to true democracy. "[P]rotecting the poor against the tyranny of the rich" is the most important of all government tasks, and it is really already too late to do that once there are very rich and very poor people around. Far better "to prevent extreme inequality of fortunes" in the first place, to manage a society's political economy so that no one will be very poor (DPE 146–147).

So the distribution of property enters into Rousseau's concerns indirectly, via his understanding of citizenship. Rousseau is concerned with the poor person *insofar as he or she is a citizen,* not insofar as he or she is, simply, a human being. Perhaps, if we consider people's political identity to be their most important identity, or to embrace all their other identities, this is the best approach to poverty. But if we consider human beings to have lives quite outside politics, if we consider citizenship to be but one, and often not the most important, part of everyone's life, then we may see great poverty as an unjustifiable harm in itself, independent of its effect on citizenship. For that insight, we need to move from Rousseau to Adam Smith.

2. Changing Our Picture of the Poor: Smith

Contrast, with the extended passage on the rich and the poor I quoted from Rousseau, the following lines from Smith (quoted also in Chapter 1, Section 3):

> Of 10,000 families which are supported by each other, 100 perhaps labour not at all and do nothing to the common support. The others have them to maintain beside themselves, and . . . have a far less share of ease, convenience, and abundance than those who work not at all. The rich and opulent merchant who does nothing but give a few directions, lives in far greater state and luxury and ease . . . than his clerks, who do all the business. They, too, excepting their confinement, are in a state of ease and plenty far superior to that of the artizan by whose labour these commodities were furnished. The labour of this man too is pretty tollerable; he works under cover protected from the inclemency in the weather, and has his livelihood in no uncomfortable way if we compare him with the poor labourer. He has all the inconveniencies of the soil and the season to struggle with, is continually exposed to the inclemency of the weather and the most severe labour at the same time. Thus he who as it were supports the whole frame of society and furnishes the means of the convenience and ease of all the rest is himself possessed of a very small share and is buried in obscurity. He bears on his shoulders the whole of mankind, and unable to sustain the load is buried by the weight of it and thrust down into the lowest parts of the earth. (LJ 341)

It is Smith, not Rousseau, who first drew widespread attention to the harm done by poverty to the poor's private lives, rather than just the harm done by the distinction between wealth and poverty to their lives as citizens. I originally quoted this passage in Chapter 1 as part of an argument against those who regard Smith as an opponent of distributive justice in its modern sense. To go in the other direction and proclaim him a "founding father" of the notion may seem a little extreme. And it would be wrong to call Smith, alone, the inventor of the concept—no single person ever really invents a concept with the complexity and historical importance of this one, and in any case, Smith must share the honor here at least with Rousseau and Kant. But he contributed far more to the birth of what today we call distributive justice than is usually noticed.

There are two main ways in which he did this. The first, and less important, is that he made some distributivist recommendations in the *Wealth of Nations*. Wealth can be redistributed in at least three ways: (1) by a direct transfer of property from the rich to the poor, (2) by taxing the rich at a higher rate than the poor, or (3) by using tax revenues, gathered from rich and poor alike, to provide public resources that will mostly benefit the poor. Smith makes proposals that fall under both the second and the third headings.

The most important of these is the advocacy of public schooling. Smith describes the mind-numbing nature of certain kinds of labor as one of the greatest dangers of an advanced economy and says that the state should take steps to insure that the laboring poor have an education giving them the capacity for moral and political judgment (WN 782–788). Building on institutions that already existed in Scotland, he recommends that states underwrite local schools that teach reading, writing, and "the elementary parts of geometry and mechanicks" (WN 785). But using public funds to support such institutions would in effect take monies from the rich and transfer them to the poor.

In addition to this proposal, Smith suggests that luxury vehicles pay a higher road toll than freight vehicles so that "the indolence and vanity of the rich [can be] made to contribute in a[n] . . . easy manner to the relief of the poor" (WN 725). He also advocates a tax on house rents, in part because it would fall heaviest on the rich. In making the rich contribute proportionately more than the poor do to public revenue, "there would not, perhaps, be any thing very unreasonable" (WN 842). Finally, as Gertrude Himmelfarb has pointed out, although Smith harshly criticizes the Act of Settlement, he "conspicuously did not . . . challenge" the English Poor Law—the most significant government program to help the poor in his day and one that came under criticism, then and later, as being too expensive and as sapping the poor's incentives to labor.[13]

This is about all one can find in Smith in the way of positive programs to help the poor. He advocates the lifting of apprenticeship statutes, residence requirements for poor laborers, and sumptuary laws, but these are all negative proposals, aimed to remove obstacles to people's freedom rather than to provide them with material goods. If his positive proposals seem a bit meager to us, we should remember that he was writing at a time when common wisdom held that the poor needed to be *kept poor*, else they would not work, that they were a class of people so given to indolence that only necessity would keep them from wasting their time in drink and debauchery. Most writers also held that poor people needed to be restrained from luxury spending and taught habits of deference so that they remained in their proper social place and did not "ape" their superiors. In this context, to propose *any* government programs that would allow wages to rise and poor people to aspire to the goods and learning of the middle and upper classes was to swim mightily upstream.

Which brings us to the second, more important way in which Smith was a founder of modern distributive justice: almost single-handedly, he *changed the attitudes* that underwrote the restrictive, disdainful policies by which the poor were kept poor. "More important than this or that policy [in Smith]," Himmelfarb rightly says, "was the image of the poor implicit in those policies,"[14] and she sums up a consensus among scholars when she writes, "[I]f the *Wealth of Nations* was less than novel in its theories of money, trade, or value, it was genuinely revolutionary in its view of poverty and its attitude towards the poor."[15]

Smith's picture of the poor may be one we take for granted now, but that is in good part the effect of his work. It certainly inverted the common attitudes of his time. Smith has changed our notion of what "the poverty problem" *is;* his predecessors regarded "the poverty problem" as the problem, primarily, of how to cope with the vice and criminality of the lower classes. Few people before Smith thought that the world should, much less could, do without a class of poor people. Until the late eighteenth century, most Christians believed that God had ordained a hierarchical organization for society with the truly virtuous people occupying positions of wealth and power at the top and "the poor and inferior sort" at the bottom.[16] Of course, the people at the top were supposed to help those at the bottom—but not enough to raise them above their proper place. Almsgiving was understood as a means to redemption, and the existence of poor people was seen as an integral part of God's plan for human life.[17] As late as 1728, the humanitarian Isaac Watts could say that "Great God has wisely ordained . . . that among Mankind there should be some Rich, and some Poor: and the same Providence hath alloted to the Poor the meaner Services."[18] As Daniel Baugh writes:

> In summing up the situation in 1750, we may observe that there were two widely held attitudes toward the poor. . . . The dominant one sup-

posed that the poor should never have misery lifted from them, nor their children be encouraged to look beyond the plough or loom. It reflected traditional notions of social hierarchy and was reinforced by economic theories about labor and motivation. The other attitude was derived chiefly from Christian ethics. It held that the duty of the rich was to treat the poor with kindness and compassion, and to aid them in times of distress. This benevolent attitude did not provide a suitable basis for policy-making; rather it was a reminder of conscience, of the fact that the ill-clad, filthy laboring masses habitually viewed with contempt by their betters, were equally God's creatures, whom a Christian community could neither exclude nor ignore.[19]

The major breakthrough in getting beyond these two attitudes, says Baugh, "came in 1776, when a philosopher of great learning, penetration, and literary persuasiveness published his *Inquiry into the Nature and Causes of the Wealth of Nations.*"[20] Smith combated both the explicit condescension of the first view and the implicit condescension of the second one. He was a virulent opponent of the notion that the poor are inferior in any way to the well-off. Over and over again in the *Wealth of Nations,* Smith pricks the vanity upholding a contemptuous picture of the virtues and skills of the poor. He presents the poor as people with the same native abilities as everyone else: "The difference in natural talents in different men is, in reality, much less than we are aware of," he says. Habit and education make for most of that supposedly great gap between the philosopher and the common street porter, even though "the vanity of the philosopher is willing to acknowledge scarce any resemblance" between the two.[21] To those who complain that the poor are naturally indolent,[22] Smith declares that, on the contrary, they are "very apt to overwork themselves" (WN 100). To those—and these were legion, even among the advocates of the poor—who saw indulgence in drink as a vice characteristic of poor people,[23] Smith replies that "[m]an is an anxious animal and must have his care swept off by something that can exhilarate the spirits" (LJ 497).[24] To those who complained that the poor were affecting the manners of their "betters" and should be prevented from buying luxury goods in the name of natural social hierarchy,[25] Smith says that it is "but equity" for the lower ranks of society to have a good share in the food, clothes, and housing they themselves produce (WN 96). And to those who claimed to be protecting the poor from their own prodigality, he says it is "the highest impertinence and presumption, ... in kings and ministers, to pretend to watch over the economy of private people." He adds, about these kings and ministers, "They are themselves, always, and without any exception, the greatest spendthrifts in the society" (WN 346).

This is not the end of the list. Smith defends poor people's religious choices against the contempt and fear of his Enlightenment colleagues, pointing out that the religious sects that urban poor people tend to join, while sometimes "disagreeably rigorous and unsocial," provide them with community and moral guidance (WN 794–796). He repeatedly praises the virtues and accomplishments of independent laborers, maintaining that it is unnecessary as well as inappropriate to monitor and control the lives of the poor (WN 101–102, 335–336, 412–420). He even tries to excuse, if not quite to justify, the mob violence characteristic of workers in their struggles with their employers (WN 84).

Smith thus presents a remarkably dignified picture of the poor, a picture in which they make choices every bit as respectable as those of their social superiors—a picture, therefore, in which there are no true "inferiors" and "superiors" at all. Individual people may be good or bad, of course, but Smith urges his (mostly well-off) readers to see the average poor person as just like their friends, their relatives, or themselves: equal in intelligence, virtue, ambition, and interests with every other human being and hence equal in rights and desert, in dignity. It is this picture of the poor person as equal in dignity to everyone else and as deserving, therefore, of whatever any of us would give to our friends and acquaintances that sets up the possibility of seeing poverty itself as a harm, as something that, since we would not have it inflicted on anyone we liked or respected, we should not be willing to have inflicted on anyone at all. The possibility that people might have a right not to be poor, that the state, in the course of enforcing human rights, should attempt to abolish poverty, is one that could open up only once Smith's dignified portrayal of the poor replaced the view, which had reigned unquestioned for centuries, by which poverty went with a difference in kinds of people, not merely a difference in luck.

Now, first, it is deeply appropriate if, as Himmelfarb suggests, the dignified picture of the poor is Smith's most novel contribution in the *Wealth of Nations*. For then the book's greatest triumph is a shift in our moral imaginations—it leads its readers to *imagine* the poor person differently— and it was the central teaching of Smith's *Theory of Moral Sentiments* that our imaginations are what most profoundly shape our characters and moral attitudes. Only by imagining ourselves in others' situations can we come to share their feelings and thereby develop benevolence, respect, or any other moral attitude toward them. In the *Wealth of Nations* Smith puts us, vividly and in detail, into the poor's situation and thereby overturns ancient stereotypes against them. Thomas Laqueur has written that in the eighteenth century "a new cluster of narratives came to speak in extraordinarily detailed fashion about the pains and deaths of ordinary people in such a way as to make apparent the causal chains that might connect the actions of its readers with the suffering of its subjects."[26] Laqueur uses the phrase "humanitarian narrative" for these texts and argues that the realistic novel, the autopsy, the clinical report, and the social inquiry could all be instances of this humanitarian narrative. One perfect example of the genre is Adam Smith's *Wealth of Nations*.

Second, we can now see how Smith's picture of the poor helped to bring about the modern notion of distributive justice. It is essential to this notion that one believe the poor *deserve* certain kinds of aid, but one is unlikely to believe that if one takes poor people to be naturally or divinely appointed to the bottom of a social hierarchy, or to be inherently vicious and indolent. Seeing the poor as just like one's friends and acquaintances, by contrast, invites the question, "don't they deserve not to *be* poor?" One would rather one's friends and acquaintances work from choice rather than need, that they have a buffer against starvation or homelessness should they lose their jobs, and that they have enough education, health, and financial resources to be able to escape a miserable social condition. It becomes natural to ask why everyone cannot be protected against great need, why there cannot be education, health care, unemployment insurance, and the like for everyone. And once one does ask this question, especially if one also loses the optimism Smith had about a free economy employing everyone (WN 469–470), some sort of welfare state comes to seem morally necessary.

I do not mean to imply that Smith himself would necessarily have defended the modern welfare state, let alone modern socialism, or that his latter-day followers are wrong to invoke him when they complain about welfare programs administered by large bureaucracies. Smith does prefer government to work through a small number of clear, general laws rather than to empower officials to make ad hoc decisions; he worries about both the inefficiency and the danger to liberty of anything that involves interference in people's lives on a daily basis. But he does not say, nor would it be true, that all attempts to redistribute resources require bureaucratic power in this way, and he did not think that redirecting resources to help the poor was in principle beyond either the capability or the rightful province of the state. On the contrary, he made such proposals himself. And his conception of the poor and of what the poor deserve helped bring about the peculiarly modern view that it is a duty, and not an act of grace, for the state to alleviate or abolish poverty.

3. The Equal Worth of Human Beings: Kant

Kant is a curious figure in the history of distributive justice. He is both the author of the strictest account of property rights to be found in philosophical literature up to his time and the first major thinker to argue explicitly that care for the poor ought to be a matter for the state rather than a private obligation. It would be nice if he also had a clear, powerful argument for how these two things can and should go together, but he did not. Rather, what Kant says on both subjects, as on much else about politics, is scattered around a few of his less well-known texts and comes with arguments that are either obscure or considerably less plausible than one expects from this careful philosopher. Kant took a limited and discontinuous interest in politics. He wrote several short pamphlets on political subjects, arguing for freedom of speech and conscience, for a modified social contract conception of the state, and, tentatively, for republicanism. He also put these arguments, along with an extended consideration of property and contracts, into more or less systematic form in the first half of his *Metaphysics of Morals*. But he never developed a full-scale critique of politics comparable to his works on epistemology, moral philosophy, philosophy of religion, and aesthetics.[27] His interest in politics was, moreover, mostly derivative from certain of his moral concerns, and his contribution to the notion that aid to the poor should be handled by the state turns out to lie more in certain aspects of his moral philosophy than in what he said directly on the subject.

What Kant said directly on both property rights and welfare programs is confusing. To begin with, when he uses the phrase "distributive justice," he gives it an odd meaning. Public justice consists in "protective justice," "commutative justice," and "distributive justice," he says. One might imagine that the first two of these phrases split up the jobs done by

Aristotle's "corrective justice" or Grotius's "expletive justice" while the third corresponds either to Aristotle's "distributive" or to Grotius's "attributive" justice. In fact, however, Kant is trying to proceed, as he so often does, on the model of the epistemological trichotomies he had introduced in the *Critique of Pure Reason*, such that the three kinds of justice will correspond to the "possibility," the "actuality," and the "necessity" of law, respectively (MM 120–121). Protective justice is supposed to give us the form of law (what makes law possible), commutative justice the content of law (its actuality), and distributive justice the mechanism by which laws are enforced (made "necessary"). Accordingly, distributive justice consists in the use of courts to apply laws in particular cases, and the presence of distributive justice, in this sense, is what marks the difference between having a government and living in the state of nature (MM 121). Where there is no one to enforce laws, the acquisition of property "is still only *provisional*... since it is not determined by public (distributive) justice and secured by an authority putting this right into effect" (MM 124). For Kant, it would be ridiculous to suggest that distributive justice might be unenforceable: distributive justice *is* the enforcement of laws. It is a little difficult to see why the word "distributive" should characterize this aspect of justice, but perhaps what Kant has in mind is that courts "distribute" to each of us the rights we would otherwise have only in principle. I take the fact that Kant so stretches the traditional meaning of "distributive justice"—that his usage is so out of line with both the Aristotelian and the Grotian traditions about how to understand that phrase—to be evidence that he was poorly acquainted with the classic works of legal and political philosophy to which most of his contemporaries would have turned.[28]

The same inattention to the jurisprudential tradition to which he was supposedly contributing helps explain Kant's peculiarly strong conception of property rights. As one might expect from Kant's moral philosophy—but not from the complex arguments by which property rights were justified in, say, Aquinas, Grotius, or Hutcheson—the principle of right for Kant can have no exceptions, and the justification of property, which for Kant as for his predecessors is the paradigm case of a right, must grant a person ownership of a thing against all other possible claimants, in all possible situations. His aversion to qualifying, or allowing exceptions to, the basic principles of right and property comes out in a remarkable dismissal of the "right of necessity" as the product of a "strange confusion [among] jurists" (MM 60). Kant concedes that it might be impossible to deter someone who needs to violate the usual order of justice in order to survive[29] but maintains that such violations will still be wrong and should be recognized as such by the law.

Kant is therefore a good source for a strict libertarian view of law and politics and is indeed cited as a source by some contemporary libertarians.[30] Unlike contemporary libertarians, however, he displays no worry either about a possible general tension between property rights and taxation or about the possibility that the use of tax monies for redistributive purposes might conflict with the state's obligation to maintain everyone's property rights. On the contrary, he urges the state to run schools, hospitals, and other institutions for the sick or orphaned poor and, in addition, to provide direct poor relief, all at the expense of the taxpayer.[31] Indeed, he says explicitly that support for these institutions should be compulsory for all citizens, not voluntary, and that it should come through taxation rather than through state lotteries (MM 136). Kant may, therefore, offer arguments of value to the most extreme libertarian right on today's political spectrum, but his policy proposals place him to the left even of many welfare liberals.

In part, this seeming contradiction is paved over by an embarrassingly bad argument. To defend state support for the poor, what Kant needs to do is show that such support is required by justice. But in what sense does justice require aid to the poor? We have seen that Kant understood justice to be concerned primarily with the protection of a very strict notion of property rights. Where is there room for state aid to the poor here? Well, one might make room by suggesting that people are poor only because their property rights have in the past been invaded by those who are now rich. This is precisely what Kant does. What was called by Kant's predecessors "commutative justice" demands redistributive programs for the poor, he says, since riches and poverty can come about only by way of fraud or theft:

> Although we may be entirely within our rights, according to the laws of the land and the rules of our social structure, we may nevertheless be participating in general injustice, and in giving to an unfortunate man we do not give him a gratuity but only help to return to him that of which the general injustice of our system has deprived him. For if none of us drew to himself a greater share of the world's wealth than his neighbour, there would be no rich and no poor. (LE 194)[32]

The thought seems to be that the goods provided to us by nature come in a fixed amount, so if they were divided up fairly, everyone would get an equal share of them. Wealth, then, is only possible if some people cheat others out of what is rightfully theirs. One might call this the "all wealth is robbery" thesis.[33] The thesis depends on regarding economics as a zero-sum game, such that one person's gains can come only at the cost of another person's losses. Someone who holds such a view would seem to be entirely unaware of the possibility of economic growth, of the fact that a person can increase what he or she has in ways that, far from taking from someone else, increase the total number of goods available in the world. And if unequal distributions of goods foster such growth, they can benefit the worst off and therefore be agreed to by everyone. Where there is more to go around, everyone's standard of living, including that of the worst off, can improve. It was precisely this point that Smith was at pains to demonstrate in the opening chapters of the *Wealth of Nations*. Kant was not only a contemporary but an avid reader of Smith.[34] Yet even after reading the *Wealth of Nations*, he maintained the "all wealth is robbery" thesis.

If we turn now from economics, where Kant made no contribution, to moral theory, where he made a very substantial one, we can find a more interesting argument for placing aid to the poor in the hands of the state. Indeed, the weakness of Kant's "all wealth is robbery" argument is itself an indication, I think, that something else lies behind his attempt to construe aid to the poor as a matter of justice. That something is a fascinating critique of the virtue of charity. Kant notes that giving alms "flatters the giver's pride" while "degrad[ing]" those to whom the alms are given. "It would be better," he says, "to see whether the poor man could not be helped in some other way which would not entail his being degraded by accepting alms" (LE 236). State-run provision of the poor, on Kant's view, has *moral* advantages over private charity. Kant sees moral corruption in the private relationships by which well-off people bestow of their bounty to the needy and looks to the state to provide for a more respectful relationship between rich and poor.[35]

It is worth pausing over the details of Kant's view here, both because it has become an influential one and because it is surprising in the context of a moral tradition that had long lauded the virtue of generosity. Philosophers from Aristotle to Hutcheson had given the fact that one needs one's own means in order to display generosity, and to experience the pleasures of being generous, as an important reason for private property.

For Kant, one should not in general be virtuous in order to gain pleasure by doing so, and a person who performs good deeds only when they are pleasurable is not virtuous at all. As regards generosity in particular, Kant notes that a truly moral person should seek to cultivate "good-will from principles" rather than mere "kindliness of heart and temper" since the latter is unreliable and subject to the mercies of whatever accidental factors happen to shape one's emotions: "Such a man will be charitable, by inclination, to all and sundry; and then, if someone takes advantage of his kind heart, in sheer disgust he will decide from then onwards to give up doing good to others."[36]

But the deeper problem with "charity from inclination" is the implicit hierarchy it sets up between giver and recipient. When I give charity, I flatter myself that I am better than the person I am helping. I thereby morally degrade the recipient of my aid even as I help him or her materially. Virtuous acts should not express, much less create, such a hierarchy. On the contrary, it belongs to the essence of all virtue, for Kant, that it express and help create a community of *equal* rational beings, a community that respects the equal, absolute worth of every individual within it. I violate something fundamental to morality when I regard myself as superior to others; I must instead regard every other human being as an end in him- or herself, as having exactly as much right to a good life as I do. It is therefore better that I focus on the *rights* of others rather than on their *needs* (LE 193), and Kant considers a proper respect for such rights to be the primary duty of beneficence (LE 193–194; compare also G 423). Every human being "has an equal *right* to the good things which nature has provided," he says (LE 192, my italics), from which it is supposed to follow that even the duty of material aid to others should be construed as a response to people's rights. Charity should be seen "as a debt of honour rather than as an exhibition of kindness and generosity" and indeed as a "trifl[ing] . . . repayment of our indebtedness" to others (LE 236):

> All moralists and teachers should . . . see to it that, so far as possible, they represent acts of benevolence to be acts of obligation, and reduce them to a matter of right. A man should not be flattered for performing acts of kindness, for then his heart inflames with generosity and he wants all his actions to be of that kind. (LE 193)[37]

We should see morality in general as a matter of a law—the categorical imperative—that humbles us all equally, not as an activity in which there are some experts and some poor players. The traditional presentation of charity as a virtue at which some excel and for which others should be grateful is a misconstrual of the way virtue works, and of the attitude toward other human beings that a virtuous person should take.

Given these views, it is easy to see why Kant would favor state-run provisions for the poor. Where the state taxes everybody to provide for the poor, everyone comes to have an obligation to contribute,[38] and the provision for the poor becomes a right, not a favor. In his lectures on ethics in the 1770s and 1780s, Kant restricts himself to suggesting that it "would be better to see whether the poor man cannot be helped in some way other" than by private alms.[39] In his 1797 *Metaphysics of Morals*, published after the French Revolution had introduced radical ideas about what the state can do, Kant called explicitly for the state to provide that "other way" of taking care of the poor. It was part of the social contract establishing a state, he said, that the government "constrain the wealthy to provide the means of sustenance to those who are unable to provide for their most necessary natural needs" (MM 136). This argument is well suited to a vision by which care for the poor should be part of everyone's obligations to one another, a part of the duties moral equals have to one another, rather than an expression of the special virtues of some. On Kant's justification for state provisions for the poor, everyone should equally see him- or herself as part of a community that supports the others, and respect for the rights of each should replace gratitude, on the one hand, and self-flattery, on the other, as the basis of this mutual support. Small wonder that many supporters of a welfare state, even today, look back to Kant as a source of inspiration.

Two final implications of Kant before we move on: First, more clearly and explicitly than any of his predecessors, Kant proclaims the equal worth of all human beings. That claim is indeed one of the most famous elements of his *Foundations of the Metaphysics of Morals*. Every human being, and indeed every rational being, "exists as an end in himself and not merely as a means," Kant says (G 428), and must be so regarded within the deliberations of every other rational being. Every human being is of "absolute worth" (G 428, 435)—hence of equal worth.

With this claim in place, we can supply the premise for distributive justice that we found so difficult to make sense of on Aristotelian grounds (premise 2 in my list of premises in the introduction). People are not worthy now merely because they have "virtues," where that word refers to excellences in the Aristotelian sense. They are worthy in themselves, and all equally so, by way of possessing rationality. This does not rule out the possibility that some people, by performing good deeds or working hard, may acquire superior worth over others in some respects, may become more deserving of some honors or goods than their less moral or lazier peers. But at a fundamental level all people are equally worthy, equally deserving of a good life. To aid them in achieving that good life, to aid them at least to the extent of ensuring that they have the minimal goods they need in order to exercise their rational wills, becomes now a duty rather than an act of mere kindness. And Kant in fact uses the duty to aid other rational beings as the fourth of his examples of moral action in the *Foundations* (G 423, 430).

Second, Kant construes human nature such that we all have a set of potentials for fully free action that we can realize only if we live in favorable natural and social circumstances. In the third of Kant's examples of moral action in the *Foundations,* he speaks of the obligation we all have to develop our "talents" or "gifts" (G 423). This provides a moral foundation for what, in the *Critique of Judgment,* he will call "Cultur":[40] the bringing of all human capacities, by way of political, economic, and educational progress, to their fullest form. The *Critique of Judgment* was Kant's most immediately successful book, influencing an entire generation of German thinkers—Humboldt, Schiller, Goethe, Hegel—who differed on many things but all held up an ideal of human "cultivation" as the ultimate purpose of society. That ideal is still very much with us today, even as many other of these German thinkers' beliefs have faded. When William O. Douglas wrote, in his dissent in *Wisconsin v. Yoder,* that a person's "entire life may be stunted and deformed" if she is not educated such that she has a chance to become "a pianist or an astronaut or an oceanographer,"[41] he was echoing, although surely unwittingly, the Romantic German view of human nature that has one of its main sources in Kant.

This view has important consequences for distributive justice, for the development of people's potentials may require a large number of material goods and social institutions. So if the value of a person's life requires the development of his or her potentials, then it may be necessary for society to provide the material circumstances for developing those potentials to everyone who would not otherwise have them. Certainly, it will need to make sure that everyone is at least given the education and opportunities necessary to see *what* potentials they have. (This is what

Douglas was calling for in *Wisconsin v. Yoder.*) Human beings will not have an adequate life, on this view, if they merely fulfill a set of static tasks and duties pointed out to them as good by their society. They need instead freely to develop and live out a rich "life plan" of their own, in which they can play out all the capabilities they find valuable.

Kant does not fully develop this thought, but he does maintain that the process of bringing ourselves to "greater perfection," of bringing all that is potentially excellent in us to actuality, is morally required of us (G 430). Where society can help in this process, and especially where individuals cannot make progress in their self-development without so-cietal help, it would seem that the society is likewise morally required, not merely permitted, to provide such help. This extends the obligation to help the poor far beyond the provision of what they need in order to survive or even to have a minimal level of health and self-respect. If the goal of human life is the bringing of our talents to a possibly unlimited level of perfection, then the obligation of society to help the poor is potentially endless. Participation in a "playing field" where talents can be developed now becomes essential to human life, and a society in which the possibilities for self-development increase over time will need to keep readjusting resources and institutions so as to "level the playing field." Latent in Kant's stress on the duty to develop our talents is therefore a demanding conception of the good human life, one which in turn can come to require a great deal of society. As I will show in the next chapter, the political philosophies of John Rawls, Amartya Sen, and Martha Nuss-baum owe a lot to this aspect of Kant.

4. To the Vendôme *Palais de Justice:* Babeuf

Kant gets extremely close to the modern notion of distributive justice, but he does not state it explicitly. He never quite says that the state is required by justice to provide for the poor, merely that such provision is part of the social contract. And he makes this remark in the course of a very brief paragraph on state duties to the poor; the whole issue is mar-ginal to his main concerns. So while it is right to see later promoters of distributive justice as looking back to Kant, it is not quite right to see Kant himself as having proclaimed that notion.

It was in the decade after Kant had published most of his major works, and after Adam Smith and Rousseau were dead, that the modern notion of distributive justice was born. Rousseau, Smith, and Kant were all heroes of the French Revolution; the first two, especially, were cited admiringly by many revolutionaries. Rousseau's presence pervades the revolutionary period, although he had passed away in 1778. Smith died in 1790, as the revolution was just beginning, and we know of no explicit comment by him about it.[42] Only Kant, of the three, had so much as the opportunity to contribute directly to the revolution, and he restricted himself to making a couple of ambiguous remarks about it.[43] So if modern distributive justice was born during the wild throes of the French Revolution, when the state came to be seen as capable of solving all social problems, the three eighteenth-century philosophers I have examined thus far can only be precursors to the notion. Instead, it was "Gracchus" Babeuf, the leader of an abortive coup attempt in 1796, at the very end of the revolution, who first explicitly proclaimed that justice requires the state to redistribute goods to the poor.[44] Even Babeuf, as far as I know, does not seem to have used the phrase "distributive justice" in its modern sense, but he did attribute to everyone a full-fledged right—a perfect, strict, enforceable right—to an equal share in all wealth, and justice has been treated by the natural law tradition since Grotius as correlative with perfect rights claims.

The idea that at least some goods should be distributed to everyone had already made an appearance in the 1780s in the land redistribution proposals of Thomas Spence and William Ogilvie, both of whom referred to the "natural and equal rights" of all mankind to property in land.[45] Then Thomas Paine introduced a ground-breaking poverty program for the state to undertake in his 1792 *Rights of Man*. Yet even Paine did not quite say that *justice* demanded the institution of his program. The program for dealing with poverty in the *Rights of Man* consists, primarily, of five proposals: a remission of sales taxes to the poor, a grant to poor families to be used for the education of their children, a provision for the elderly, the establishment of shelters in cities that would provide food and lodging in return for a certain amount of work per day, and the establishment of a progressive estate tax.[46] About one of these proposals—the provision for the elderly—Paine says that it is "not a matter of grace and favour, but of right."[47] So here we have an explicit statement that a certain kind of aid to the poor is demanded by justice rather than charity. But only one kind of such aid. Only about his proto–social security plan does Paine say this, not about his proposals for the education of children, for the remission of sales taxes, or for the establishment of work shelters. Why this difference between the provision for the elderly and his other proposals? Because the elderly, says Paine, have *earned* that provision. Every person in England spends a lifetime paying taxes to the government. As they do this, they lose not only the money itself, but the interest on the money, which they might otherwise have saved for their retirement.[48] Paine says that his proposal restores to each of them, after the age of fifty, "little more than the legal interest of the nett money he has paid."[49] The indigent elderly, that is, deserve their pension as a rebate on excessive payments they have already made, not because they are unable to work, much less because they are human and all humans deserve not to be poor.

I think we can safely assume that if Paine, one of the most unabashedly radical of eighteenth-century writers, had thought that his readers would accept the claim that *all* human beings deserve to be raised out of poverty "not as a matter of grace and favour, but of right," he would have made such a claim instead of the roundabout, and not terribly plausible, argument that the elderly poor deserve government aid as a rebate on past taxes. So even among radicals in 1792, we may take it that the notion of aid to the poor being a matter of distributive justice, the notion that justice might demand a distribution of goods so as to alleviate or abolish poverty, was practically unheard-of.

Consider now a speech given one year later. Armand de la Meuse, speaking before the French National Convention on April 17, 1793, declared that

there cannot be . . . a more dangerous, absurd, and immoral contradiction than political equality without social and economic equality. To enjoy equality in law but to be deprived of it in life is an odious injustice. . . . There is no need to raise the question here as to whether . . . under [natural law] all men possess an equal right to the fruits of the earth. This is a truth about which we can entertain no doubts at all. The real issue is this: granted that in society the public convenience admits of a right to private property, is there not also an obligation to limit those rights and not to abandon their use to the caprice of the property owner?[50]

Babeuf, on trial for his life, was to quote this speech at length, as one of the clear forerunners to his own teaching. Armand does state, unequivocally, that everyone has a natural right to an equal share in "the fruits of the earth." On the other hand, his argument for economic equality depends heavily on the notion that economic equality underwrites political equality and is thus not necessarily important in itself. He also allows for a distinction between what holds in the state of nature and what societies must grant their citizens. Armand grants that "in society the public convenience admits of a right to property," although in nature no such right exists, and implies strongly that some economic inequality is likewise acceptable in society.

Babeuf went a step further, drawing a direct line from the natural right of equal wealth to the demand that society equalize wealth. That nature gives everyone "an equal right to the enjoyment of all wealth" was the first principle in the twelve-point summary by which Babeuf's views were disseminated, and the second was that "[t]he aim of society is to defend this equality, often attacked by the strong and the wicked in the state of nature, and to increase, by the co-operation of all, this enjoyment."[51] So Locke's basic argument for the purpose of all states—that the state can enhance and better preserve the rights we have in the state of nature— is here applied to one right that Locke himself never considered as such: the right to equal economic status. Given the Lockean view of legitimate government, it would follow that only communist states can be legitimate. One cannot find an argument like this anywhere in the earlier writings of the Western political tradition.

One cannot even find it in Rousseau, as we have seen. Rousseau sharply separated the state of nature from the state of human beings in society, and he never said that justice demanded that society remake itself in the image of the state of nature. But his followers eventually said just that. The line between presocial fantasy and political recommendation became more and more blurred as the French Revolution pursued its fevered course. Babeuf saw Rousseau's state of nature as setting the standard for all human rights, for what we may demand in the name of justice, and drew the conclusion that everyone by *right* should be able to enjoy all the products of the earth. Once one measures the distribution of goods in a society by the standard of an imagined presocial paradise, however, the society is bound to look wildly unjust and to require revolution rather than mere reform. It will be difficult to see why one should "respect the sacred bonds" of one's society, as Rousseau said he wanted to do, or "scrupulously obey" its laws. Instead, those laws and bonds will start to appear as the greatest obstacle to the achievement of justice, deserving not respect, but a comprehensive overhaul. The distance between Rousseau, who considered it foolish to want to "annihilate mine and thine," and Babeuf, who proclaimed in Rousseau's name that we need to do exactly that, is a great one, too often overlooked by both Rousseau's admirers and his critics.

Many later distributivists would not share Babeuf's revolutionary inclinations. Nor would they all join his call for strict equality and the abolition of property. However, these aspects of Babouvism are not what matters for our purposes. For our purposes, what matters is that Babeuf made not living in poverty into a political right, that he put on the political agenda, for the first time, a right of all people to a certain socioeconomic status—not because poverty gets in the way of people's ability to be good citizens, but because poverty is an affront, indeed a justiciable injury, to people as human beings. It would be a long time before many states made an effort to implement any such right, but the notion of distributive justice, in its modern form, had finally arrived.

3

From Babeuf to Rawls

TANNER: Are you all Socialists here, may I ask?

MENDOZA [*repudiating this humiliating misconception*]: Oh no, no, no: nothing of the kind, I assure you. We naturally have modern views as to the injustice of the existing distribution of wealth: otherwise we should lose our self-respect. But nothing that you could take exception to, except two or three faddists.

TANNER: I had no intention of suggesting anything discreditable. In fact, I am a bit of a Socialist myself.

STRAKER [*drily*]: Most rich men are, I notice.

MENDOZA: Quite so. It has reached us, I admit. It is in the air of the century.

— GEORGE BERNARD SHAW, *MAN AND SUPERMAN*
(1901–1903)

After Babeuf, the concept of distributive justice entered political discourse, but it remained at the margins of respectability for some time. There are any number of nineteenth-century books with the title "Distribution of Wealth," or some close variant thereof.[1] There were also a number of political movements in the nineteenth century that saw the redistribution of wealth as a principal task for government. Yet the phrase "distributive justice" seems not to have become widespread until after the second World War, and it took a surprisingly long time before philosophers and political theorists began to describe themselves as developing accounts of it.

It did not take so long for a doctrine that deserved that name to begin to become part of everyday life. E. P. Thompson has documented how the unruly and seemingly apolitical "mob" of the eighteenth century transformed itself into the far more organized and politically self-conscious "working class" by the beginning of the nineteenth century,[2] and this change was almost precisely paralleled by a subtle shift, among workers and their advocates, toward regarding not just poor relief but measures designed to bring an end to poverty itself as a right. In 1765, workers in East Anglia proclaimed their right to be relieved in their own parishes, as opposed to a policy that consolidated the poor of several parishes into centralized workhouses. In 1795, a mob demanded, instead, to "live better," and a group of laborers in Kent pressured an overseer to take political steps that might bring about higher wages.[3] And when protests against workhouses again broke out after the Poor Law of 1834, the banners called for "England, home, and liberty: local rights, wholesome food, and no separation in bastilles!"[4] As in 1765, the poor wanted relief in their own parishes and did not want to be confined in order to get relief, but this time they also regarded "wholesome food" as a right and made an unsubtle allusion to the French Revolution to place their social and economic demands on the same level with the political demands that had brought down the French monarchy. This politicization of poverty in fact got under way in Britain at the time of the French Revolution, spurred on not only by the French example, but by a severe local food crisis. Popular seizures of grain during the 1794–1796 crisis took on a far more political character than they ever had before, with workers forming committees to demand or provide help for the hungry.[5] After the Speenhamland system was adopted in 1795, moreover, people came to look on a subsistence income as something to which they were entitled; Arthur Young noted ominously in 1797 that "[t]hat relief which formerly was and still ought to be petitioned for as a favour, is now frequently demanded as a right."[6] In 1796, William Pitt called for Parliament to "make relief in cases where there are a number of children a right and an honour" and drew up a bill that, had it passed, would have supplied Britain with a far more expansive array of social insurance programs than any other nation had ever had.[7]

These are but a few signs of the rapid spread, after the French Revolution, of an ideology according to which the poor should have a legal right to improved economic conditions, not merely a right to survive alongside a moral claim on rich people's charity. In the 1820s, the English poet John Clare attacked parish officials who, in depriving the poor of maintenance, "take that away which as their right they call"; he looked forward also to a world in which the poor were treated "as equals not as slaves," where masters and servants were seated at table "without distinction."[8] In 1834, William Cobbett wrote that both laborers and those unable to labor have "a right to subsistence out of the land," and York-shire demonstrators in 1837 proclaimed that "[t]he poor have a right to subsistence from the land."⁹ Across the Atlantic, Judge David Brewer of the Kansas Supreme Court declared in 1875 that "the relief of the poor—the care of those who are unable to care for themselves—is among the unquestioned objects of public duty."¹⁰ Norwegian law briefly contained a claim that the poor had a legal right to relief in the nineteenth century, and in the early twentieth century, Norway, Sweden, and Finland all clas-sified minimum relief for the poor as "mandatory assistance."¹¹ It is worth dwelling on Judge Brewer's emphasis on "those who are unable to care for themselves," however: for most of the nineteenth century, both in law and among even the more radical social agitators, only those unable to labor were regarded as having a right to aid from the state. Correlatively, the laboring poor were said to deserve a greater share of material goods *only by virtue of their labor* by radicals such as Cobbett, Proudhon, Thomas Hodgskin, and even Marx.¹² The notion that being human alone, independent of laboring, might entitle one to some goods, that people might deserve something to help them when they could not find work or to help them "get started" in life—that poor children, for instance, might deserve aid from the state if their parents could not supply them with adequate food, clothing, and shelter (let alone education and health care)—was not yet seen as part of justice. Distributive justice at most called for a greater reward for labor and for meeting the basic needs of those who could not labor.

By the beginning of the twentieth century, a more expansive notion of distributive justice was in place. The first pages of Alfred Marshall's 1890 *Principles of Economics* declare that the possibility of getting rid of poverty altogether is what "gives to economic studies their chief and their highest interest," and Marshall tells us that the possibility he has in mind is one in which "all should start in the world with a fair chance of leading a cultured life, free from the pains of poverty and the stagnating influences of excessive mechanical toil."¹³ Franklin Roosevelt's New Deal provided "social security" to every citizen above a certain age, and his Aid to Fam-ilies with Dependent Children (AFDC) was meant to offer means of op-portunity precisely to people who had not yet earned those means by labor. Roosevelt proposed a "second bill of rights" in his 1944 State of the Union address, which would have included a right to a home, a job with an adequate wage, medical care, "a good education," and "adequate protection from the economic fears of old age, sickness, accident and unemployment."[14] His widow, Eleanor Roosevelt, helped craft the United Nations's 1948 *Universal Declaration of Human Rights* (UDHR), which included rights to "social security," to the "economic, social and cultural [goods] indispensable for [every person's] dignity and the free development of his personality," to protection against unemployment, and to "food, clothing, housing, and health care" (UDHR Articles 22, 23, and 25). This extravagant set of economic rights has never been supported, in any country, by a legal framework allowing those deprived of the rights to sue for relief. Still, the fact that the international community adopted such a declaration shows that the notion of distributive or social justice was firmly entrenched by the middle of the twentieth century.

Firmly entrenched in *popular* moral consciousness, that is. Only when John Rawls began developing his theory of justice in the 1950s and '60s did philosophers and political theorists begin to take seriously the individual right to well-being that Babeuf had proclaimed in 1796. The dominant schools of political philosophy and political economy in the nineteenth and early twentieth centuries were either opposed to the redistribution of wealth or supported such redistribution while eschewing the language of justice. In this chapter, I will consider some of the reasons why each of four major schools of thought kept distributive justice off the philosophical table for so long, then turn more briefly to the important contribution Rawls made to bringing it to that table, and close with an even briefer glance at the work of some of his successors.

1. Reaction

In an uncannily precise illustration of the Hegelian principle that a thesis always brings about its own antithesis, theories and movements that utterly rejected the new notion of distributive justice sprang up at almost exactly the same moment that that notion first appeared.[15] Joseph Townsend insisted on the intrinsic inferiority of poor people and railed against the public provision of poor aid within a decade after the publication of Smith's *Wealth of Nations*. Like Mandeville, Townsend saw hunger as useful in motivating poor people and called for the abolition of the poor laws. He was followed in this, over the next decade, by Patrick Colquhoun, Thomas Malthus, and Edmund Burke.[16] (All still thought there was an appropriate place for private charity, but they tended to welcome, rather than regret, the fact that private charity was unlikely ever fully to relieve hunger.) The idea that the poor are *not* the same as other people—the idea, which I shall call "poor-person exceptionalism," that Smith had so energetically disputed—returns here with a vengeance. Townsend thinks of the poor as inherently "indolent and vicious," properly suited to "vile" labor.[17] In one form or another, this idea has never really gone away; it still reappears, every once in a while, as an argument against welfare policies. It is an idea that richly deserves the label "reactionary" since it represents the bringing back of a premodern notion that the later Enlightenment worked to get rid of and a notion at odds with the whole Enlightenment commitment to human equality.

Yet at the same time Townsend, Colquhoun, Malthus, and Burke—and Mandeville before them—are very much *products* of the Enlightenment. Indeed, there is something subtly reflective of Enlightenment progressivism in their very opposition to the poor laws. For it is quite a new and not a traditional idea that the poor laws should be abolished and that the hunger of the poor should be welcomed. The premodern version of poor-person exceptionalism had gone along with a Christian belief that all human beings were equal "in the eyes of God," if not necessarily in one another's eyes, and as such deserved Christian charity. It was therefore neither appropriate to celebrate the poor's hunger nor wrong for the state, in the name of charity, to help alleviate that hunger. Mandeville had scandalized faithful Christians by pointing out the advantages to society of the poor's suffering,[18] and Townsend and the rest, although they were committed Christians (both Townsend and Malthus were ministers), were no less breaking with traditional attitudes in calling for the end of the poor laws.[19] They show their Enlightenment heritage in their attempt to give secular, naturalistic reasons for their proposals and to reason unflinchingly from their first principles to a conclusion that contradicted popular prejudices. The Enlightenment delight in seeing things clearly for what they are combines here with the inegalitarianism of the premodern Christian world to make for a new callousness, an unprecedented harshness toward the poor. A truly rational person had no time for sentiment when investigating a scientific problem; it was a mark of the impartiality, the cool rationality, needed to do good science that one could free oneself of any feelings that might cloud one's objective judgment. Or so some of the Enlightenment's children thought.

This scientific coldness was nowhere demonstrated more vividly than in Arthur Young's 1774 *Political Arithmetic*, in which the author declared a preference for the poor to be killed in war than to "be constantly increasing, and remain a dead weight on the industrious; and my humanity [*sic*] prompts me to the idea, because I apprehend, population would suffer less in the former than in the latter case. . . . In a word, when the maxims of a pernicious government have forced a class of the people to be idle, the greatest favour you can do them, is to range them before a battery of the enemy's cannon."[20] Earlier in the century, Jonathan Swift had hoped to shock people into recognizing the callousness of their attitudes toward the poor with a sardonic proposal for eating poor babies; now Young was making an equally horrific suggestion in perfect seriousness.

Still, as Keith Snell remarks, "[t]his was not a commonly held proposal" in the eighteenth century.[21] In the nineteenth century, the thinking behind the proposal, if not the proposal itself, became an important element in the movement calling for the abolition of poor aid. After Malthus had argued that the human competition for food and other basic resources necessitates that people will die of hunger and disease in every generation, some came to consider it a kindness to society as a whole to let as many poor people as possible die off quickly. Malthus himself did not advocate letting the poor die. He was one of the first to call for the abolition of all public aid to the poor, but he thought that private charity was a good thing and that it would adequately meet the most basic needs of the poor. Not even Young advocated, nor were even the most extreme of social Darwinists to advocate, the abolition of private charity: they acknowledged the importance and decency of the human impulse to help the needy. But they also maintained that any sort of aid to this particular class was disadvantageous in that it delayed the dying-off of a group of people who were a drain on society and, in the long run, could not survive in any case.[22]

The Mandevillian belief in "the utility of poverty" is here taken a step further than Mandeville himself was willing to go.[23] For Mandeville, hunger was useful in that it spurred the poor to labor. But this makes hunger useful both to society as a whole and to the poor themselves: once they labored, they would eat, and if they did not have the spur of hunger, they would waste and drink away their lives. For the social Darwinists, the hunger of the poor was useful to the rest of society, but it was not useful to the poor themselves—they, perhaps unfortunately, had simply to die off. Again, we see a coldness that extends pre-Enlightenment dismissive attitudes toward the poor in a way that the Enlightenment itself made possible. No traditional Christian (or Jew or Muslim or Hindu or Buddhist) had ever held such a view toward the poor, had ever been willing simply to write off the lives of an entire group of people who had not committed any crime.

The question of greatest interest to the story I am telling is whether or not this "let them die" attitude played a significant role in the opposition to distributive justice from the nineteenth century on. It might be just a curious fact that some opponents of distributive justice believed the survival of the fittest entailed that poor people die off in the short run. Need we assume that that belief is essential to the arguments against the legitimacy of distributive justice, to the arguments against the feasibility of welfare programs, or against the right of the state to use tax revenues for such purposes? Surely social Darwinism is but one strain in the complex of ideas opposing distributive justice, which can easily be separated from the libertarian arguments that stress the importance and absoluteness of property rights.

Many libertarians will argue this. I believe the separation is not as easy as they suppose. It is instructive to look at the thought of the most influential social Darwinist of them all, a founder of libertarianism and one of the most important figures in the entire nineteenth-century intellectual world: Herbert Spencer.

Spencer put together a comprehensive system of epistemology, metaphysics, ethics, politics, and philosophy of religion that for its range alone competed with the works of Plato, Aristotle, Kant, and Hegel. His "Synthetic Philosophy" was widely regarded as a comforting replacement for Christianity, and it won disciples all over Europe and America.[24] "As it seems to me," wrote one disciple, "we have in Herbert Spencer not only the profoundest thinker of our time, but the most capacious and most powerful intellect of all time. Aristotle and his master were no more beyond the pygmies who preceded them than he is beyond Aristotle. Kant, Hegel, Fichte, and Schelling are gropers in the dark by the side of him. In all the history of science, there is but one name which can be compared to his, and that is Newton's."[25] If nothing else, as this tribute indicates, Spencer was a grand systematist. And while Spencer's system does not necessarily hold together in every respect, he did make a strong case that a belief in social evolution, in the absoluteness of property rights, and in the inefficacy and moral corruption of welfare programs are tightly interwoven parts of one worldview.

Spencer introduced something much like evolution by natural selection in his first book, *Social Statics*, originally published in 1851, eight years before Darwin's *Origin of Species*. (Ironically, Darwin himself was not a "social Darwinist" in the ordinary sense of that term. It is Spencer, not Darwin, who was responsible for the phrase "survival of the fittest" and for the notion that political programs should not "interfere" with the struggle for survival.[26]) In *Social Statics*, Spencer argued against all state aid to the poor—"not only poor laws, but also state-supported education, sanitary supervision other than the suppression of nuisances, regulation of housing conditions, and even state protection of the ignorant from medical quacks"[27]—on the grounds that the poor were unfit to survive and should be eliminated: "Why the whole effort of nature is to get rid of such—to clear the world of them, and make room for better" (SS 379). People were poor because of moral, mental, or physical failings, and even where their failings were nonmoral ones—stupidity or physical weakness or an inborn tendency to indolence—it was a mistake, a matter of misguided pity, to try to keep them alive: "Beings thus imperfect are nature's failures, and are recalled by her laws when found to be such. . . . If they are sufficiently complete to live, they *do* live, and it is well they should live. If they are not sufficiently complete to live, they die, and it is best they should die" (SS 380). Poverty is a useful condition, weeding out the unfit from the human species just as disease and drought do for other animal species: "The poverty of the incapable, the distresses that come upon the imprudent, the starvation of the idle, and those shoulderings aside of the weak by the strong, which leave so many 'in shallows and in miseries,' are the decrees of a large, far-seeing benevolence" (SS 323). Under "the natural order of things," society will "constantly excret[e] its unhealthy, imbecile, slow, vacillating, faithless members," and state aid to the poor merely "stops the purifying process" (SS 324). Spencer did not oppose private charity—that, he felt, was a natural and good expression of the virtues of the fit—but he thought even that was disadvantageous insofar as it prolonged the survival of the unfit. He was particularly concerned to keep down breeding among the poor. Nothing should be done, he maintained, that would encourage "the multiplication of the reckless and incompetent" (SS 324). Then poverty might die out in a generation or two.[28]

So far, Spencer the social Darwinist. But Spencer's arguments against state programs to help the poor did not rely solely on the claim that the poor should be allowed to die off. In the first place, he demonstrated, like Adam Smith, the immense complexity of society and how very difficult, therefore, it was for anyone to predict how any given social project would play itself out. Individual human beings never *create* social forms: "What Sir James Mackintosh says of constitutions—that they are not made but grow—applies to all social arrangements" (SS 263). Spencer, who was a founder of sociology, considered that science of great importance because it could "awaken [people] to the enormous complexity of the social organism and put an end to hasty legislative panaceas."[29] The purpose of social science was "not to guide the conscious control of societal evolution, but rather to show that such control is an absolute impossibility."[30]

In the second place, Spencer argued that the goal of distributivist programs was, necessarily, unclear. Ask someone like William Cobbett what exactly he means by saying that everyone has "a right to maintenance," Spencer suggested:

> Inquire, "What is a maintenance?" "Is it," say you, "potatoes and salt, with rags and a mud cabin? or is it bread and bacon, in a two-roomed cottage?... will tea, coffee, and tobacco be expected? and if so, how many ounces of each?... Are shoes considered essential? Or will the Scotch practice [of going barefoot] be approved? Shall the clothing be of fustian? if not, of what quality must the broadcloth be? In short, just point out where, between the two extremes of starvation and luxury, this something called a maintenance lies." (SS 312)

There is no possible answer, Spencer maintains. This is not the sort of thing that can be settled in a precise way. But law requires precise definitions, so the absence of a definitive mark for where necessity ends and luxury begins will lead those who try to enforce the provision of necessities into endless difficulties.

Third, Spencer reverses, with astute psychological insight, the type of argument Kant had offered for the superiority of state aid to the poor to private charity (see Chapter 2, Section 3):

> "The quality of mercy (or pity) is not strained," says the poet. But a poor-law tries to make men pitiful by force.... "It blesses him that

gives, and him that takes," adds the poet. A poor-law makes it curse both; the one with discontent and recklessness, the other with complainings and often-renewed bitterness. . . . Watch a ratepayer when the collector's name is announced. You will observe no kindling of the eye at the thought of happiness to be conferred—no softening of the voice to tell of compassionate emotion: no, none of these; but rather will you see contracted features, a clouded brow, a sudden disappearance of what habitual kindliness of expression there may be. . . . The purse comes slowly from the pocket, and after the collector, who is treated with bare civility, has made his exit, some little time passes before the usual equanimity is regained. Is there anything in this to remind us of the virtue which is "twice blessed"? Note, again, how this act-of-parliament charity perpetually supersedes men's better sentiments. Here is a respectable citizen with enough and to spare: a man of some feeling; liberal, if there is need; generous, even, if his pity is excited. A beggar knocks at his door; or he is accosted in his walk by some way-worn tramp. What does he do? Does he listen, investigate, and, if proper, assist? No; he commonly cuts short the tale with—"I have nothing for you, my good man; you must go to your parish." And then he shuts the door, or walks on, as the case may be, with evident unconcern. Thus does the consciousness that there exists a legal provision for the indigent, act as an opiate to the yearnings of sympathy. (SS 318–320)

State aid to the poor is not, as Kant had described it, an act of justice expressing respect for every citizen, but "act-of-parliament charity," which squelches the capacity for private charity and nurtures in the poor "complainings and . . . bitterness."

Finally, for Spencer, justice itself not only does not require but *disallows* state-run aid for the poor. Spencer is as uncompromising a believer in the primacy and absoluteness of property rights as one can find anywhere. His first principle of politics is what has come to be known as the basic libertarian one—"Every man has freedom to do all that he wills, provided he infringes not the equal freedom of any other man" (SS 103; see also 75–102)—and he understands the right to property to be an integral part of this freedom. "What is this property?" he has a citizen ask the government; "Is it not that . . . on which I depend for the exercise of most of my faculties?" But the whole purpose of government is "to guarantee to each the fullest freedom for the exercise of his faculties compatible with the equal freedom of all others," so for government to tax property for any purpose other than the guarantee of freedom itself is inadmissible. To diminish "the liberty of each man to pursue the objects of his desires" will always be wrong, except where necessary to guarantee that everyone else has a like liberty (SS 277–278). Taxation always lies under suspicion, as a potential violation of the very purpose of government, and can be justified only where it serves such liberty-preserving purposes as the protection of citizens against uses of force, not where it gives one citizen goods belonging to another. Government can legitimately be used to prevent *harm* but not to promote *good:* forcing one citizen, through the tax code, to support others' ways of living is no more justifiable than forcing one citizen to support others' religious beliefs. "Most of the objections raised by the dissenter to an established religion," says Spencer, "tell with equal force against established charity. He asserts that it is unjust to tax him for the support of a creed he does not believe. May not another as reasonably protest against being taxed for the maintenance of a system of relief he disapproves?" (SS 317).

It is difficult to separate this argument from Spencer's social evolutionist attitude toward poverty. Consider one immediate response to what he says: if the property owner requires his property "for the exercise of most of his faculties," one might say, then propertyless people surely need to *have* some property if they are to exercise most of their faculties. Equal liberty for all would then seem to demand some redistribution of wealth rather than ruling it out. What blocks such an easy retort, for Spencer, is that he considers freedom, and hence property, a good only because in the end it will promote the existence of the "perfect man," the best kind of human being, and will wipe out the evils due to the existence of inferior people. Morality must be based on what perfect people would do, he says, and cannot make any compromise with the conditions that generate evil (SS 55–56). Consequently, it will never be acceptable to infringe on superior people's freedom to support their inferiors: "For is it not cruel to increase the sufferings of the better that the sufferings of the worse may be decreased?"[31]

We therefore cannot easily extract Spencer's libertarianism from his social Darwinism. Indeed, it seems likely that his absolutism about property rights is more a *product* of his opposition to distributivist programs than its source. As I have noted, it is not easy to find a good argument to support the claim that property rights are more essential to property owners' freedom than a redistribution of property is to those without property, and it is even harder to find much of a precedent for this claim in the natural rights tradition on which Spencer relies. Even Kant combined his strict view of property rights with an insistence on the legitimacy of state-run poverty programs. Spencer's supremely absolutist view of property rights can only be entertained once one has already dismissed the possibility that justice might call for poverty programs. Libertarians after Spencer will sometimes weigh the good of protecting property rights against the good of helping the poor and conclude, with at least a show of reluctance, that the former trumps the latter. Other liberals who respect the importance of property rights will weigh the two and conclude, also with some reluctance, that the latter trumps the former. For Spencer, there is simply no contest between the two: that the poor are more likely to die out without state aid is an *advantage,* not a disadvantage, of a strict insistence on the sanctity of property rights.

Now the strong emphasis on the sanctity of property rights in the nineteenth century had other roots besides Spencer's work. The so-called "Manchester liberals," under the leadership of Richard Cobden, passionately defended free-trade policies without making any appeal to social evolution. However, free trade was for Cobden, as it had been for Smith, above all a matter of lifting import and export restrictions, not of avoiding aid to the poor, and he regarded it (as, again, did Smith) as part of a wider commitment to internationalism and world peace. Naively or not, Cobden sincerely believed that government interventions would almost always hurt the poor, and he supported government help whenever it was clear to him that it would prevent suffering among the poor. Thus he always supported the poor rates, scorned the harsh Poor Law of 1834 (an icon for many laissez-faire ideologues), and was a strong advocate of government relief efforts during the cotton famine of 1862–63.[32] In 1910, the eleventh edition of the *Encyclopedia Britannica* indeed ranged socialism and free trade together, contrasting them both with economic nationalism:

Socialism, like free trade, is cosmopolitan in its aims, and is indifferent to patriotism and hostile to militarism. Socialism, like free trade, insists on material welfare as the primary object to be aimed at in any policy, and like free trade, socialism tests welfare by reference to possibilities of consumption. In one respect there is a difference; throughout Cobden's attack on the governing classes there are signs of his jealousy of the superior status of the landed gentry, but socialism has a somewhat wider range of view and demands "equality of opportunity" with the capitalist as well.[33]

In *one* respect there is a difference. And socialism makes just "somewhat" wider demands than Richard Cobden did? Once the Russian Revolution broke out, seven years after this was written, socialists and capitalists alike would find a characterization like this extraordinary. So we might not want to go all the way with this author in lumping Manchesterism and socialism together. But it is certainly true that advocacy of free trade did not necessarily go together with an opposition to social welfare legislation in the mid-nineteenth century. There were in fact radical advocates of the poor who supported free trade. William Thompson sounds much like Cobden when railing against monopolies and bounties or calling for full freedom of exchange and free use of labor.[34] Cobden and the Manchester liberals do not really belong under the heading of the "reaction" to distributive justice, therefore, and are not nearly as clear ancestors as Spencer is of twentieth-century libertarianism, which has been practically defined by its opposition to government programs that redistribute goods to the poor.[35]

We therefore need to bear Spencer's case against distributivism in mind when we read later versions of the libertarian position. To recapitulate, Spencer believes the state should avoid helping the poor because (1) the poor are composed of a group of people unfit for survival who cannot be helped much anyway; (2) the process of social evolution, in which the unfit die out, will if left alone vanquish poverty; (3) society is uncontrollable, so government attempts to solve the problem of poverty are likely to fail; (4) such government attempts will corrode the virtue of charity; (5) such attempts will lead to all sorts of legal problems since their goal is necessarily unclear; and (6) such attempts will override property rights, which it is the prime purpose of government to protect. The third, fourth, fifth, and sixth arguments have been extracted by later libertarians, most famously by Ludwig von Mises and Friedrich Hayek (both of whom stressed the third argument) and by Milton Friedman and Robert Nozick (both of whom stressed the sixth argument). Some notion of social evolution is important to most of these later thinkers as well—especially Hayek[36]—if only because it is the notion that society develops by an evolutionary process, and not by conscious change, that underlies the claim that conscious social planning is likely to fail (argument 3). This version of social evolutionism, however, does not involve any suggestion that the poor make up a special, inferior class of people, much less that it would be better if they died off (none of the later figures I have mentioned hold either of those views).[37] Yet if one rejects these unpalatable claims, what justification does one have for saying that the difficulties of precisely defining distributive justice (argument 5) or the limitation on freedom involved in taxing one person's property to benefit someone else (argument 6) are so important that they always trump the good that can be done by government help to the poor?

The use of property rights to rule out distributive justice, the claim that justice *forbids* using tax monies to help the poor, is particularly mysterious without the Spencerian framework. The claim that property rights are "sacred," "inviolate," or "absolute," in Locke, Hume, Smith, and their natural law antecedents, was always such that it could be trumped by important state purposes. The question was simply whether a particular purpose was important enough to do the trumping. For Spencer, as we have seen, state aid to the poor certainly did not meet that threshold since it was not a good at all. Contemporary libertarians are likely to say that the goal of such aid is a good but one that can be achieved in other ways (e.g., through a fully free market together with private charity) or that it is not good *enough* to override people's rights to do what they want with their property. But if the poor are truly equal to everyone else, why should their freedom to exercise their faculties, for which they need to have property, never override the freedom of the better-off to exercise theirs? And if evolution cannot be trusted to solve the problem of poverty, then is it not unacceptably cruel for a society to turn its back on the poor, generation after generation? Spencer combined an extremely pessimistic view of the poor with an extremely optimistic view of social evolution, so that he could reasonably say that his opposition to welfare was at bottom humanitarian: if we just let the present poor die out, in a generation everyone will be comfortably off. If one does not believe that, if one does not hold that all evolutionary processes, including the sufferings of the poor, are "the decrees of a large, far-seeing benevolence," then it is much harder to make the end of social welfare programs look remotely humanitarian.

My point is not that all opponents of distributivism have been secret

Spencerians. On the contrary, neither Hayek nor Friedman nor Nozick accepted Spencer's inegalitarianism about human nature; all started instead from the assumption that every human being equally deserves freedom. But some of their most important positions nevertheless make best sense within the Spencerian framework. In particular, the absolutist conception of property rights, which is a philosophical oddity, not easily justified on its own and with only weak roots in the natural law tradition, makes better sense in the context of Spencer's evolutionary system than it does in any of its later, kinder and gentler incarnations.

2. Positivists

It is of course to be expected that people who oppose state redistribution of wealth would not develop a theory of distributive justice. Far more surprising, many thinkers who *supported* the redistribution of wealth, often quite fervently, refused to use "distributive justice" to describe their aim. For at least three very important schools of nineteenth-century philosophy, there were reasons to avoid the language of justice altogether.

The first obstacle that nineteenth-century philosophy threw in the way of the emerging notion of distributive justice was positivism, a doctrine that cast suspicion on moral talk of all sorts, including talk of justice. Mark Blaug, a modern economist and historian of economics, writes that the great nineteenth-century economist John Bates Clark regarded his theory of marginal productivity "as providing a normative principle of distributive justice." But Clark did not express himself in these terms. On the contrary, in his massive *Distribution of Wealth* (1899), he described himself as concerned with "the *science* of distribution" and said that the question of whether states *should* override property rights to give people economic goods in accordance with need "lies outside our inquiry, for it is a matter of pure ethics." He preferred to focus on "issue[s] of pure fact"—drawing the sharp divide, characteristic of positivism, between "ethical" and "factual" issues.[38]

"Positivism" is a catchall label for a variety of views, which have in common an extremely high appraisal of science and a corresponding tendency either to reduce every other mode of thinking (ethics, religion, metaphysics) to a scientific enterprise or to deride that mode as irrational or empty. The term was coined by the comte de Saint-Simon and his follower, Auguste Comte, both of whom aligned themselves with proto-socialist critiques of capitalism's emphasis on the individual and callous treatment of the poor. Both they and the positivists who came after them, however, preferred developing a social science that might tell policy makers *how* to transform the society they saw around them over putting effort into analyzing exactly *why* that society was morally objectionable.

Comte and Saint-Simon understood science to be rooted in observable facts rather than the idealistic methodology favored by their contemporary Hegel. They looked back to the British empiricists in this, although they did not necessarily share the empiricists' conception of facts as pure sensations. They differed most sharply with the Hegelians over the *separability* of facts: even where, as Comte did, they saw one science as building on others, they were atomists, convinced that the building blocks of science could be known each on its own and not simply as part of an overarching system of thought. In this, the positivists of the twentieth century were their true heirs. Positivism has always been atomistic and has regarded observation rather than abstract thought as the paradigmatic, if not the only, way of grasping each individual fact.

Positivists have not all believed, however, that ethics and religion are irredeemably irrational. Saint-Simon felt that the moral principles of Christianity were worthy of continued respect and allegiance even if Christianity's theology and metaphysics should be abandoned.[39] Comte proposed a new positivist religion and looked forward to a scientific ethics. Jeremy Bentham and James and John Stuart Mill developed what they regarded as just such a scientific ethics. Only in the twentieth century did the so-called "logical positivists," particularly Moritz Schlick and Alfred Ayer, maintain that ethical and religious statements were meaningless.

At the same time, positivists have always held that ethics must either be put on a sound, scientific footing or abandoned and have always been a bit suspicious of what philosophers do under the heading of "ethical theory." It is difficult to construe the foundational principles of most ethical theories as observable facts, after all. Neither the intuitions into the *telos* of human beings that informed ethics from Plato and Aristotle through Thomas Aquinas, nor the deliverances of Kant's transcendental will, nor even the expressions of sentiment that govern the ethics of Hutcheson, Hume, and Smith are publically sharable, testable bits of data of the sort that positivists so love. Utilitarians such as Bentham suggested that one could construe ethics as a sort of technology in the service of a maximization of human happiness and reduce all ethical questions to the respectable scientific form "does action X maximize human happiness more than any of its alternatives?" This proposal, while subjected to a withering critique by twentieth-century positivists, was enough to keep ethics within the domain of science for most of their predecessors. Such an approach to ethics, however, does not encourage close examination of, say, the fine distinctions among various virtues—the difference between "justice" and "charity," to take a nonrandom example—or spending many pages on such questions as whether it is morally acceptable for the state to enforce charity. Needless to say, arguments over whether justice properly comprises a "distributive" as well as a "commutative" element fell into the category of pointless debates. It was neither well suited for treatment by positivist science nor conducive to the technological and political progress that the positivists wanted to foster. It was indeed precisely the sort of issue the positivists had hoped to leave behind. Again, we should not forget that both Saint-Simon and Comte, along with many of their followers, were founders of socialism: they strongly favored a redistribution of wealth by the state. But it did not suit their intellectual predilections to present this proposal under the rubric of justice.

3. Marx

Karl Marx is by far the most influential figure ever to decry the distinction between rich and poor. He also developed certain notions that were to become of great importance to the full flowering of distributive justice in its modern sense—above all, a view of human nature as largely the product of human societies and a view of those societies as capable of radical change. But it is a mistake to see Marx himself as a defender of distributive justice. He did not put his critique of capitalism in those terms. Some say that is because he believed communism would bring an abundance of goods and, like Hume, recognized that issues of justice arise only where there is scarcity.[40] Others argue that he saw the entire language of "justice" as a baleful historical relic, more likely to impede than to help the proletariat in its struggle with the bourgeoisie. Debate over why Marx avoided couching his critique of capitalism in terms of justice has raged among his commentators for years.[41] We need not address this dispute here—it suffices for our purposes that Marx was not an explicit proponent of distributive justice. However, it is worthwhile to spend a little time elaborating Marx's stated objections to justice talk, both because these remarks have played an important role among some of Marx's followers and because they are interesting in their own right.[42]

Marx most sharply indicates that justice is an unsuitable tool for socialist thought in "On the Jewish Question," which criticizes the notion of individual rights, and in his critique of the Gotha Program, which describes appeals to rights as "bourgeois phrases" and "ideological nonsense" (MER 526, 531). In the latter, Marx also rejects the social democratic call for a redistribution of goods, rejects, indeed, the "presentation of socialism as turning principally on distribution" (532). Both of these pieces are examples of Marx's seemingly irrepressible urge to attack everyone he knew and worked with (Bruno Bauer and Ferdinand Lassalle in these two cases),[43] but they also contain one of the most astute critiques of the traditional idea of justice ever penned.

Let us suspend Marx's critique of the concept of justice in general for a moment. Even if he had wanted to hold on to some elements of that concept, it is doubtful that he would have embraced *distributive* justice, given the second of his complaints against Lassalle: that socialism should not be presented as "turning principally on distribution." Marx held that it was a mistake to treat economic distribution separately from production. In the first place, among the most significant goods to be distributed are the means of production. To treat distribution purely as "the distribution of products," he says, is to have a shallow view of economic activity. Before food, clothing, and shelter can be distributed, land, tools, and other capital goods first need to be distributed (MER 232–233). And the balance of power in any society will be determined far more by the distribution of these factors of production than by the distribution of consumer goods. Those who own land or capital goods will have a control over the distribution of consumer goods that those who live by labor will lack. Hence, "[t]he structure of distribution is completely determined by the structure of production" (232–233).

In addition, the suffering and dehumanization of workers that Marx sees in the capitalist system comes about at least as much because of the circumstances under which they carry out the production of goods as because of the skimpy number of those goods they are able to purchase. A justly famous stretch of Marx's 1844 *Economic and Philosophic Manuscripts* analyzes the multiple forms of "alienation" workers undergo when they lack control over their products and working conditions (MER 70–

81). The worker whose labor is bought by an owner of capital, says Marx, is alienated from the product of his labor, from his employer, from his fellow workers, and above all from his "producing activity itself." Marx believes that human beings naturally love to produce things—they are creative beings, beings who find their self-realization in making things—and when their production is controlled by others, and becomes simply a means to a life outside of production, they lose an essential part of their humanity. The worker under capitalism

> is at home when he is not working, and when he is working he is not at home. His labour is therefore not voluntary, but coerced. . . . As a result, . . . man (the worker) no longer feels himself to be freely active in any but his animal functions—eating, drinking, procreating, or at most in his dwelling and in dressing-up, etc.; and in his human functions he no longer feels himself to be anything but an animal. What is animal becomes human and what is human becomes animal. (74)

The goal of socialism, then, is to humanize production as much as distribution—or rather, since the two are inseparable, to humanize *economic activity*.

To "humanize" or "socialize" (the two are practically identical for Marx, as we shall see) economic activity—not to make it "fairer" or more "just." "What is 'a fair distribution' " of goods? Marx asks rhetorically (MER 528). The capitalists consider their mode of distributing goods "fair," socialists have many different notions of "fairness," and there is no good way of resolving these differences. It is also a mistake to suppose that legal notions such as fairness or justice can be used to determine economic relations: rather, legal relations and the notions governing them "arise from economic ones." Allen Wood has argued that Marx considered the exploitation of workers under capitalism to be just, that he regarded "justice" as a term for whatever legal relations conduced to the maintenance of a particular mode of production, and that under that definition, all institutions contributing to the flourishing of capitalism deserve to be called "just."[44]

But to say this is not to praise capitalism; it is to challenge the idea that "justice" is a useful norm. Marx's conception of human nature is radically at odds with the presupposition, basic to justice, that human beings should be regarded as first and foremost *individuals* rather than members of a social group. Marx directs great ire at the notion of individual rights so central to justice. He notes that the notion of people as having rights—as in "the proceeds of labour belong . . . with equal right to all members of society" (the first sentence of the Gotha program and a clear descendant of the opening lines of Babeuf's *Manifeste des Egaux*)[45]—is (1) strongly individualistic, (2) a product primarily of certain developments in eighteenth-century European thought, and (3) part and parcel of a vision, exalting the individual, in which there is a sharp division between the political and the private realms, the purpose of the political realm is to protect individual freedom in the private one, and it is only in the private realm that human beings live out their highest aspirations.

All of these claims are quite correct. The various French and American eighteenth-century declarations of rights (Marx considers the declarations in several American state constitutions as well as in the federal one) are indeed founded, as Marx says, "upon the separation of man from man"; they do indeed attempt to establish and protect a way of regarding each person as "separated from other men and from the community" (MER 42). And the notion of the "isolated individual" in these declarations is indeed a product of the moral and political thought of those "eighteenth century prophets, in whose imaginations [the] eighteenth century individual . . . appear[ed] as an ideal."[46]

Finally, it is true that the same eighteenth-century thinkers who thus exalted the individual conceived of human nature as best flourishing in a private sphere wherein they wished to place religious practice as well as commerce (MER 34, 45). Proclamations of rights were part of a more general move toward what Marx calls the "decomposition" of human being (MER 35) or what we today call, more moderately, the "compartmentalization" of our lives. Since the eighteenth century, especially in the West but now, increasingly, all over the world, it has become more and more possible to separate one's religious life from one's political life, both of these from one's commercial life, and to separate one's recreational, artistic, or sexual life from the previous three. One can be a Hindu while simultaneously holding American citizenship, working for a Japanese-based multinational corporation, and devoting most of one's free time to an international community—possibly aided by the Internet—of bridge players or opera lovers. One thing this means is that citizenship need not integrate or permeate the rest of our identities and certainly need not be seen, as it was by Aristotle (to whom Marx looks back at many points), as the fullest or highest form of our identity. The political realm, the realm in which we must work together and try to understand one another's concerns, was intended by most eighteenth-century thinkers to be primarily a means for protecting our ability to live out our beliefs and interests in the private sphere—"a mere means," as Marx derisively puts it, "for preserving these so-called rights of man" (43).

Granting all this to Marx is not to grant also that he was right to portray all these eighteenth-century developments as baleful ones, not to grant that there is something terribly wrong, something corrosive of our humanity, in the compartmentalization of our identities and the subordination of the political realm to the fulfillment of individual projects. I happen myself to be sympathetic to the liberal vision that Marx rejects, to endorse its attempt to carve out a private sphere as the prime arena for expressing our humanity and its tendency to regard politics as a mere means for protecting that private sphere. Even those of us sympathetic to this liberal view, however, can learn from Marx's demonstration that that view is not simply the natural way of looking at the world, held by all rational and unprejudiced people since the beginning of time, but a product of a particular historical time period and a view that contrasts sharply with many important earlier conceptions of human nature, including that of Aristotle. Marx is useful in showing that what the eighteenth century called the "rights of man" are only that on a particular, quite controversial understanding of what "man" is—and that humanity can be, and has been, defined such that the very notion of rights is contemptible or unthinkable.

Marx himself holds precisely such an understanding of humanity. According to him, we human beings are "species beings," which means both that we think in terms of universals (of kinds or "species" rather than of particular objects) and that we most fully and freely express our nature by acting as members of our species rather than acting as if we were isolated individuals. These points are closely related: since we think about everything in universal terms, we think of ourselves in universal terms too, and we therefore distort our own conception of ourselves when we treat ourselves as isolated individuals. Instead, we should see ourselves as instances of the universal *kind,* "human being."[47] In the ideal Marxist world, we would not sacrifice our individuality for the greater social whole—putting the point that way is to hold on to an opposition between individual and society. Rather, the very distinction between individual and society would disappear, and societies would act for their individual members even while those members acted to promote the good of the society. Like the three musketeers, all would be for one and one would be for all.[48]

In practice, I take it, this means that it would become natural for each person to have the good of others in mind even when he prepared food, sought partners for procreation, or took care of his health—but all the while his neighbors would likewise be taking care in their daily life to look out for his health and happiness. Such apparently quintessential private acts as eating, drinking, and procreating are "genuinely human functions," says Marx, only when they are integrated with all other human activity and that activity is carried out in a social way, not just by and for one's own, isolated, biological unit (MER 74). There is even a properly human, which is to say a social, way of *sensing*—of "seeing, hearing, smelling, tasting, feeling" (87). "[T]he senses of the social man are *other* senses than those of the non-social man" (88). Consequently, we fail to achieve both the highest form of art (sensual gratification) and the best empirical science where we remain stuck in individualistic rather than socialized ways of living (88–91). Finally, individualistic ways of living can be endorsed only by people who blind themselves to the very condition making such endorsement possible: we can and do endorse individualism if and only if the norms of our society have encouraged us to do so. For it is *impossible* for us to be anything other than the products of our social relationships, and individualism itself is but a doctrine born of a certain social history. In fact, says Marx, "the epoch which produces this standpoint, that of the isolated individual, is also precisely that of the hitherto most developed social . . . relations" (223).

It is this thoroughly socialized conception of human beings that has had the most profound impact on the subsequent history of distributive justice. Many thinkers who otherwise differ strongly with Marx have shared his belief that practically all features of what might seem to be our nature are in fact instilled in us by the structure of our society. The idea of an unchanging, substantial human nature underlying human history has had little traction since Marx's day, and it is considered unremarkable when even a liberal, distinctly non-Marxist thinker such as John Rawls treats a person's talents and willingness "to make an effort" as a product largely of social influences.[49] More than anyone before him, Marx brought out the immense power of society over each of us, the immense degree to which social forms, and not just laws or governments, shape individuals.

But if society has this power over human nature, then surely it has power over itself as well. Society seems to be an immense force, on Marx's view of it, and it, rather than each individual, seems to be the true locus of human freedom. For Marx, as for Rousseau, what society has done, it can undo.[50] Hence society should be able to change those features of human nature that, in the opinion of earlier thinkers, made socioeconomic equality impossible. A communist, says Marx, need not believe all the supposed scientific evidence against the possibility of communism: that evidence is merely a product of capitalist science. Marx emphatically believes that communism is possible, and his confidence in society's ability to change itself helped to buttress the fourth of the premises necessary for modern distributive justice, as listed in the introduction to this book.

Yet Marx himself was no promoter of "justice" in any sense of the term. Having rejected the rights focus of traditional notions of justice, he made no attempt to develop a new meaning for the notion more appropriate to communism. Indeed, he had little use for moral terms in general. Marx considered moral language dehumanizing. We might say, although he would have rejected this way of putting his point, that he condemned moral language for moral reasons. If art, science, and the way in which we carry out our most basic daily activities can be corrupted by unhealthy social systems, morality can be similarly corrupted. Marx appears to have believed that all morality is corrupted in this way because norms receive the label "moral" only when they appear to us as something alien, underwritten by God or some similarly supernatural being or principle standing over us. Even Kant's justification of morality by way of freedom removes moral norms too far from us for Marx, given the nonnaturalistic character Kant attributed to freedom. The apparent distance of moral norms from ourselves makes them easy tools for domination, and we tend to use morality to beat each other over the head with, to coerce or cajole other people into doing what we want them to do.[51] A properly humanized set of social norms will appear to us as our own norms, as something we create and daily shape—each of us, in conjunction with our neighbors—not as something that comes to us from the outside.

Justice partakes of the alienated, threatening, heteronomous form characteristic of morality, and in addition, it promotes the alienating force of individualism. So in the ideal society there would be no justice. There might be norms bearing some sort of family resemblance to what today we call "fairness," but they would not carry the awe-inspiring freight of the word "justice"; they would pay no attention to rights; and they would not, in that or any other way, set up an opposition between individuals and their society. For Marx, as for Plato and Rousseau, there would be no need for justice in the ideal society. There would be no need, therefore, for distributive justice.

4. Utilitarians

From its inception, utilitarianism was extremely concerned with the suffering of the poor. Its founder, Jeremy Bentham, is known for proposing one of the earliest welfare programs. A little later, William Thompson used utilitarian premises to examine in great depth what he called the alarming "tendency to poverty on the part of the many, [and] to the ostentation of excessive wealth on the part of the few."[52] John Stuart Mill was a prominent advocate of government programs to aid the poor, and Alfred Marshall, whose philosophical views were heavily influenced by Mill's, claimed that the prospect of ending poverty was what gave economics its "chief and highest interest."[53] In both the nineteenth and the twentieth centuries, many utilitarians argued that socialism was the best way to achieve the greatest happiness for the greatest number of people, although other utilitarians defended free-market economics on the same grounds. The fundamental principle of utilitarianism is of course open to such varying uses, depending on how one views the facts of a given situation. Nevertheless, I would venture to guess that there have been more utilitarian socialists than utilitarian free marketeers—if only because the utilitarian criterion for right action is one that easily overcomes claims about the inviolability of property rights.

Utilitarianism is not a doctrine friendly to the idea that individuals have any absolute rights. The emphasis on the absolute importance of individual human beings, and of their freedom rather than their happiness, does not sit well with the utilitarian emphasis on spreading happiness among as many people as possible. Bentham was famously suspicious of "natural rights"; he could see no reason why the good of any one individual should trump the greater good of many others.[54] His successors would have trouble making good sense of the notion that justice might constitute a virtue separate from and irreducible to other virtues—that it might legitimately make demands of us contrary to the greatest happiness of the greatest number. The very impetus to utilitarianism, for many of its adherents, was that it offered a comprehensive account of all our different virtues and norms, such that no virtue need any longer be treated with unquestioning reverence and no ethical rule need any longer be worshipped.[55] Rather, we can ask of any purported virtue or moral norm, "does this virtue or norm conduce to greater human happiness, or does it perpetuate suffering?" And if we conclude that the virtue or norm perpetuates suffering, we see immediately that it can and should be altered or dismissed. The traditional reverence given to property rights, and to a conception of justice to which property rights are central, is a perfect example of something that utilitarians want to submit to this test. It is difficult for utilitarians to countenance deep and long-lasting suffering for any segment of society, especially when it seems that that suffering could be relieved at a relatively minor cost in happiness for people who are already well-off. To the extent that an insistence on individual rights preserves such a condition, that insistence appears to utilitarians as a sanctimonious cover for cruelty. On these sorts of grounds, utilitarians have had little use for traditional conceptions of justice. Consequently, while utilitarians have contributed a great deal to the nexus of claims that constitute modern distributive justice, they have tended not to couch their proposals in those terms.

To begin, however, with their positive contributions:

Perhaps more than any other ethical doctrine, utilitarianism has a scientific cast, and its exponents have without exception been concerned to solve moral problems rather than merely to reflect on them. That means both that utilitarians have sought a decision procedure by which apparent moral conflicts can be settled—hence their obsession with a single principle at the root of all moral thinking—and have sought to redirect moral philosophy from the lofty but unproductive terrain of value exploration to the scientific and political activities by which pressing causes of human suffering might be alleviated or eliminated. "[E]very political and moral question ought to be [put] upon the issue of fact," says Bentham,[56] at the beginning of the tradition, and two centuries later, J. J. C. Smart commends utilitarianism for its "empirical attitude to questions of means and ends," its "congenial[ity] to the scientific temper."[57] People are drawn to utilitarianism when they want to stop talking and act, when they find debate over the exact moral justification for ending slavery or illiteracy or war wearying and pointless and would rather put their energies into the medical research, educational programs, or political movements that might actually solve the relevant problem.

We should not take this attitude for granted, common as it may have been over the past two centuries. Aristotle, Cicero, Augustine, and Aquinas did not direct most of their attention to the solution of long-entrenched human problems. They did not see their work, or any other human effort, as *capable* of solving most of these problems and assumed instead that they lived in a more or less static universe—or that God alone could work the great changes needed to improve the human condition. The purpose of moral philosophy was far more to achieve some sort of self-understanding on the part of the person engaging in the philosophy than to change his or her social environment. This view of moral philosophy continues to dominate the work of more modern writers such as Hutcheson, Joseph Butler, Hume, and Kant. Kant did believe that moral philosophy could help reduce or end international conflicts, and Locke, of course, thought that moral philosophy could help people know when resistance to a government was justified. But the idea that the world might be radically revised, that practically any human problem could be solved given enough ingenuity and goodwill, is a new one, a product of the optimism that came with the scientific developments of the seventeenth and eighteenth centuries and of the French Revolution, in which for the first time it seemed as if one could entirely remake the state, and as if a well-made state might be practically omnipotent, capable of curing any social disease.

This view of society as capable of curing practically any of its own ills is implicit in Henry Sidgwick's way of posing the basic question of justice: "Are there any clear principles from which we may work out an ideally just distribution of rights and privileges, burdens and pains, among human beings as such?"[58] It is presumed here that we can and do carry out such distributions, and need principles to guide us in the process. Note that Sidgwick clearly presumes that justice is centrally concerned with matters of distribution rather than with the protection of already-distributed rights, or the maintenance of a naturally or divinely given social order. Although, like other utilitarians, he did not emphasize the individual nor develop much of an account of justice as a distinct virtue, he clearly takes distributive rather than commutative justice to define the terrain covered by that virtue. The more important presupposition at the moment, however, is that all privileges and all pains—all "good and evil," indeed, according to another version of this question appearing slightly earlier on the same page—*can* be "distributed" across human beings, that it is reasonable to conceive of society as if it were capable of giving each individual the basic components of happiness. Aristotle asked about the proper distribution of political status among citizens, as did his followers in the natural law tradition, but it did not occur to practically any political thinker, at least when they were making serious proposals rather than dreaming up utopias, to think of society as an agent that might take "the right distribution of good and evil" as its end.

It is this immense sense of the power human beings can wield over their institutions that inspires utilitarian writers, and they display boundless optimism about the resolution of hitherto irremediable problems. Utilitarians were pioneers in the development of all the social sciences and in the attempt to use these sciences to improve public policy. They were leaders of movements for public education and public health, for shorter working hours and better working conditions, for greater public access to art and to sources of natural beauty, and for many other progressive causes. Maximizing happiness had a very concrete meaning for them, and it inspired reform movement after reform movement, many of which have had long-lasting success.

In particular, utilitarians have been among the prime movers in movements promoting a welfare state. One may see the very formulation of the utilitarian basic principle as a way of urging the redistribution of material goods. Hutcheson was the first to proclaim that the goal of moral action was "the greatest happiness for the greatest number," but for him aiming at this goal was pointless unless one did so out of benevolence, and he devoted far more attention to how one could encourage people to express benevolence than to how the greatest happiness criterion could be used.[59] By contrast, when Bentham took over the criterion, he wanted precisely to use it as the basis of a practical decision procedure—a procedure by which, above all, to test laws. "No law ought to be made," he said, "that does not add more to the general mass of felicity than it takes from it."[60] And in the context of his day, where in practically every country the vast majority of the people were poor, adding to "the general mass of felicity" would inevitably mean improving the situation of the poor. Where the overwhelming majority of a society is poor, redistributing goods from the wealthy to the poor will almost always increase both the total and the average societal happiness.

In more recent times, however, the utilitarian principle has been less squarely on the side of redistribution. Since the 1940s, the vast majority of people in Western democracies have become quite comfortable, and the question of poverty has turned into a question about how to get the *majority* to give of their goods to a suffering *minority*. In these circumstances, it is unclear whether either the total or the average happiness in a society will be enhanced by a movement of goods from rich to poor.

To that objection, modern utilitarians who favor redistribution have the following response: Given the diminishing marginal utility of most goods, and of the total package of goods sought by most people, it will generally be the case that the next increment of each good—and especially of necessities or of whatever can be exchanged for a necessity—will most increase the happiness of the least well-off person. At any point in the distribution of goods, therefore, we should be giving to the poorest person, and we should continue to distribute to that person until his or her marginal utility becomes less than the marginal utility of the next poorest person. At that point, whoever hitherto was the next poorest person becomes the recipient of choice, and so on until everyone has roughly equal marginal utility. Thus does utilitarianism tend toward equality.[61]

We should note that this argument depends on the assumption of diminishing marginal utility, which does not hold for all goods (if I am putting together a stamp collection, the stamp that completes a certain set may well be *more* valuable to me than its predecessors); that it assumes that goods can be neatly individuated (how do we decide how much education to distribute to each person?) and that each good can be distributed independently of the others (does it make sense to distribute a Shakespeare subscription to someone who is barely literate rather than to an English major?); and that it assumes that happiness or "utility" can be fairly well correlated with material goods. All of these assumptions are questionable, which is one reason why contemporary promoters of distributive justice often prefer to base their claims on a moral philosophy other than utilitarianism.

But there is a deeper reason for that preference: the difficulty, already mentioned, of making any place at all for justice in the fundamental framework of utilitarianism. Mill devoted a full chapter of *Utilitarianism*—more than a third of the book—to the problem of how justice can be accounted for in utilitarian terms, and J. J. C. Smart added a section on that problem to his mid-twentieth-century monograph on utilitarianism, since he came to regard it as the greatest challenge to utilitarianism. As Mill describes the problem, it is that "people find it difficult to see in justice only a particular kind or branch of general utility."[62] The solution, he says, is to recognize that justice describes a particularly *urgent* kind of utility, a kind that almost always must be satisfied before any other types of utility are addressed. But Mill understates the problem. Justice has traditionally been *contrasted* with utility, such that one famous tag would have justice served even if the world has to perish *(fiat justitia et pereat mundus),* and even those who find this sentiment outlandish are inclined to describe justice as a virtue that protects certain good things against being sacrificed for the sake of expediency. In particular, as I have emphasized from the beginning of this book, justice is supposed to pro-tect *individual human beings* against being sacrificed for any societal greater good. But this focus on individuals is something that utilitarians typically have had difficulty grasping. That individuals should have any claim against the greater good of society simply does not make sense to Bentham—hence his dismissal of "natural rights"—and even Mill, who placed great stress on what he called "individuality," had to struggle to reconcile this emphasis with his stated loyalty to the utilitarian calculus.

The difficulty in recognizing the importance of individuals runs deep for utilitarians. In its purest, Benthamite form, the form that most con-duces to setting up a calculus that might settle all ethical questions, util-itarianism aims at pleasure and the avoidance of pain, where "pleasure" and "pain" refer strictly and simply to feelings. But feelings are states that exist for a moment, a limited period of time, and then are succeeded by other feelings. *As* beings who simply experience feelings—as "sentient" beings—we ourselves therefore consist just of one moment followed by another; we are simply collections of such moments. It is no wonder that Bentham should have regarded Hume, for whom the self was a "bundle of perceptions," as his primary precursor, nor that Kant should have resisted both Hume's moral theory and his conception of the self, and developed instead a moral theory whose fundamental premise was that our selves are enduring entities of absolute value.

Consider what it means, after all, to maximize happiness in a society if happiness is just a sum of moments containing pleasure or lacking pain. How can it matter, in that case, *who* has the pleasures or lacks the pains? Can we even make good sense of this "who" that might have a pleasure or lack a pain? Are we confident that we can identify individual consciousnesses if they are simply equivalent to the pains and pleasures they experience? Smart asks, "if it is rational for me to choose the pain of a visit to the dentist in order to prevent the pain of toothache, why is it not rational of me to choose a pain for Jones, similar to that of my visit to the dentist, if that is the only way in which I can prevent a pain, equal to that of my toothache, for Robinson?"[63] Individual consciousnesses dissolve on this approach to ethical questions; we worry about the distribution of certain sensory states without needing to worry about whom they "belong" to. But in that case we are surely not going to worry about a virtue that purports to protect the ability of each individual to make choices even when those choices impose a cost in net pleasure to the society as a whole. Utilitarians find it difficult to accept John Rawls's claim that "[e]ach person possesses an inviolability founded on justice that even the welfare of society as a whole cannot override" (TJ 3), but that is because, as Rawls also says, "[u]tilitarianism does not take seriously the distinction between persons" (TJ 27).

As I have stressed, this theoretical problem should not lead us to overlook the many contributions that utilitarians have made to actual programs for the redistribution of social resources. Moreover, John Stuart Mill, who in many ways tried to mitigate Benthamite utilitarianism, did manage to come up with a doctrine of justice that resembles the traditional one in most respects. And he and his followers, who include Marshall and Sidgwick, saw the distribution of social resources to help the poor as very much a question of justice. But their ethical philosophy was not well suited to the idea of justice—or, consequently, to the development of the idea of distributive justice.

5. Rawls

We have now surveyed four major political and philosophical movements that for various reasons either rejected or played down the notion of distributive justice. The reactionaries I have described were opposed to state aid to the poor and believed that justice did not properly have a distributive component. Positivists wanted to clear moral language of all sorts out of social science and to grapple with social problems as much as possible from a purely scientific perspective rather than a moral one. Marx also wanted to abolish the language of "morality," and especially of "justice," although not for scientific reasons. The utilitarians were happy with moral language, but they reduced all morality to one principle, and a principle by which the good of society was supposed to trump the good of individuals; they therefore had little room for the special virtue of justice.

To get a clear picture of the importance of John Rawls, it is helpful to realize that almost all serious work in political philosophy from the beginning of the nineteenth century right up to the publication of *A Theory of Justice* in 1971 fell into one of these four categories.[64] When Rawls started writing, pretty much *only* Marxists and utilitarians were willing to develop normative accounts of political issues, and even they were under constant siege by the upholders of the reigning positivist paradigm, for whom all normative declarations were expressions of emotion and did not belong in scientific or philosophical analysis. What Rawls did was to make moral philosophy in a nonutilitarian key respectable again. The revolution he accomplished here was truly astonishing: within ten years of the publication of the *Theory of Justice,* utilitarianism went into decline and a plethora of moral systems were once again in business. Rawls accomplished this in good part by borrowing a great deal of what had made utilitarianism attractive, and accepting much of the critique of traditional moral theory to be found among Marxists and positivists, while showing that his own trimmed-down Kantianism could meet the demands of these critiques.

To be more precise: Rawls shares the aversion of his rivals to quasi-mystical views of morality, by which moral systems seem to stand over us as if issued forth from a divine being. For him, as for the Marxists, positivists, and utilitarians, moral systems are creations of human societies, designed to solve problems that arise when people live together. For him in addition, as especially for the utilitarians, a moral system is useless unless it can issue in concrete proposals for resolving controversial issues: unless it comes with some sort of decision procedure. Rawls inserts into his work some judicious warnings against the expectation that moral philosophers will be able to offer solutions to all the specific problems that arise among people; he says that "settl[ing] the question of social justice, understood as the justice of the basic structure [of society]" will be easier than "settl[ing] hard cases in everyday life" (DJ 156). Yet, with the justice of the basic structure settled, Rawls seems to think that everyday life will be far less prone to present a stream of hard cases. So his object is in the end not unlike that of rule utilitarians such as Mill. In any case, he expresses admiration for utilitarianism and proposes "to work out a contractarian alternative" that has "comparable if not all the same virtues"

(DJ 132; cf. TJ 52). His motto, we might say, is "Everything Mill can do I can do better."

Where Rawls differs sharply from utilitarianism, and from the other paradigms of moral and political philosophy in his day, is in his strong emphasis on the importance of the individual. The very first page of the *Theory of Justice* declares that "[e]ach person possesses an inviolability founded on justice that even the welfare of society as a whole cannot override" (3; see also DJ 131),[65] and this point is used throughout the book against utilitarianism. Utilitarianism, he says, employs a methodology by which "many persons are fused into one" (TJ 27). We ought, by contrast, to start by assuming "that the plurality of distinct persons with separate systems of ends is an essential feature of human societies" (TJ 29). Note in this last quotation the connection between "distinct persons" and "separate systems of ends": because Rawls takes the distinction between persons so seriously, he also resists utilitarianism's tendency to reduce all human ends to one homogeneous type of thing (pleasure). This leads to one of Rawls's most interesting suggestions: that justice ought to be concerned only with the distribution of "primary goods"—goods that are necessary for the pursuit of practically any human end—and should set aside the question of what constitutes the ultimate human good.

So Rawls's grounding intuition picks up on precisely what we have identified as utilitarianism's greatest difficulty in making sense of justice. By strongly affirming the importance of human individuality and the need, consequently, for society to protect individuals against even its own greater interests, Rawls starts in the right place to define, finally, the modern notion of distributive justice. The concept had been playing a prominent but inchoate role in political debate for almost two centuries. Now it was at last to receive a clear formulation.

Rawls's most concise account of the project that became the *Theory of Justice* is to be found in an article he published a few years earlier titled "Distributive Justice." The article begins by echoing Sidgwick: "A conception of justice is a set of principles for choosing between the social arrangements which determine [the] division [of benefits produced by a society] and for underwriting a consensus as to the proper distributive shares" (DJ 130). For Rawls, as for Sidgwick, the distribution of benefits occupies the entire space described by the virtue of justice; distributive justice no longer needs to scrounge around looking for some place it can call its own in the middle of a virtue devoted primarily to other tasks (preserving order, protecting people from harm, inflicting retribution for harm, and the like).[66] And for Rawls, also as for Sidgwick, society as a whole is a joint project with rules and ways of acting that its members can control. Rawls makes this conception of society quite explicit: "a society is a cooperative venture for mutual advantage" (TJ 4; see also 11, 13).

In addition to echoes of Sidgwick, there are echoes of Marx. For Rawls, as for Marx, human nature is more a product of society than a determinant of it. The social system will always "affect the wants and preferences that persons come to have," so "one must choose between social systems in part according to the desires and needs which they generate and encourage" (DJ 157; cf. TJ 259, which cites Marx on this point). Our "life-prospects" will also be shaped in large part by the political and social structure we inhabit (DJ 134), and our talents and skills will be significantly shaped by our society. "[A]ll kinds of social conditions and class attitudes" will affect the degree to which our natural capacities "develop and reach fruition," such that "even the willingness to make an effort, to try, and to be deserving in the ordinary sense is ... dependent on fortunate family and social circumstances" (DJ 162; cf. TJ 103–104, 311–312). And because our "personal characteristics" are so shaped by society, because we have so little control over them, they must be set aside when considering principles for a fair distribution of goods. Desert, which defined distributive justice and marked it off from corrective justice for Aristotle, has now entirely disappeared from that concept.[67] In distributive justice, says Rawls, as opposed to retributive justice, "the precept of need is emphasized" and "moral worth is ignored" (TJ 312; see also 314–315). This almost exactly reverses the way Aristotle saw the two kinds of justice. And while this move is implicitly present already in Kant's account of human worth and attribution of absolute, hence equal, worth to everyone, it is Marx's argument that character is mostly a product of society that clinches the point for Rawls. If our talents and moral energy are really just products of our society, then it is silly to hold us, as individuals, responsible for having them or not having them.

But if Rawls incorporates some insights from Marx into his work, he is far more concerned to show positivists and utilitarians that his individualist approach can be as rigorous and as scientifically respectable as theirs. The utilitarians had managed to win some grudging respect even from positivists by making use of a minimal number of normative assumptions, proclaiming the compatibility of both their normative assumptions and their approach to decision making with the going picture of human nature in social science—the picture of human beings as "rational choosers" concerned to maximize the satisfaction of their desires—and giving their decision procedure an apparently rigorous mathematical shape. Utilitarianism commends itself to people with "a scientific... frame of mind," as Smart says: "it is congenial to the scientific temper."[68] Rawls's approach to morality differs in a fundamental way from that of the utilitarians, but at the time he wrote *Theory of Justice*, he admired these quasi-scientific features of utilitarianism. He said then that "the theory of justice, and indeed ethics itself, is part of the general theory of rational choice" (DJ 132; cf. TJ 16) and tried to work, as the utilitarians did, with a minimal set of normative assumptions and a scientifically acceptable picture of human nature. He also was very concerned to show that his more individualist morality could meet the challenge of offering a clear and rigorous decision procedure. "The philosophical appeal of utilitarianism," he said, "is that it seems to offer a single principle on the basis of which a consistent and complete conception of right can be developed. The problem is to work out a contractarian alternative in such a way that it has comparable if not all the same virtues" (DJ 132). Both the argument for the selection of the two principles of justice in the original position and the lexical ordering of those principles so that they yield consistent and plausible results are attempts by Rawls to show how a nonutilitarian philosophy can determine an answer to difficult ethical choices with the same rigor as utilitarianism.[69]

Along the same lines, Rawls wants to show that his basic principles are themselves "well defined," in more or less the sense that mathematicians would use that term. The essay "Distributive Justice" shows this mathematical bent particularly clearly, although the same points can be made about *Theory of Justice*. Rawls tells us that he is looking for a "consistent and complete" conception of justice. These are terms normally used to describe logical systems. It is essential to such systems to be consistent and they seek as much as possible to be "complete," to be such that one can prove true or false all statements that are well formulated in the systems' terms. Rawls defines his principles, moreover, and delineates their domain of application, with a mathematician's precision (DJ 133–134). He then takes up a definition of societal well-being that had already been given mathematical definition—Pareto optimality—and in the course of discussing it makes use of such familiar notions from set theory as "classes" and different kinds of "orderings" (134–137). It is against this background that he introduces his own preferred standard for judging societies (137–138), in which a society will be just if and only if it is that Pareto-optimal society that maximizes the expectations of a representative of its worst-off group. In the course of defending this standard, Rawls brings in additional mathematical terms: "chain-connectedness," "pair-wise comparisons," "close-knitness" (139). With them in hand, he refines his standard and demonstrates how it gives an interpretation of what it means for a society to work to "everyone's" advantage. This process is repeated in greater detail in *Theory of Justice*, where Rawls offers several versions of his famous two principles of justice until finally he arrives at what he claims is their full formulation:

1. Each person is to have an equal right to the most extensive total system of equal basic liberties compatible with a similar system of liberty for all.
2. Social and economic inequalities are to be arranged so that they are both:
    (a) to the greatest benefit of the least advantaged, consistent with the just savings principle, and
    (b) attached to offices and positions open to all under conditions of fair equality of opportunity [the Difference Principle]. (TJ 302)[70]

As the voluminous literature on Rawls suggests, there is much to be said about both the content of these principles and the argument that is supposed to lead us to them. What I want to stress here is just that they amount, as a whole, to a remarkably precise *definition* of "distributive justice" in its modern sense and that the phrase had lacked any such definition before. Rawls himself stresses this aspect of his project. In several places, he notes that such widely cited maxims of distributive justice as the slogan, "From each according to his abilities; to each according to his needs," are, as such, merely unjustified intuitions that cannot serve as a complete theory of justice and that we have no way of rationally balancing when they compete with one another (TJ 304–309). One of Rawls's main reasons for offering a "theory" of justice is precisely to help settle such disputes, to place common sense maxims about justice into a more rigorous intellectual framework.

We can clarify this point by focusing on the slogan about distribution in accordance with needs. One problem with this particular slogan is that it competes, even among socialists, with the quite different slogan, "From each according to his abilities; to each according to his contribution,"[71] and little reason is given for preferring one slogan over the other. Another problem is that "needs" goes undefined in the first slogan. It is also unclear *what* we are distributing "to each." Finally, no account is taken, in this slogan or its competitors, of the potential conflict between liberty and such distributions, of the potential danger that a distributive state poses to freedom. Rawls's two principles, by contrast, together with the argument for them, provide a comprehensive account of (1) what goods should be distributed, (2) what needs those goods satisfy, (3) why needs should be favored over contribution, and (4) how distribution should be balanced against liberty (such that the "distribution" of liberty takes priority over all distribution of economic and social goods). Rawls *organizes* and *explains* the disparate, conflicting intuitions people had had for over a century about the just distribution of goods and thereby provides, for the first time, a sharp definition of distributive justice. This is a major philosophical achievement, comparable to the work of Giuseppe Peano, Richard Dedekind, and Georg Cantor in helping us define natural, real, and transfinite numbers or of Cantor in helping us define sets. In each case, ordinary intuitions about a notion were brought together by a mode of construction that enabled one to account for each element of those intuitions and that illuminated the central properties holding the intuitions together. The thought experiment Rawls proposes in which principles of justice are chosen in an "Original Position" is such a mode of construction, and it organizes and accounts for the otherwise vague and conflicting intuitions we have about distributive justice.

This view of Rawls as like Dedekind or Cantor is quite different from the more common view of him as like Plato or Locke. Plato and Locke provided highly original defenses of a controversial notion of justice; Rawls, as I see him, was more concerned to explicate a notion of justice that in its fundamentals is not particularly controversial. That has certainly been the effect of his work, whether or not it was the intention. Rawls has been tremendously influential even while his attempt to defend the two principles of justice has been widely regarded as unsuccessful. The influence, I think, comes from the fact that he provided such a clear definition of what people were already talking about in the past two centuries, when they talked about "distributive justice."

What Rawls did not do was provide an account of what "justice" has always and everywhere meant. Rawls himself obscures this point when he says that "it is one of the fixed points of our moral judgments that no one deserves his place in the distribution of natural assets [or] . . . his initial starting place in society" (TJ 311; see also 74, 104). If "our," here, refers to "modern Westerners," the sentence may be true (although even that is not so clear). But if the "our" is supposed to be timeless, as it seems to be, if it is supposed to be such that any rational group of human beings could stand in for it at any point in history, then the sentence is false. What I have tried to do in this book is show the history by which the belief that people do not deserve their socioeconomic place has *become* a "fixed point" in most modern people's moral convictions, the history behind a moral intuition that Rawls seems to take as simply given to any rational being. Rawls was superb at clearly defining a notion that rested, until he wrote, mostly on vague intuitions. He was not so good at indicating how those intuitions arose—or that they have arisen, that they have a history, at all.

6. After Rawls

In the past thirty years, there has been an outpouring of writing on distributive justice, mostly responding in some way to Rawls. Even Robert Nozick, whose own work on this subject was devoted to undermining the *Theory of Justice*, said that "[p]olitical philosophers now must either work within Rawls' theory or explain why not" (ASU 183). I will end this history with a very brief look at some of the major directions in which Rawls's work has been taken.

THE SCOPE OF DISTRIBUTION (1): HOW MUCH OF WHAT GOODS?   The two questions that have most preoccupied political theorists working on distributive justice since Rawls are (1) what goods ought to be distributed, and (2) how much of these goods everyone ought to have. These questions are linked. It is fairly obvious that everyone ought to have an equal share of *some* goods (e.g., civil rights) and that it makes no sense to seek an equal distribution of some other goods (e.g., chocolate bars). Once the goods to be distributed are specified in a certain way, however—as units of utility, primary goods, and so on—there remains a question about whether the Difference Principle adequately captures the demands of distributive justice. Perhaps one ought to aim instead either for stricter equality or for some sort of "guaranteed minimum" of these goods, by which no one would fall below a certain level but the inequalities in society could range further than the Difference Principle would allow.[72] Thinkers to Rawls's left have argued that only strict equality allows for equal citizenship in a democracy or properly reflects the equal worth of every human being, while thinkers to Rawls's right have argued that only a guaranteed minimum is required by equal respect for all human beings and that inequalities above that baseline have a variety of social or moral advantages. Other positions about the appropriate level of distribution have also been defended, including Ronald Dworkin's suggestion that the ideal would be a world in which no one envies the "package of resources" anyone else possesses over the course of a lifetime.[73]

A yet livelier debate continues to rage over *what* should be distributed. Should we be distributing what Dworkin calls "resources," or Rawls's primary goods, or should we return to the older notion that the proper object of distribution is happiness (now often called "welfare" or "utility")? Recognizing, with Rawls, that the attempt to distribute happiness (or welfare or utility) is fraught with definitional questions (what exactly *is* "welfare"? to what degree does it depend on what people think they want?), most theorists seek some set of political and material means that we can all agree everyone needs, whatever their ultimate goals. So far, of course, they agree with Rawls; the main reason for Rawls's introduction of primary goods was to shift the focus of distributivist concern from happiness or welfare to the things rational people want whatever else they want (TJ 62, 92). But the post-Rawlsian theorists are unconvinced that "primary goods" are the right substitute for happiness or welfare. Gerald Cohen argues that societies should aim to equalize everybody's "access to advantage."[74] Amartya Sen and Martha Nussbaum maintain that societies ought to be aiming their distributivist policies toward an equalization of people's basic "capabilities."

Dworkin, Cohen, Sen, and Nussbaum can all be described as working within Rawls's project, broadly construed, but Sen and Nussbaum engage with that project more closely than the others. In a 1979 lecture titled, "Equality of What?" Sen launched a trenchant critique of Rawls for not going far enough in recognizing the differences among people: "If people were basically very similar, then an index of primary goods might be quite a good way of judging advantage. But, in fact, people seem to have very different needs varying with health, longevity, climatic conditions, location, work conditions, temperament, and even body size (affecting food and clothing requirements)."[75] Sen agrees with Rawls about the importance of recognizing the heterogeneity of human ends but argues that a focus on primary goods does not adequately do that. Moreover, says Sen, a focus on goods of any sort is a distraction from the central question of what people *do* with those goods: "it can be argued that there is, in fact, an element of 'fetishism' in the Rawlsian framework. Rawls takes primary goods as the embodiment of advantage rather than taking advantage to be a *relationship* between persons and goods."[76] For a Kantian thinker such as Rawls, especially, this is a surprisingly passive construal of "advantage." If we want to emphasize human agency, as Rawls does, we need to be concerned not so much with the goods people have as with their capacities to act. To this, their possession of certain goods may be relevant, but it will not be the whole story. From this insight arises the approach to distribution Sen calls "basic capability equality."[77] A few years later, Martha Nussbaum showed how Aristotle's conception of human nature—modified, somewhat, to overcome the illiberal aspects of Aristotle's thought—could be used to underwrite and enrich this approach,[78] and she has since worked out a list of human capabilities at whose development distributive justice ought to aim.[79] Among other things, she has used this list to combat cultural relativism and demonstrated how a focus on the capacities people ought to have can enable one to address certain deeply entrenched forms of cultural oppression, which distort the very conception individuals may have of their own needs. Nussbaum thereby holds cultures, and not merely states, up to norms of justice.[80]

Sen and Nussbaum's emphasis on agency, like Rawls's, obviously owes a lot to Kant, and we can see in Nussbaum in particular much of the conception of human beings as fraught with potential that I have traced to Kant. Nussbaum herself acknowledges a debt to Marx for his conception of human nature as requiring more than the satisfaction of our animal needs,[81] and I would suggest that she uses, and extends, Marx in her recognition of the many ways that culture, and not merely political or socioeconomic arrangements, can shape human nature. Unlike others who follow Marx in this regard, however, Nussbaum has no tendency to *dissolve* the individual into his or her cultural and social circumstances; her emphasis on individual agency keeps her from that. She is therefore able to make her normative case comfortably in the language of "justice," to use Marxist notions as tools for the development of distributive justice.

THE SCOPE OF DISTRIBUTION (II): WHOSE NEEDS ARE WE RESPONSIBLE FOR? A third question about the scope of distribution concerns the set of people to whom goods ought to be distributed, whatever those goods may be. Rawls assumes that duties of distributive justice are duties that a state owes to its own citizens. This leaves open tricky questions about how states ought to handle the needs of resident aliens or whether a state with a rich welfare program may restrict immigration, and it implicitly denies that anyone owes duties of aid to people across the world. Some writers have preferred to see duties of distributive justice as intrinsically international ones, such that each of us owes aid to poor people everywhere, and have taken Rawls to task for his willingness to work with the nation-state as the basic subject of distributive justice.[82]

THE LIBERTARIAN CHALLENGE   In *Anarchy, State and Utopia*, which appeared a bare three years after *A Theory of Justice*, Robert Nozick offered a view of justice diametrically opposed to Rawls's. Nobody has a right to any material goods other than those she has acquired as private property, Nozick said. Nobody has any right, in particular, to goods designed to place her in a particular material condition:

> The major objection to speaking of everyone's having a right *to* various things such as equality of opportunity, life, and so on, and enforcing this right, is that these "rights" require a substructure of things and materials and actions; and *other* people may have rights and entitlements over these. No one has a right to something whose realization requires certain uses of things and activities that other people have rights and entitlements over. . . . No rights exist in conflict with this substructure of particular rights. . . . The particular rights over things fill the space of rights, leaving no room for general rights to be in a certain material condition. (ASU 238)

Nozick offered a battery of arguments against the concept of distributive justice in general, and against Rawls's conception of distributive justice in particular.[83] Of particular interest is that he pointed out, and put sharply into question, the assumption we have seen running through

Marx, Sidgwick, and Rawls: that society is to be conceived as a "scheme of co-operation" rather than an unplanned, less than fully voluntary coming together of different individuals (ASU 149–150, 183–197, 223). Why should individuals be seen as "shar[ing] one another's fate" (TJ 102)— much less as responsible for what happens to everyone else around them? That person A is well-off and person B badly off need not mean, Nozick points out, that A is well-off *because* B is badly off, much less that A has done anything to *make* B badly off (ASU 191). So it is not clear why A owes anything to B—has a duty of justice to give some of his goods to B—although of course A might freely help B out of kindness or charity.

Nozick also trenchantly argues that any redistributive plan will be constantly disturbed by free gifts and exchanges, hence that redistribution will be impossible without constant interference in people's ability to give and exchange goods. The tension between redistribution and liberty is for Nozick not just an empirical matter, as it was for Hayek and Friedman, arising from the need for redistributing governments to give too much power to bureaucrats, but something rooted in the very goals that distributive justice sets for itself. Nozick distinguishes between "historical" and "patterned" principles of justice: the latter try to shoehorn society into some pattern, some ideal end-state, rather than letting it alone for the individuals who compose it to find their own way to their own different end-states. It is better, if one truly values liberty, to stick to historical principles of justice, principles that govern merely what means people take to their various ends. But "[a]lmost every suggested principle of distributive justice is patterned," which alone gives us reason to avoid those principles (ASU 156).

Nozick's arguments are of varying quality, but some, including the ones I have mentioned, are very strong. What he does not do is provide a strong positive argument for his own notion of justice as giving us rights to particular things on the basis of what we have originally acquired in a Lockean way or received by way of legitimate exchange, gift, and so on. He does not directly defend the claim, embodied in the passage quoted above, that one person's right over the property she already owns must always take precedence over other people's rights to own some minimal level of property, that historical property rights "fill the space of rights." What gives the Nozickean "substructure of particular rights" such absolute priority over all claims *to* various things—some of which may be essential to the claimant's freedom? Why should justice require such a strict conception of property rights?—a far stricter one than traditional natural law theorists ever held.

Nozick is of course continuing a line of thinking that has roots going back a century and more before his work. Earlier I considered the writings of Herbert Spencer, the first philosophical spokesperson for libertarianism, and after Spencer, the economists Mises, Hayek, and Friedman all gave expression to ideas much like those of Nozick. But Nozick is to the libertarianism that preceded him somewhat as Rawls is to the advocates of distributive justice who preceded him: the first person to provide a clear articulation of the position at stake and its implications. He simply does not provide much of an argument to convince anyone of the libertarian position who was not already convinced before reading him. Libertarians have been tremendously inspired by Nozick's work, but they themselves sometimes complain that he did not provide an argument for the fundamental importance of property rights to justice and liberty.[84] No other libertarian has thus far improved much on Nozick in this regard, however. No other libertarian has indeed been nearly as persuasive as Nozick has to nonlibertarians.

EXTENSIONS OF DISTRIBUTIVE JUSTICE   Rawls, his followers, and his critics have all been primarily concerned with the distribution of rights and material goods. In recent years, thinkers of various stripes have begun to ask whether justice might not require some sort of fair distribution of goods quite different from either rights or material things. Inspired, perhaps, by Rawls's intriguing suggestion that the most important primary good is "the social basis of self-respect" (TJ 62, 440), some people have suggested that we need to consider the distribution of *symbolic* goods as well as political and material ones. If the reason we believe in distributive justice, after all, is that we think each individual must have the means to realize his or her capacities for action, then we may need to be concerned about, say, whether an agent who identifies with a particular culture has the linguistic training to express his cultural identification or whether an agent who identifies as lesbian has access to a public space where she can freely express her sexual orientation. Even more important, if we take seriously the notion that people's psychological capacity for making choices can be hindered when society strongly disapproves of some of their options, is the degree to which educational and entertainment institutions create a public environment allowing minorities to feel safe and unashamed in their cultural or other group identities. Hence there may be a serious question of justice about the distribution of educational and media resources.

So, at least, a number of people have argued. Will Kymlicka has called cultural membership a "primary good" and given a Rawlsian argument for liberal states to help preserve disadvantaged minority cultures.[85] Yael Tamir has recommended, on similarly Rawlsian grounds, that states distribute cultural resources equally among their citizens.[86] James Tully notes that when struggles for political recognition succeed, the change in the way the state treats the relevant group "will itself constitute a redistribution of 'recognition capital' (status, respect, and esteem)."[87] Members of the group in question will experience an increase in their psychological well-being, which in itself will help them in their quest for economic and political power. They will in addition find economic and political opportunities newly open to them:

> For example, struggles over equity policies for women, visible minorities, persons with disabilities, Aboriginal people, and immigrants in the public and private sectors over the last thirty years, where successful, not only gave these citizens a form of public recognition. By challenging deeply sedimented racist, sexist, and xenophobic social norms of recognition, they also redistribute access to universities, jobs, promotions, and the corresponding relations of economic power.[88]

The argument that individuals can realize their freedom only when their society provides them with favorable conditions for the development of their capacities can justify a call for a redistribution of "recognition capital" as well as a call for a redistribution of land, income, capital, or primary goods.

In some recent literature, this same argument has been used to suggest that even our *genes* might come to be a subject for distributive justice. As we get closer and closer to being able to clone people and as our genetic engineering holds out the promise of prenatal remedies for many diseases, both physical and mental, a question arises about whether there would be something unjust about wealthy people being able to create better children for themselves while the less well-off remain stuck with the luck of the draw. Norman Daniels has argued that distributive justice makes strong demands on the delivery of health care, and he and others maintain that the benefits of genetic engineering are just like other aspects of health care in this respect.[89] If we are going to have genetic engineering at all, say these theorists, we are going to have to distribute its benefits equally, or at least in accordance with Rawls's Difference Principle. Otherwise, we will have a society in which there will be injustice in the distribution of human "nature" itself.

I report all these developments without comment; I do not mean to endorse them. I do, however, believe that each of them flows from the basic complex of arguments that allowed for Rawls's formulation of distributive justice. If (as Smith, Rousseau, and Kant stressed) all human beings are equally deserving of respect, and if (as Kant argued) respecting human beings means promoting their free agency, and if (as Kant also argued) all human beings have capacities for agency that need development, and if (as Marx maintained) society shapes the degree to which they can develop these capacities and does so in particular by making resources available to them, and if, finally (as Marx and Sidgwick and many others maintained), society is a cooperative effort that we can shape and reshape if we wish, then we *can* remake the distribution of resources in our society so that it better helps all its members develop their capacities, and our obligation to respect other human beings entails that we *should* do so. But once we accept this line of argument, then what resources we redistribute will depend simply on what capacities we regard as essential to human agency. If we think that cultural identification is essential to making choices, then we will need to make sure all citizens have the resources enabling them to form a cultural identity. If we take sexual expression to be a crucial exercise of agency, then distributing the resources necessary for choosing among sexual options will be a concern for justice. If we think that any of the things that genetic engineering promises to accomplish (better health, better looks, better athletic or musical skills) are essential to full freedom, then distributing the resources for everyone to get a good set of genes will also be a task for justice. If, on the other hand, we think that basic liberal rights, education, and protection against poverty are all that an individual needs in order to be free—as I tend to think[90]—then we will not extend distributive justice to symbolic goods, much less to genes.

It will not be altogether easy to settle the debate between those who want a more constricted and those who want a more expansive notion of distributive justice, however, for that debate turns on fundamental issues about the nature of agency and humanity that have not shown themselves readily amenable to philosophical resolution. Moreover, the notion of distributive justice that Rawls finally harvested from the seeds sown by Babeuf is flexible enough to lend itself both to those who want to limit it and to those who want it to grow ever larger and more comprehensive. The task of this book has been to show that this last debate, like its many predecessors, cannot be settled by looking to the content of "distributive justice," stripped of its history, alone.

Epilogue

What have we gained by this short survey of the history of distributive justice? Well, first, it is always interesting to know one's history. It is especially interesting, or so it seems to me, to realize that there have really been *two* notions of "distributive justice" in Western political philosophy, not one, and that the one that begins with Aristotle and peters out in the late eighteenth century contrasts quite sharply with the one formulated, out of a bundle of intuitions that arose in the nineteenth and early twentieth centuries, by John Rawls. But what, more precisely, have we gained *philosophically* by looking at the history of distributive justice? How, if at all, does the history of an idea ever help us understand that idea and defend or criticize it?

I think we do gain something philosophically by examining the history of ideas. First, by looking at the development of the notion of distributive justice, we have had a chance to see just how complex that notion is, how many different ideas needed to be pulled together for it to be fully in place. Until I began to look into the history of the notion, it did not occur to me that to believe in distributive justice one needed to be an individualist *and* to see the poor as deserving of the same social and economic status as everyone else *and* to see society as responsible for the condition of the poor and capable of radically changing it *and* to have secular, rather than religious, justifications for all this. I now think all these pieces do belong to the idea of distributive justice, and while I am ready to believe that some of the figures whose beliefs I have discussed might turn out, on further consideration, to be closer to or farther from the modern notion of distributive justice than I have said, I am fairly confident that the outlines of what we need to look for, when we ask about a person's commitment to distributive justice, are more or less as I have described them. That will, I hope, be an aid to further historical research, but it should also contribute to clarifying the idea of distributive justice for us today.

Second, we gain some insight into the nature of present-day debates about the justification for distributive justice by discovering that the main obstacle to the rise of the modern notion was not, as one might suppose, a belief in the absolutism of property rights, but a belief in the value of keeping the poor in poverty. This is a useful fact historically, but it is also useful insofar as it puts pressure on those who suppose that the case for absolute property rights—vis-à-vis welfare policies in particular—was made long ago and need no longer be defended by those who inherit the liberal tradition. We can see the burdens of argument in this arena more clearly, can see in particular that the strict conception of property rights is not an obvious one, and it needs more defense than it usually receives.

Third, we have seen that in certain crucial respects the development that led to the modern notion of distributive justice was a change in people's sensibilities, not a change in what they knew, how they argued, or what moral theories they held. It was not new arguments or factual discoveries that led people to have a more sympathetic attitude toward the difficulties of the poor, but new ways of presenting the circumstances of poverty, beginning with the writings of Adam Smith and continuing into the explosion of literature about poor people in the nineteenth century. The importance of imaginative literature here, and the priority of changes in sensibility to changes in belief, suggest an intriguing model for how progress in ethical matters comes about. And that model might lead us to think twice about how helpful the sort of thing that today passes for "applied ethics" really is to the solution of ethical problems.

Finally, and a bit more controversially, I believe that by learning the history of a moral idea we gain a better understanding of why we ourselves endorse or reject it. I have argued elsewhere that for most of us, most of the time—even those of us who congratulate ourselves with the name "philosophers"—moral intuitions come down to us from our past with an aura of authority, and we do not actively question them.[1] Others have made much the same point balefully: it is a terrible problem, they think, that we do not examine our lives more fully and subject all our beliefs, especially our moral beliefs, to the test of reason. They see invidious prejudices lurking in this acceptance of moral attitudes on authority;

they see bigotry and small-mindedness. I believe the authoritative passing down of moral beliefs is not normally baleful and is in any case necessary to moral thought—is inevitable and something without which moral discourse would, even in principle, be impossible. We do need to watch out for bigotry and small-mindedness, however, and one of the best ways of doing that is to examine the history of our beliefs.

Systematic moral arguments, whether of the utilitarian, Kantian, or intuitionist variety, normally proceed *from* some of the author's favorite prejudices *to* some of the author's other prejudices (or to a counterintuitive position that one suspects the author holds purely for academic "show"). By failing to confront the authoritative roots of moral belief, such arguments tend merely to reinforce those beliefs. By contrast, learning the history of our ideas estranges them from us and thereby gives us some measure of critical distance from the authority with which they appear to us. That means both that the discovery that a particular idea has roots in something morally ugly may lead us to feel suspicious of it— a good deal of modern-day discomfort with eugenics proposals comes, justifiably I think, from the degree to which eugenics has its origins in programs promoted by social Darwinists in America and Nazis in Europe—and that discovering noble or otherwise admirable sources for an idea may increase our attachment to it. We want to know how fully we can endorse the process by which an idea has reached us, and the discovery that it has roots in a particularly heroic struggle against oppression, say, normally strengthens our endorsement of it.

In the case of distributive justice, specifically, it seems to me that there are moments in its history that we ought to embrace as well as moments that should give us pause. I find the movement of Western culture from an attitude of contempt for the poor to a recognition that they are "just like the rest of us" an unmixed good. The notion that people need certain material means to develop their capacities seems also a wise one to me, and one that has become increasingly true as society and technology have become more complex. The notion that everyone has endless capacities that they need to bring to realization seems to me more problematic, however, part of an excessively demanding conception of the free and happy self. This aspect of the history of distributive justice has also led to more and more expansive claims for what the state ought to do to help people, which may help account for the increasing disfavor with which even minimal versions of distributive justice have been met in recent years. Finally, the notion that society and government are responsible for all suffering and can solve all of it is one that I think we should reject. Surely some aspects of our lives are due simply to luck and some to our individual virtues and vices. In addition, it is unclear to what degree "society" can reasonably be regarded as a conscious agent that can deliberately correct its mistakes or indeed aim coherently at any goal whatsoever. The critique already implicit in Adam Smith, and developed by Hayek, of the very idea that society moves by way of deliberate actions, of the very idea that future states of any society can be successfully predicted, let alone controlled, in any detail, is a powerful one and needs to be borne in mind by those of us who want to help the poor.

Of course, believers in distributive justice do not necessarily endorse every one of its historical connotations. The meaning of an idea is never identical with its genealogy. But ideas tend to be couched in terms that carry connotations from the past in addition to, and independent of, the way they get "officially" defined in each period of their history. Political ideas also serve many functions at the same time. People are drawn to a cause—a slogan, a candidate, a party or movement—by a host of differing concerns and experiences. They might become socialists because they are sickened by the condition of the poor, but they might also become socialists because they dislike the consumerism they associate with capitalism; or because they are pacifists, and the socialists they know portray capitalism as a source of war; or because they see socialism as allied to movements working for racial or gender equality or for free love; or simply because the socialists they know seem "modern" or "enlightened" or "deep." Socialism has in fact been a movement critical of consumerism, war, racial and gender inequality, marriage, and bourgeois culture, partly because there have actually been many different socialisms and partly because the thinkers who have tried most thoroughly to develop a full-blown theory of socialism have argued, rightly or not, that all these seemingly different causes belong together. When someone now proclaims herself a socialist, or, conversely, attacks socialism or particular socialist policies, it is a mistake to assess her claim solely by way of some presumed essential doctrine, some "essence" of socialism. Rather, the word is used properly for a cluster of projects, related to one another by what Wittgenstein called "family resemblance" and not enclosed by any definite border.[2] Something similar goes for free-trade doctrines and for any other political movement. The ideas these movements uphold are linked to one another in complex ways, and it is never entirely clear which particular views are "the" reasons for a given person's belief in the movement, even to the believer him or herself. Socialism "is" all the different ideas that more or less cling together under its rubric, although clearly some are more important to it than others (helping the poor over free love, for instance). Any particular debate between socialists and their opponents may focus more on one issue than another, moreover, and within these contexts "socialism" may mean something that is peripheral to what it means elsewhere; it may mean free love in some contexts, for instance, even though elsewhere there are plenty of socialists who reject free love. So the actual debates in which people enlist a particular political doctrine are crucial to what that doctrine means. (A Wittgensteinian argument can be made that debate brings out what *every* idea means, that *all* claims gain meaning only by what, in practice, they rule out.) Without knowing the particular debates in which they have been used, then, we do not really know our political terms.

One might object that the term "socialism" is a poor example for the point I have been trying to make since it is the name of a movement and movements naturally put together alliances of different causes. However, the same sort of point goes, mutatis mutandis, for all political terms, including our favorite in this book, "distributive justice." The meaning of such terms (again, a Wittgensteinian might reasonably say, "the meaning of *all* terms") is inextricably bound up with their use, and in politics, use is bound up with an array of ever-changing polemics, for or against various laws and institutions. A person comes, often at a young age, to conclude that she believes strongly in distributive justice—or, having been strongly impressed by Spencer or Friedman or Nozick, that she *doesn't* believe in distributive justice—and then files that belief somewhere in her evaluative repertoire, to be taken out, normally without further reflection, when she needs to make decisions about participating in political activities of a certain sort. She might need to make such decisions all the time, if she becomes a full-time politician or political activist—but even then, she is likely to be far too busy with actual vote-getting or demonstrating to have much time to think further about her basic ideas—or these issues may only occasionally come up for her, if most of her life is taken up with, say, business or laboratory science. In either case, she is unlikely to examine and re-examine the nature or justification of distributive justice. Unless she takes up political philosophy as a profession, she is likely to consider the idea in any depth only at that first moment when she embraces or rejects it.

What might she think at that decisive moment? That distributive justice makes sense only if one believes in the moral equality of all human beings, the need of all human beings for individual freedom, the dependence of such freedom on certain material goods, and the feasibility of having the state guarantee the distribution of these goods? Unlikely. Most people will be struck by, for instance, the oppressive circumstances of poor people in the American inner city and, in their sympathy, find "distributive justice" to be a good way of expressing what they would like to see done for these people. Or they will feel angry at pictures of homeless children or at stories in the newspapers about people dying of easily cured illnesses because they have no health care. Or they will be disgusted by the outrageous wealth flaunted by some people in Beverly Hills or Manhattan. And what do they *mean*, then, by the "distributive justice" they embrace? They may not know exactly. They certainly mean that people ought not to live, generation after generation, in the conditions that the poor have to put up with in American cities, that all children should have a roof over their heads, or that enormous luxury is unjustifiable where others are barely surviving, but they need not have any worked-out theory of how the evils they see connect to one another or should be cured. As each person joins the historical chain of those who have believed in distributive justice (or disbelieved in it), she need not know exactly what she has connected herself to. The history of the idea, as well as its broader use at the moment she grabs onto it, give it connotations that she need not consciously share.

I do not mean by this to endorse a fully emotivist conception of our moral commitments, but a large part of the truth about what we believe morally is, surely, that we *feel* that certain goals or actions or principles are good ones and that others are evil. We do not, however, regard as morally good something that we merely feel positively about at one moment; we condemn some of our own feelings of approval as misguided. To approve of something morally, we need both to feel that it is good and to endorse our own feeling, on reflection, as a well-informed, decent feeling to have. It is here that the history both of our individual feelings, and of the feelings that have produced a value across our society can be very important. If I reflect on my love for a person, a movement, or an idea and feel that it is the product of my own self-loathing, alcoholism, or ignorance, then I will probably turn against the feelings that led me to endow that person, movement, or idea with worth. I may be able to pick out these emotive failures fairly easily in my own individual life. Far subtler are the feelings of which I *would* disapprove if I knew their genealogy but in which the problems with the feeling's source lie in my society's past. My feelings are in large part shaped by the feelings of those around me, so even when I think I have come to a particular value in a clear-eyed and healthy manner, it may be that I have merely absorbed the prejudices or pathologies of my friends and neighbors. When I discover that the feelings leading most people in my society, and me by way of the influence of others, to endorse a certain value—a condemnation of homosexuality, say, or of Muslims or Jews—are ill informed or shaped by a narrow fear, then I am likely to withdraw my endorsement of those feelings. I am likely to feel that those feelings are unworthy of me and that I should try not to have them. When I discover, on the contrary, that the history of a feeling endorsed by my society is an admirable one, my own endorsement of it will probably be strengthened.

Of course, it can always turn out that a value that started out expressing one feeling and endorsing one type of action later comes to express and endorse something quite different. Values, like institutions, may shift their social role once they have been established. The survival of values and institutions is overdetermined, and they can easily outlive their original functions. But at the least we want to know how any given value has come to mean what we thought we accepted when we embraced it. If, on studying its history, we see it consistently expressing feelings or serving purposes different from those we took it to have, then we may need to conclude that we misunderstood it—that it is either a different value from what we took it to be or a blind taboo that now survives in our society's consciousness despite the fact that it lacks any morally useful function. On my account of how values are passed down—such that the transmission process is largely a blind, not a rational one—values should quite often drift from their original function without most of us even noticing. History provides a good corrective to this blindness, letting us know what has happened to our values while we have had our backs turned to them. We wake up from the semiconscious obeisance that we give in our ordinary lives to the importance of distributive justice—or to its unimportance if we are semiblind libertarians instead of semiblind welfare liberals—when we look at the notion's history, when we see how that value has arrived in our midst. We learn something about who we are as evaluative beings, what factors have, without our being fully aware of them, drifted into our evaluative framework. And then, whether we begin to question the idea or we embrace it more fully, we are clearer about *what* we believe.

If all this is correct, however, it will be a serious error for systematic moral philosophers to ignore the history of moral philosophy. I take for granted that all moral philosophers need somehow to mesh their theories with our pretheoretic moral intuitions. But in that case, when a moral philosopher sets out to draw, for instance, a rigorous theory of distributive justice out of the intuitions we already have on that subject, he is liable to two major difficulties if he simply takes those intuitions as they appear to him. First, he may mistake the *content* of the idea he is trying to explain: the history of the idea might have let him know that rather different intuitions go into it than he supposed, that he, like the rest of the society from which he has imbibed the idea, has taken on board thoughts and attitudes of which he is at best only dimly aware. Second, he may mistake the way in which the idea *works,* the larger moral view into which this particular value fits. Thus if we invoke "distributive justice" to express our dismay about lazy heirs living high on the hog while hard-working people live in penury, it is surely true, as Rawls supposes, that we implicitly have a general principle according to which luck should not determine one's life chances. But it may or may not be true, as Rawls also supposes, that we therefore regard people's talents and willingness to work hard in the same light as their inherited wealth. We may or may not extend our intuitions in this way, may or may not regard genetic inheritance as we do capital inheritance.

A look at the history out of which we came to reject the notion that the heirs of the rich and powerful are automatically entitled to wealth and power in fact does not support the Rawlsian extension of that intuition. Those, such as Smith, Kant, and Beaumarchais, who were most opposed to inherited social status, were at the same time enthusiastic about a society in which "talent, industry, and luck" would be the primary basis for social and economic advancement.[3] This does not show that Rawls is *wrong* to regard talent and the impulse to industry as arbitrary, morally irrelevant characteristics, but it does suggest that he needs to provide an argument to move us from our shared intuitions about the arbitrariness of inherited wealth to his own intuition about the arbitrariness of inherited skills. He should not merely assume, as he does, that we already share his intuition.

The systematic moral philosopher and the historian of moral philosophy need to work together. Good history must pay close attention to the arguments at work in the development of moral ideas, and good systematic moral thought needs a firm grasp on what exactly has gone into the intuitions with which it begins. This book has been devoted primarily to the way ideas arise and change, but not, I hope, at the expense of systematic concerns. The history of distributive justice is incomprehensible without the arguments that have surrounded it. But the arguments that surround it, now and in the past, are also obscured if we do not properly grasp its history.

Notes

Introduction

1. John Roemer, *Theories of Distributive Justice,* p. 1.
2. Bronislaw Geremek, *Poverty,* p. 20 (quoting from the *Life of St Eligius*).
3. On *haqq,* see Clifford Geertz, *Local Knowledge,* part 3. *Tzedek* is one of several Hebrew terms for "justice" (*mishpat* and *din* are two other important ones), all of which are usually associated, in biblical and rabbinic literature, primarily with the prevention of robbery and fraud, especially to the poor, and with fairness in court proceedings. All of the terms listed are concerned with the protection of individuals against physical harm and theft at the hands either of other individuals or of corrupt judges, but they otherwise differ in many ways.
4. Premise 2 can be characterized as saying that justice demands some distribution in accordance with needs, rather than with merits alone. This is a fairly common way of putting the point, and few people recognize the novelty of the idea that needs can give rise to a claim of justice or recognize how odd that would have sounded to the tradition of moral and political philosophy that begins with Aristotle. One philosopher who does recognize the novelty of this idea is D. D. Raphael, in *Concepts of Justice,* pp. 235–238. (I think Raphael overstates the degree to which this claim was anticipated, however, in biblical and medieval writers; both the Hebrew term *tzedakah* and the term *ius* in the particular texts he cites are best understood as what Aristotle calls "universal justice"—righteousness in general—not as justice in the strict, political and legal sense.) A philosopher who comes to grips with the oddity, conceptually, of the notion that need might be a basis of just claims is David Miller, in *Social Justice,* Chapter 4. Miller's account is both wise and perspicuous, but some of the perplexities in which he and his interlocutors find themselves could have been clarified, I think, by a historical look at the way need found its way into the notion of justice.
5. An argument that Plato's republic is fundamentally oriented toward the good of its individual citizens can be found in Rachana Kamtekar, "Social Justice."

6. Aristotle, *Politics*, I.5, 1254b20–1254b21. On Plato, see *Republic* 420b–421c, 463a–463b and Kamtekar, "Social Justice."

7. A cautionary note here about attitudes in non-Western societies. There have certainly been societies far less committed to social hierarchy than was the medieval Christian West, and in which the poor were better and more respectfully treated. In the Jewish world, for instance, poor people were understood to have a legal right to at least some forms of aid (see *Matanot Aniyim* I.8, IV.12, VII.8 in Maimonides' *Mishneh Torah*, Book Seven), inquiry into whether the poor were "deserving" or not was discouraged (P. T. *Peah* 37b [translated in Brooks, *Peah*, p. 327] but Maimonides, *Mishneh Torah*, VII.6 is somewhat less generous; contrast the Christian practices described in Chapter 1, Section 5), and Maimonides famously said that helping a poor person out of necessity altogether was the highest form of charity (ibid., X.7; contrast the attitudes toward the poor described in Chapter 2, Section 2). These practices do not mean that Jews believed in anything like the need for the state to abolish poverty, but they do suggest that one would have to tell a rather different story if one were looking at a world other than the one of European Christianity and its Greco-Roman forebears. I shall not do that; this book is a history of distributive justice in the West, both because that is what I know best and because the notion most people call "distributive justice" today, wherever they live and whatever culture they claim to uphold, is the Western one, the one that originates, according to the account I shall offer here, in late eighteenth-century France.

8. Richard Kraut takes even Aristotle's characterization of "universal justice" to be directed against Plato, and he provides nuanced and deep ways to distinguish Aristotle's universal justice from what the *Republic* calls "justice" (Kraut, *Aristotle*, pp. 121–122; see also pp. 102–125 as a whole, which constitute the best analysis I have seen of universal justice). But I think he overdoes the distinction. It is true but misleading to say that for Plato justice "at bottom . . . exists entirely within each person" (121, 100) or to suggest that for Aristotle but not for Plato justice "is a virtue that by its nature bears on one's relations to others" (121). In the *Republic* justice is rooted in a state of one's soul, and it is on that basis that Plato can respond to Glaucon's and Adeimantus's challenge that acting unjustly might be good for the unjust agent. But Plato takes pains to justify his intrapersonal definition of justice by arguing that it is precisely and only an agent with the internal state he describes who will consistently behave toward others in ways that accord with the more common, interpersonal meaning of "justice" (442e–444a). So, for Plato as for Aristotle, justice by its nature bears on one's relations to others, and for Aristotle as for Plato, an internal state of full virtue is the best guarantee that one's relations with others will be just. It therefore seems

reasonable to me to take Aristotle's characterization of universal justice as "complete virtue" (NE V.1, 1129b26–1130a13)—which occurs in a paragraph that alludes to the *Republic*—to be mostly a nod toward Plato rather than a criticism of him. The beginning of *Nichomachean Ethics* V.2 then marks a sharp break with Plato, as Aristotle announces that what we generally mean by "justice" is not complete virtue but a particular element of it, and proceeds to investigate this "particular" justice in the rest of Book V with nary another mention of universal justice (it returns briefly in Chapter 11).

Even if Kraut is entirely right, moreover, Aristotle's "universal justice" will be broad enough to include charity among its constituents. Thus when Aristotle's Christian followers say that universal justice requires giving sustenance to the poor, they mean nothing more than that *charity* requires giving such sustenance.

9. Augustine, *City of God*, Book XIX, Chapter 21, pp. 951–952.

10. Vitoria, "On the American Indians," Question 2, Article 4, Question 3, Article 5 (pp. 265–272, 287–288).

11. *Metaphysics of Morals*, Part 1, Introduction, §C; Rawls, *Political Liberalism*, especially Lectures I, IV, and VI.

12. See discussion of these slogans in Chapter 3, Sections 3 and 5.

13. Terence Irwin, who translates *axia* as "worth," comments: "I may deserve and be entitled to unemployment pay because I am out of work, but being out of work is hardly part of my worth" (Irwin, *Nicomachean Ethics*, p. 326).

14. Chapter 2, §3. For Kant's use of the language of "merit" or "worth," see his *Foundations of the Metaphysics of Morals*, pp. 435–436.

15. Wittgenstein, *Philosophical Investigations*, §69.

16. "[T]he men who fight and die for Italy enjoy the common air and light, indeed, but little else; houseless and homeless they wander about with their wives and children. . . . [T]hey fight and die to support others in wealth and luxury, and though they are styled masters of the world, they have not a single clod of earth that is their own" (Plutarch, *Tiberius Gracchus*, pp. 165–166). Of course, Gracchus's argument here can easily be couched in terms of Aristotelian distributive justice—the soldiers deserve land because of their service to the state; their neediness alone would not give them a rightful claim. Still, this recognition of merits in the poor, and appeal to fairness as a ground for state distribution of material resources, is very unusual in the premodern world. (I thank Dan Brudney for stressing the importance of this quotation to me.)

    On More, see Chapter 1, Section 4.

17. Wittgenstein, *Philosophical Investigations*, §67.

1. From Aristotle to Adam Smith

1. See *Theory of Moral Sentiments*, p. 269 and the footnote on that page.
2. Winch, *Riches and Poverty*, p. 100.
3. Griswold, *Adam Smith and the Virtues of Enlightenment*, p. 250.
4. Strictly speaking, this first sense of justice for Aristotle incorporates all virtuous actions that relate to *other people*, thus including brave and temperate acts insofar as they affect other people but excluding those and other virtues insofar as they simply lead us to develop ourselves. But this refinement will not matter to us here.

   For an argument that Aristotle's "universal justice" is importantly different from what Plato calls "justice," see Kraut, *Aristotle*.
5. Aristotle may have intended to have yet a third kind of particular justice: what he calls "reciprocal justice" in Book V, Chapter 5. Reciprocal justice is supposed to apply to market exchanges, and it is indeed under this heading that the medieval notion of a "just price" developed. But medieval thinkers tended to assimilate reciprocal to corrective justice, calling them together "commutative justice" (justice in exchange, where market activity was voluntary exchange and crime was, for one party certainly, involuntary exchange). In any case, reciprocal justice would not belong under distributive justice: either it is sui generis or it belongs under corrective justice. See the excellent discussions in J. W. Baldwin, *Medieval Theories of the Just Price*, pp. 11–12, 63–64; D. D. Raphael, *Concepts of Justice*, pp. 57–58; and Sarah Broadie and Christopher Rowe, *Aristotle*, pp. 339, 343.
6. In Rawls's terms (see Introduction), the Aristotelian concept of distributive justice requires distribution according to merit, and the conceptions under it differ over the kind of merit relevant to, for example, political distributions.

   Kraut says that "Aristotle... ignores the point that sometimes distributions are based not on merit, but on some other criterion" (Kraut, *Aristotle*, p. 146). According to Kraut, "If food and other resources are available for distribution to the needy, then justice requires that larger amounts be given to those who have greater needs." But it is not quite right to say that Aristotle simply ignores this point, as if he would have accepted it had he thought to discuss it. The texts suggest strongly, rather, that he would not have accepted it, that distributive justice, for him, is *essentially* tied to merit and not to need. Christian followers of Aristotle certainly took distributive justice to be governed by a norm of merit rather than need: if A needed shoes more badly than B, but B was more virtuous than A, then it was B, not A, who was considered to "deserve" the shoes. And a straightforward reading of what Aristotle says about distributive justice suggests that he would have endorsed this account.

7. See, for instance, *Politics* III.6–13 and VI.2–3.

8. He discusses other proposals for distributing property in II.7 and again does not consider them under the rubric of justice.

9. It may seem that what I say here is in tension with Martha Nussbaum's argument that for Aristotle "[t]he aim of political planning is the distribution to the city's individual people of the conditions in which a good human life can be chosen and lived" (Nussbaum, "Nature, Function, and Capability," p. 145). But Nussbaum's emphasis, when explicating Aristotle as opposed to developing her own view of distributive justice, is on the claims (1) that a conception of the good human life is necessary for politics, and (2) that Aristotle often, and perhaps generally, maintains that states should aim at helping each individual and not the society taken as some sort of organic whole (ibid., pp. 155–160). She does not mean to say that Aristotle favored a redistribution of property and indeed warns against reading any such modern agenda into her interpretation of Aristotle. Defending her use of the term "distributive conception" for her view of Aristotle, she says, " 'Distributive' seems therefore the best word that can be found. But it is certainly not ideal; among other things, it might be taken to contain the suggestion that the goods to be arranged belong to the government, or to the lawgiver, antecedently, and that he or she is in consequence playing the role of beneficent donor. It also might be taken to suggest that the end result will be some sort of private ownership of the goods in question. Both of these suggestions would be misleading where Aristotle's theory is concerned. His view about the antecedent situation of the goods is extremely unclear, but he certainly does not take them to belong to the 'state'; and he investigates as candidates numerous forms of arrangement that involve at least some common ownership and/or common use" (ibid., p. 147, note 2).

10. Cicero, *De Officiis*, I.20–59, III.21–28.

11. Nussbaum, "Duties of Justice, Duties of Material Aid," now a chapter in *The Cosmopolitan Tradition*.

12. Nussbaum, "Duties," 189–191.

13. *De Officiis*, 1.20.

14. *De Officiis*, 1.51–52 and *De Finibus*, II.117, III.62–63.

15. *Summa Theologiae*, II-II, Q 61, A2; see also A1 and A3.

16. Jerome Schneewind (*Invention of Autonomy*, pp. 78–80) and Knud Haakonssen (*Natural Law and Moral Philosophy*, pp. 26–30) both claim that Grotius introduced the distinction between "perfect" and "imperfect" rights. Grotius does lay out the basis for this distinction (LWP 35–36) but never quite uses the terms "perfect right" and "imperfect right." He talks instead of "a legal right properly or strictly so called" and something less than that, which he calls an "aptitude." Is the something less meant to be a right as

well, just not a legal one, or not a "proper or strict" legal one? Or is it supposed to be something different in kind—a moral claim that could not, in principle, enter the legal realm? Grotius does not say, and does not use the word "right" for his aptitudes. The latter seem, however, not to be rights at all, just to be a sort of moral quality that, *if perfected,* would count as a "faculty" and hence as a right (I.I.iv–v). There are, we might say, only perfect rights for Grotius, along with moral claims that do not quite rise to the status of a right. So to call the latter "imperfect rights" is misleading: it looks too much as if they have some sort of legal status, which is precisely what Grotius wants to deny them. For Grotius, a claim either is or is not a "right"; the phrase "perfect right" is redundant, and he does not use it. It is Pufendorf who first uses the phrases "perfect right" and "imperfect right"—and he intends for the latter to have a quasi-legal status (see my discussion later in this chapter).

17. Schneewind, *Invention,* pp. 79–80.
18. *Law of War and Peace,* I:3, 37; II.xii.ix.2, 347–348; II.xxv.ii.3, 579; III.xiii.iv.1, 759–760.
19. Ibid., I.ii.viii.2–10, 71–75; II.i.xiii.1, 182.
20. *Law of Nature and Nations,* I.i.3–4, 5–6. All "moral entities" must be imposed on reality, for Pufendorf, although some are imposed by human beings and some by God. See also Schneewind, *Invention,* 121–122.
21. Pufendorf is the first to make the so-called "right of necessity" an extension of beneficence rather than a matter of strict justice. Hont and Ignatieff rightly point this out in "Needs and Justice," pp. 30–31. But they fail to note that Pufendorf also brings beneficence in general closer to justice—makes it more of a law-governed virtue—than his predecessors had done. So he does not weaken the right of necessity as much as it may appear.
22. Locke's account of property rights, by which labor provides the original and primary basis of all claims to property, was to be embraced fervently by eighteenth- and nineteenth-century worker advocates. The claim that property can be traced to labor does lend itself to arguments that the working poor deserve more than they receive. Locke himself, far more interested in the rights of landowners than the rights of workers, argued in the opposite direction: that anyone who received any sort of goods, from the state or from charitable individuals, needed to be made to work. His idea of a solution to the poverty problem was to make England's poor laws yet harsher and more punitive than they already were, to set up institutions that would make sure everyone on relief worked, including children over the age of three; see his "Draft of a Representation Containing a Scheme of Methods for the Employment of the Poor." (A. J. Simmons discusses Locke's view of charity

thoughtfully, and more sympathetically than I have done, in *Lockean Theory of Rights*, Chapter 6.)

Still, Locke contributed, if unwittingly, to an important change in the notion of merit. The sort of merit that Aristotle had in mind when he discussed the distribution of goods was aristocratic merit: virtuous achievement, by which one might deserve honor, or political skill (*phronesis*), by which one might deserve political office. To a lesser extent, he may have considered the merits by which artists claim honors and the "merit" that accrues to one member of a business partnership when he or she puts more capital or effort into the joint venture in question. The sorts of things that laborers did were, however, demeaning rather than meritorious, on the Aristotelian view, and were certainly not a primary, let alone the sole, basis on which claims to social status and material goods should be based. Locke, implicitly at least, upends this aristocratic conception of merit.

Note that Lockean merit will still give at most the working poor a claim on a certain share of material goods. That anyone, by virtue of being human, could merit material support is a notion that did not receive wide acceptance until the twentieth century. Only the latter, however, will give children, the disabled, and the unemployed a right to aid. (See also Introduction, p. 14.)

23. As Dan Brudney has pointed out to me, Locke speaks of an individualized "title" to charity here and a few sentences earlier even mentions "a Right" of the needy to the "Surplusage" of wealthier people's goods. But it seems clear from context that the "title" or "right" in question is, first, a moral rather than a legal right and, second, a right merely to what a person needs to keep himself from starvation. Locke is thus talking about the right of necessity, so it is more striking that he treats even that as a matter of "charity" than that he speaks of it as a right (although his claim that it is a matter of "charity" accords with Pufendorf's view; see note 21).

Confusion about this passage in Locke thus arises if one fails to notice that he is talking about what natural law theorists call the "right of necessity" (see this chapter, Section 2). A similar confusion can arise with other early modern writers. Thomas Hobbes declares it to be against a law of nature "to strive to retain those things which to himselfe are superfluous, and to others necessary" (*Leviathan*, Chapter 15, ¶ 17) but makes clear in the next sentence that by "necessary" he means only what a person requires "for his conservation." It is not a law of nature for Hobbes that the rich should in general support the poor, simply that they should give of their abundance when a poor person would otherwise not survive. (Hobbes's views on state support for the poor are much like Locke's: see *Leviathan*, Chapter 30, ¶¶ 18 and 19.)

Similarly, Thomas Reid maintains that the natural right of property should be constrained by the "right of an innocent man to the necessaries of life," to what is needed for "present and certain necessity." He defends this claim by saying that "[a]s, in a family, justice requires that the children who are unable to labour, and those who, by sickness, are disabled, should have their necessities supplied out of the common stock, so, in the great family of God, of which all mankind are the children, justice, I think, as well as charity, requires, that the necessities of those who, by the providence of God, are disabled from supplying themselves, should be supplied from what might otherwise be stored for future wants" (*Active Powers*, V.5, pp. 423–424). D. D. Raphael takes this to be an anticipation of modern arguments for the justice of the welfare state in *Concepts of Justice*, p. 236. But while it might be useful to employ Reid's analogy today to clarify or defend what we call distributive justice, Reid himself clearly means to defend nothing more than the traditional right of necessity (this is especially clear when the passage is read in context, which argues for other, classically accepted features of the natural law account of property rights).

24. George Clarke (ed.), *John Bellers*, pp. 55, 86, 88. Born in 1654, Bellers wrote "the most detailed collection of papers on education, social and economic reform to be issued by anyone during the seventeenth century" (Clarke, *John Bellers*, p. 80), and his proposal to establish "colleges of industry"—little villages where the poor could find lodging, employment, education, fellowship, and protection against legal and medical calamities—went far beyond the almshouses and poor relief of his day. They looked forward instead to Robert Owen's utopian communities in the beginning of the nineteenth century and Ebenezer Howard's "Garden Cities" in the beginning of the twentieth. In many ways, Bellers anticipated the notion that society both can and should reorganize itself so as to eliminate the entire condition of poverty. Yet even he did not couch his proposals in the language of justice, did not appeal to any right the poor might have to the elimination of poverty. On the contrary, he called his proposals, over and over again, a better form of charity (48–49, 55, 88), noting, when speaking to his fellow Quakers, that their charitable works enabled them to "shew forth . . . the Christianity of [our] Faith" (48). He also expressed concern that "the Bodies of many poor, which might and should be Temples for the Holy Ghost to dwell in, are the Receptacles so much of Vice and Vermine" (88) and recommended his proposals by saying that they might remove "the Profaneness of Swearing, Drunkenness, etc. with the Idleness and Penury of many in the Nation; which evil Qualities of the Poor, are an Objection with some against this Undertaking, though with others a great Reason for it: For the worse they are, the more need of endeavouring to mend them" (55; see also 52). Far from proclaiming aid to

the poor to be something that the poor deserve, Bellers was only too ready to acknowledge that they were undeserving in their present state, and to hope that giving them aid might help make them more deserving. In a very Christian way, salvation precedes claims of justice for Bellers. Welfare programs can display the overflow of love Christians receive from God, and that overflow is dispensed as a blessed being bestows kindnesses on undeserving inferiors, not as one group of human beings might help their equals achieve what is owed them.

25. Hutcheson, *Short Introduction,* II.iv.v.

26. Ibid., II.ii.iii.

27. Ibid.

28. Hont and Ignatieff associate the right of necessity with distributive justice in "Needs and Justice" p. 29. It is commutative, not distributive, justice that handles matters of property in the natural law tradition (see, e.g., ST II-II Q61 A1, A3, Q62A1).

29. Aquinas does imply here, and say explicitly in *Summa Theologiae,* II-II Q66 A2, that one purpose of property rights is to enable each person to tend to the needs of others. He quotes Ambrose here, and 1 Timothy 6:17–18 in A2, to the effect that rich people owe bread to the hungry and clothing to the naked. Yet this "owing" does not amount to an obligation of justice: the rich are stewards of the world's goods, and one of the duties of their stewardship is to help the poor satisfy their needs, but since "those who suffer want are so numerous" (A7), it is up to the judgment and will of each rich person to determine to whom to give and how much to give. There is no sense in which any particular poor person, or group of poor people, has a right to the rich person's property, in normal cases, such that they can demand the use of that property or direct the rich person as to how he or she ought to use it. The duty Ambrose and Timothy impose on the rich is a duty of charity, for which one can be called to account by God and God's law, but not by human beings and their law.

30. He treats this right, structurally, very similarly to the way he treats a right to overthrow the government. The latter gets placed in a reply to an objection, at the end of an article whose general thrust is that "sedition is always a mortal sin"—and the reply argues that tyranny, because it defeats the purpose of all government, is actually not a government at all, so overthrowing it is not sedition (ST II-II, Q42, A2, R3). Again, Aquinas needs the entire normal order of justice to collapse before he dispenses with the rules that, he believes, should hold absolutely, and again, he sees himself as not really waiving those rules, since they have already lost their proper grounds and domain of application.

31. Here I have revised mildly the Blackfriars translation, which has "starving"

instead of "hungry" (the Latin is *famis*), in accordance with the translation to be found in *The Political Ideas of St. Thomas Aquinas,* since "starving" means "dying of hunger" in ordinary English, which is precisely the case where Aquinas thinks the right of necessity *does* apply.

32. It is not entirely clear what justification he is giving for this claim since it is not entirely clear what justification he gives for the entire order of property. At times he implies that, like Aquinas, he sees individual ownership as justified by its effectiveness in meeting human needs, hence that such ownership is trumped when urgent and desperate needs cannot be met via normally owned goods. But there are also strong hints of a Hobbesian justification of property, as a sort of concession to human ambition and selfishness made to prevent constant struggle (II.ii.3–5, 188–189), in which case the reservation in cases of need is presumably made because violence would return if one insisted on property rights in such cases. "[I]n respect to all human laws— the law of ownership included," says Grotius, "supreme necessity seems to have been excepted." And he quotes Seneca: "Necessity, the great source of human weakness, breaks every [human] law" (LWP II.vi.2, 4, 193–194). On this line of reasoning, however, the justification for the right of necessity does not hang on anything peculiar to the laws of property.

33. Pufendorf incorporates the same kinds of conditions on the right of necessity: "[S]ince only an unavoidable necessity allows one to use force in claiming what is owed by an imperfect obligation, it is obvious that every effort should be made to see whether a necessity can be avoided in some other way . . . ; for instance, by seeking a magistrate, promising restitution, when once the current of our fortune begins to move more gently, or by offering our services in exchange" (LNN II.vi.6, p. 305).

34. MacIntyre, *Whose Justice? Which Rationality?,* p. 307.

35. In most of these cases, an entire society is threatened by a crisis rendering its justice system pointless, so one might think that they show nothing about whether an *individual* might ever have moral cause to set aside his or her society's rules of justice. But in one case (E 187), Hume talks of an individual "virtuous man" who falls among "ruffians" and then has, Hume thinks, a right to do whatever it takes in order to survive. So Hume does endorse the right of necessity in its traditional, individuated form, albeit for reasons that might make him loath to describe this moral permission as a "right," strictly speaking. But his view is not really far from that of Grotius, who quotes Seneca to the effect that "[n]ecessity . . . breaks every human law" and defends the right of necessity on the basis that the people who originally set up the system of property would have agreed that that system should not hold in times of great necessity (LWP 193–194; see note 32). We might say that for Grotius the suspension of property in times of necessity is just while

for Hume it is morally right for justice itself to be suspended, but given the close tie between property and justice in both writers, this is not much of a distinction.

36. I again here use the translation in *Political Ideas of St. Thomas Aquinas.* The Blackfriars translation does not have the word "communicate," although that word appears in the Latin and provides the link Aquinas wants to make to 1 Timothy.

37. The first case concerns homicide in the case of a shipwreck and the third harm caused to innocent citizens in the course of war—but these are standard cases in which the right of necessity was held to apply in the writings of Grotius and his followers. Smith clearly both knew and accepted the right of necessity in the jurisprudential tradition.

38. Hont and Ignatieff say that for post-Grotian thinkers the right of necessity was an "exception" to the rules of property rather than an ongoing, structural feature of those rules (NJ 25–26, 29), while it constituted a permanent, structural feature of justice for Aquinas. But this is not true. Necessity constituted an exception to property rules for Aquinas as well.

39. Smith of course did propose that a free market in corn would more effectively prevent famine than laws policing the grain market. However, it is false to say, as Hont and Ignatieff do, that Smith differed with James Steuart and the Abbé Galiani over whether the price of food "should be regulated, [even] in times of grave necessity . . . , by the government" (NJ 14), that Smith, unlike Galiani, insisted that any attempt to stabilize food prices in the short term would "jeopardize . . . a long-term solution to the recurring crises in agricultural productivity" (NJ 17, 14–18). In fact, he explicitly allowed for the regulation of the price of bread in some cases: "Where there is an exclusive corporation [of bakers], it may perhaps be proper to regulate the price of this first necessary of life" (WN 158). Similarly, he declared that a small country in conditions of dearth may legitimately forbid the exportation of corn (WN 539; see discussion in Fleischacker, *On Adam Smith's Wealth of Nations*).

40. "Community of goods is said to be part of the natural law, not because it requires everything to be held in common . . . : but because the distribution of property is a matter . . . [for] human agreement, which is what positive law is about" (ST II-II, Q66, A2, R1). Natural law, that is, permits individual ownership of goods but leaves it up to positive law to determine exactly how such ownership should proceed. From the standpoint of natural law alone, goods are ownerless rather than owned in common: Aquinas holds what gets called in later literature a "negative community" rather than a "positive community" view of goods in the state of nature (and Grotius, Pufendorf, and Locke follow him on this). See Richard Tuck, *Natural Rights Theories*, pp. 20–

22. According to Tuck, it was a member of Aquinas's rival Franciscan order, Duns Scotus, who most powerfully formulated the view by which natural law opposes individual property rights for people in a state of innocence (presumably it is our sinful condition—our irremediable selfishness and jealousy of one another—that requires us to split up the world in this way). Even Scotus, on Tuck's reading, does not say that originally the world was held in positive community, as a collective possession of all human beings: "Common use, for Scotus, was not common dominium: it was not the case that the human race collectively had the kind of right over the world which (say) a Benedictine monastery had over its estates. Rather each human being was simply able to take what he needed, and had no right to exclude another from what was necessary for him" (21). So even Scotus does not claim that human beings originally lived in a "positive community," and indeed, Pufendorf, who puts a good deal of effort into laying out the sources of "positive community" views, attributes them to Virgil, Seneca, Ovid, and other poets, but not to Scotus (LNN IV.iv.8–9; 542–547).

41. Tuck, *Natural Rights Theories,* p. 20.

42. Hont and Ignatieff say similarly, on p. 29, that Grotius "so reduc[ed] the scope of distributive justice that the right of theft in necessity or the right to buy grain at a fair price—rights of desert and claims of need—were theorized as exceptions, rather than as rules, as they had been in Thomist jurisprudence." Both as regards fair price and as regards the right of theft in necessity, they again get Thomas exactly wrong. Aquinas theorized the right of necessity as precisely an exception rather than a rule, and he certainly did not include it in the domain of distributive justice. Both the right of necessity and the just price belonged under the heading of commutative justice for Thomas (on "just prices," see ST II-II, Q61, A2, A3, Q77, A1, and Baldwin, *Medieval Theories,* pp. 62–63, 71–80).

43. Hont and Ignatieff note that this point appears in almost exactly the same terms in economic pamphlets of Locke's day, but that "in none of this economic pamphleteering was the paradox posed as a problem of justice—of reconciling property claims against need claims" (42). But for Locke, too, it was not a problem of justice.

44. It is worth noting that this was published four years before Rousseau's *Second Discourse.* Indeed, when Rousseau wrote the *Second Discourse,* he was still a great admirer of Hume and may have used some of Hume's terms to set up his critique of property.

45. The passage does not quite call the unequal distribution of goods, by which those who work hardest get the least, "unfair." In an early draft of the *Wealth of Nations,* however, Smith does say that "[s]upposing . . . that the produce of the labour of the multitude was to be equally and fairly divided, each indi-

vidual, we should expect, could be little better provided for than the single person who laboured alone. But with regard to the produce of the labour of a great society there is never any such thing as a fair and equal division. In a society of an hundred thousand families, there will perhaps be one hundred who don't labour at all, and who yet, either by violence or by the more orderly oppression of law, employ a greater part of the labour of the society than any other ten thousand in it" (ED 563–564).

46. Sometimes an "African" king instead, as at the end of *Wealth of Nations* I.i, but we have "an Indian prince" at *Lectures on Jurisprudence*, p. 339 and "the chief of a savage nation in North America" at "Early Draft," p. 563.

47. William Herzog, for instance: "[The displacement of poor peasants] . . . provides a context for understanding Jesus' remark, 'for you always have the poor with you, and you can show kindness to them whenever you wish' (Mark 14:7). Why are there always the poor? Because there are always ruling class oppressors fleecing the people. Far from being a saying about the prevalence of the poor, it is a wry saying about the omnipresence of oppression and exploitation" *Jesus, Justice, and the Reign of God*, p. 142. See also John Dominic Crossan and Richard Watts, *Who Is Jesus?*: "Jesus and his fellow peasants found themselves in a structured system of injustice. In situations of oppression, especially where injustice is so built into the system that it seems normal or even necessary, the only ones who are innocent or blessed are those who have been squeezed out deliberately as human junk from the operations of the system. If Jesus were to speak this message among us today, it might come out like this: 'Only the homeless are innocent.' . . . [A]s participants in social systems that are unjust, none of us has clean hands or a clean conscience" (p. 50).

48. Compare A. Gray, *Socialist Tradition*, pp. 39–40.

49. Nonetheless, the exaltation of the poor in the Gospels and the communal arrangements in Acts were to inspire some protocommunist political programs many centuries later; see Gregory Claeys (ed.), *Utopias of the British Enlightenment*, p. xviii, and A. S. P. Woodhouse (ed.), *Puritanism and Liberty*, p. 384 (for a use of Acts 4:32 by the Diggers); see also Desroche, *American Shakers*, cited in note 53.

50. As Bertrand de Jouvenel writes, "It is . . . to be noticed that [in monastic communities] material goods are shared without question because they are spurned. The members of the community are not anxious to increase their individual well-being at the expense of one another, but then they are not very anxious to increase it at all. Their appetites are not addressed to scarce material commodities, and thus competitive; they are addressed to God, who is infinite" (*Ethics of Redistribution*, pp. 14–15).

51. In 1534, a group of Anabaptists, under the leadership first of Jan Matthias

and then of Jan Bockelson (known as Jan of Leyden), came to dominate the town council in Münster. Matthias proclaimed a community of property throughout the town—in the name, importantly, of "love," not of justice (private property "offends against love," he said, and was to be abolished among the Münsterites "by the power of love and community")—and Jan of Leyden added to this a community of women (he took particular advantage of this himself, taking for himself fifteen wives during his one-year reign). Both also called for the killing of those outside the true faith; the second Jan beheaded one of his new wives with his own hand and eventually instituted execution for everyone who disagreed with him. After a yearlong siege, the town was captured by Catholic forces, and Jan of Leyden and many others were tortured and executed. The bodies of Jan of Leyden and two other leaders were placed in cages hanging from a church spire, from which bits and pieces fell out for half a century; the cages can still be seen today. In later years, the two Jans have sometimes been seen as far-sighted heroes of the class struggle who anticipated communism. In fact, they seem to have been part religious visionaries and part cruel megalomaniacs with no particular interest in the well-being of the poor. For a lively account of these events, see Anthony Arthur, *The Tailor-King*. Arthur discusses the abolition of property on pp. 53–54.

52. Also known as the "True Levellers," the Diggers were a small group of radical Protestants who believed in the complete equality of all human beings and derived from that belief commitments to pacifism and to the notion that the entire earth was the communal property of everyone. Following through on this latter belief, fifty of them set out to cultivate ("dig") St. George's Hill in 1649; hence their name. Their ideological leader, Gerard Winstanley, was an early Quaker.

It is important to note that the Diggers' mode of argument was almost entirely a religious one. For the Diggers, all claims to property in land are violations of the eighth commandment, "Thou shalt not steal." The spirit of Jacob, which they say was killed by Esau and revived by Christ, is one of meekness and sharing, one that recognizes that reason and spirit—which are but aspects of "the great Creator, who is the Spirit Reason"—make clear that true community is possible only where no one rules over anyone else and no one keeps any part of the earth from anyone else. Christ demands that all individuals have complete freedom to follow out the mandates of spirit and reason within them. The "English Israelites" needed to be released from their enslavement by wicked Normans, but the day would come soon when "the Spirit of Christ, which is the Spirit of universal community and freedom, is risen, and . . . [the] pure waters of Shiloa . . . [will] overrun . . . those banks of bondage, curse, and slavery" (Woodhouse, *Puritanism and Liberty*, p. 384).

It hardly needs to be said that this vision is not well characterized as an expression of justice. It is an eschatological vision, rooted in theological rather than secular premises, and, despite its use of the word "reason," couched in language designed to appeal only to those who share a certain faith. Justice, the virtue that expresses natural rather than divine law, the virtue that can be grasped universally, even by those who lack faith, is nowhere to be found here. The Diggers would presumably regard such a faithless virtue as a product of Esau, of those who wrongly think that human dominion is compatible with the dominion of God.

53. On the Shakers, see Edward Derning Andrews and Faith Andrews, *Work and Worship,* and Desroche, *American Shakers,* pp. 185–210; on Oneida, see Mark Rosen, "The Outer Limits of Community Self-Governance in Residential Associations, Municipalities, and Indian Country," pp. 1074–1077, and the literature cited therein.

Desroche has an excellent short survey of the whole history of Christian millenarianism (57–64) as well as good discussions, throughout, of the relationship of this current of religious thought to secular socialism.

54. See J. G. A. Pocock, *Machiavellian Moment.*

55. Woodhouse, *Puritanism and Liberty,* p. 53.

56. Even the Diggers were concerned with political rights at least as much as economic ones. Their manifesto, *The True Levellers' Standard Advanced,* complains about the fact that people have been made subject to the "rule" of other people and describes economic divisions between landowners and workers as but one manifestation of that inequality in "rule" or "dominion" (in Woodhouse, *Puritanism and Liberty,* pp. 379–380). Where the Diggers differ most from the other Levellers is that they seem to favor anarchy: "The flesh of man, being subject to Reason, his Maker, hath him to be his teacher and ruler within himself, therefore needs not run abroad after any teacher and ruler without him." It was "selfish imaginations," the covetous, carnal descendants of Esau, that "did set up one man to teach and rule over another. And thereby the Spirit was killed" (379–380). To the more mainstream Levellers, this condemnation of political rule was anathema. They abjured anarchy and bridled angrily at the suggestion that their movement promoted any such idea (Woodhouse, *Puritanism and Liberty,* 59–60; they also objected to any suggestion that they opposed private property). What distinguishes the Diggers is therefore primarily an attitude toward politics, not economics.

Of course, the Diggers also called for everyone to have an equal share in all wealth, or at least in all land (382–383), but here again, one major reason for this demand was that they considered inequality in land distribution to breed inequality in political power.

57. More, *Utopia,* pp. 129–130.

58. Ibid., pp. 131, 86–98.

59. Thomas Campanella, "City of the Sun" (1623), in Henry Morley (ed.), *Ideal Commonwealths,* p. 148.

60. George Clarke (ed.), *John Bellers,* p. 84.

61. Ibid., pp. 85, 88.

62. Translated as "Nature's Domain," in Manuel and Manuel (eds.), *French Utopias,* pp. 93–94.

63. The inhabitants of Diderot's Tahiti do the same; see "Love in Tahiti," in Manuel and Manuel (eds.), *French Utopias.*

64. Claeys (ed.), *Utopias,* p. xvii.

65. In Claeys, (ed.), *Utopias,* pp. 3–4; see also "An Account of the Cessares," in ibid., p. 121, and "Memoirs of the Planetes," ibid., p. 184.

66. Manuel and Manuel (eds.), *French Utopias,* p. 93.

67. Ibid., p. 93.

68. Morley (ed.), *Ideal Commonwealths,* p. 148.

69. Ibid., p. 149.

70. More, *Utopia,* pp. 75–76, 83–84.

71. Manuel and Manuel (eds.), *French Utopias,* pp. 106–107.

72. Article 3 of the summary of Babeuf's views says that "Nature has imposed on each man the duty to work; no one can, without committing a crime, abstain from working" (David Thomson, *Babeuf Plot,* p. 33).

73. Furet, *Revolutionary France, 1770–1880,* p. 176.

74. Trattner, *From Poor Law to Welfare State,* p. 4. Trattner's interpretation of premodern practice toward the poor seems misguided to me, but he gives a nice summary of the history of that practice; see also Brian Tierney, *Medieval Poor Law,* and F. R. Salter (ed.), *Some Early Tracts on Poor Relief.*

75. And where it was supplemented by, say, the care that guilds provided for their members, that care was also tied closely to religious principles and affiliations. Until the Reformation, the guilds "participated in religious festivals and processions and maintained their own chapels and altars in the parish churches" (Jonathan Israel, *Dutch Republic,* p. 120). The guilds could be very generous to their members, providing not only money and food to sick and elderly members, but even free "small cottages . . . for certain categories of house-bound poor." But they represented a model of care for others that resembles a modern shared insurance scheme, or at best a family that takes care of its own. Nothing about their systems of care suggests that all people deserve a helping hand, much less a share in the distribution of wealth.

76. Jan de Vries and Ad van der Woude, *First Modern Economy,* p. 654.

77. Tierney, *Medieval Poor Law,* p. 53.

78. Augustine's view on the able-bodied poor was widely shared: "The Church

ought not to provide for a man who is able to work, . . . for strong men, sure of their food without work, often do neglect justice" (Tierney, *Medieval Poor Law*, p. 58). "If one who asks is dishonest," says Rufinus in his commentary on the *Decretum*, "and especially if he is able to seek his food by his own labor and neglects to do so, so that he chooses rather to beg or steal, without doubt nothing is to be given to him but he is to be corrected . . . unless perchance he is close to perishing from want" (ibid., p. 59).

79. Of course one might alternatively see the condemnation of "idleness" and "drunkenness" that pervades eighteenth and nineteenth century political discourse on the poor to be a holdover from earlier Christian beliefs.

80. Tierney, *Medieval Poor Law*, pp. 55–57, 61.

81. Ibid., p. 151, note 46.

82. "At first, the Reformed church, as successor to the Roman Catholic church, defined its responsibilities broadly, to entail assistance to nearly all Christians. . . . [I]n the course of the first half of the seventeenth century, [however], . . . every religious denomination [came] to establish its own diaconate and to support orphanages and homes for the elderly. In the extreme case of Amsterdam, parallel poor-relief agencies existed for the Reformed, Walloon Reformed, Roman Catholics, Anabaptists, Lutherans, and Sephardi and Ashkenazi Jews. To some extent this structure arose out of fear that the Reformed church would attract converts by virtue of its superior charitable resources. But its longevity—this structure endured into the twentieth century—reflects the widespread belief that each denomination formed a natural affinity group, a 'nation' within the state, that had as a primary responsibility the caring for its own" (de Vries and van der Woude, *First Modern Economy*, p. 656).

83. Ibid., *First Modern Economy*, p. 655.

84. On Hamburg, the German Empire, and Sweden, see T. W. Fowle, *Poor Law*, p. 23.

85. In 1531, England imposed a requirement on "mayors, justices of the peace, and other local officials" to look out for the poor. At the same time, it restricted the movements of the poor in various ways, and provided for punishment of able-bodied beggars. Both the constructive and the punitive aspects of this measure have antecedents that go back as far as 1349 (Trattner, *From Poor Law to Welfare State*, pp. 8–12).

86. "The problem was to place the poor in a position where they could do no harm," says Ferdinand Braudel. "In Paris the sick and invalid had always been directed to the hospitals, and the fit, chained together in pairs, were employed at the hard, exacting and interminable task of cleaning the drains of the town. In England the Poor Laws . . . were in fact laws *against* the poor. . . . Houses for the poor and undesirable gradually appeared throughout the West, condemning their occupants to forced labour in workhouses,

Zuchthäuser or *Maison de force*" (Braudel, *Capitalism and Material Life*, p. 40). See also Trattner, *From Poor Law to Welfare State*, which quotes the 1531 statute's call for able-bodied beggars "to be tyed to the end of a carte naked and be beten with whyppes throughe out . . . tyll [their bodies] . . . be blody" (p. 8) and notes that both the 1536 Henrician Poor Law and the 1601 Elizabethan Poor Law allowed for branding, enslavement, and even execution for repeated offenses of begging (pp. 9–11). Trattner nevertheless understands these poor laws as recognizing that some needy people "deserve[d]" relief and granting them a true "legal right" to it (11). They are better understood as *managing* poverty, by a combination of sticks and carrots, in the interests of the wider society; little or nothing about them supports the claim that they granted the poor a right to relief.

87. English poor laws worked substantially through church wardens through the middle of the eighteenth century. Justices of the peace also had a role to play, already in 1531 and more and more as time went on, but not until the late eighteenth century does the law seem to have placed the whole administration of the system into the hands of secular officials. See the list of statutes in Paul Slack, *English Poor Law*, pp. 59–64.

88. Lynn Lees writes that " 'social citizenship' with a right to maintenance arrived in England and Wales with the poor laws, not with the Labour government of 1945" (*Solidarities of Strangers*, p. 39). People with a parish settlement, she says, "had a right to relief and they knew it." But Lees's account is anachronistic. The poor laws were certainly nothing like the modern welfare state, if only because they were more concerned with keeping the poor in their place and punishing the able-bodied among them rather than with granting relief.

In addition, there are methodological problems with Lees's claims. Lees says that "[m]uch of the evidence for the notion that the poor claimed a right of subsistence from their parish needs to be inferred from their behavior" (p. 79), pointing to a 1765 riot against a new law that would have replaced outdoor relief with workhouses as evidence of the poor's belief in such a right. But we have to be careful about such evidence. In the first place, Lees's example does not quite demonstrate what she says it does. The rioters who said they would "fight for their liberties" in 1765 were protesting a law that would have committed them to workhouses—the "liberties" in question were clearly "liberties" in the ordinary sense: liberties to work, live, and move around at one's will. There is no need to hypothesize an additional "liberty" or "right" to be relieved from penury.

In the second place, a "right of subsistence" is not the same as the "right of social maintenance" that the Labour party of 1945 attempted to institute by way of a comprehensive welfare program. The most that the poor laws granted was *relief* from life-threatening needs—and that, too, only to people who could not work, not to able-bodied people who had difficulty finding a job.

In the third place, even if people under the poor law did see the relief granted them as a *legal* right, that does not tell us whether they believed that *justice* requires nations to set up systems of poor relief. It is crucial to distinguish between legal and moral rights. That something is recognized as a legal right does not yet mean it is recognized as required by justice. On many conceptions of politics, the state may legitimately pursue other ends than justice. Thus the state might pursue national glory and in the course of that pursuit offer certain perks to people who sign up with the military. Then, if you sign up, you will have a right to those perks under the law, but it cannot be said that *justice* requires you to have such privileges. Similarly, an established church may wind up investing its clergy with many legal rights, but even the members of that clergy may agree that it is not by virtue of justice that they have such rights.

To say that people have a moral, as opposed to a merely legal, right to something is to say that if the law does not grant this something, it ought to do so. If you have a moral right to X, then you ought to have a legal right to it as well. A state that fails to grant such a legal right, to enact the relevant laws, will be unjust in this respect. Perhaps the injustice will be great enough to warrant civil disobedience or even rebellion; perhaps it is too minor for that. By contrast, if you have a legal right to X, you may or may not have a moral right to it as well. The legal right might be independent of moral rights, as in the cases of military and clerical privileges; it might reflect a moral right, as does the right to freedom of worship, or it might *violate* moral rights, the rights granted by justice, as did the rights granted by the antebellum United States to slave-owners over their slaves.

This is an important point to clarify because it is characteristic of evidence brought from the behavior of people unschooled in moral and legal theory, such as the people Lees discusses, that one cannot tell whether legal or moral rights are at stake—and therefore whether the evidence testifies to a conception of justice or not. From the fact that poor people often tried to gain whatever they could from the poor laws, we cannot tell whether they would have regarded their nation as unjust if it did not have such laws. Similarly, when E. P. Thompson shows how crowds of the poor in the eighteenth century enforced old traditions against exporting corn from the province in which it was grown or demanded the opening of storehouses in times of scarcity, it seems likely, from his own account, that the reason the crowds thought they had a "right" to do this is that they remembered *laws* giving them such a right, not that they had a conception of justice under which this ought to be the law whether it was or not ("The Moral Economy of the English Crowd," in Thompson, *Customs in Common*). It is hard to tell, however, since the poor did not write treatises explaining the theoretical basis for their actions. As Thompson notes acidly, "They were not philosophers" ("Moral Economy Reviewed," in *Customs in Common*, p. 275).

So the behavioral evidence Lees adduces is insufficient to make the claims she wants to make—that a notion of social justice existed, at least in embryo, among ordinary English people as far back as the early seventeenth century. What would suffice to show that? Well, she reports that in the anti–poor law demonstrations of 1837 and 1838 people held up signs saying "The poor have a right to subsistence from the land" and "God, Nature, and the Laws have said that men shall not die of want in the midst of plenty" (*Solidarities of Strangers*, p. 164). These people clearly did regard poor relief as a moral, not merely a legal, right and saw a guarantee of subsistence, at least, as something justice requires of every state. If we had evidence of people expressing views like these in the sixteenth, seventeenth, and early eighteenth centuries, then we could fairly conclude that a real notion of social justice "arrived [in England and Wales] with the poor laws, not with the Labour government of 1945" (p. 39). But Lees offers us no such evidence.

89. Edith Abbott, *Public Assistance*, vol. 1, pp. 6, 74, my emphasis.
90. T. H. Marshall, *Right to Welfare*, p. 84. See also Mary Ann Glendon, "Rights in Twentieth-Century Constitutions."

2. The Eighteenth Century

1. Neil McKendrick, "Home Demand and Economic Growth," pp. 191–194. The quotations come from a 1750 piece by Henry Fielding and a 1756 piece by J. Hanway, respectively, and can be found in McKendrick, pp. 191–192.
2. Gordon Wood, *Radicalism of the American Revolution*, pp. 32, 235–241.
3. See Benedict Anderson, *Imagined Communities*, and Thomas Laqueur, "Bodies, Details, and the Humanitarian Narrative."
4. John Wood, editor's introduction, Beaumarchais's *Barber of Seville and the Marriage of Figaro*, p. 23.
5. Ak 20:44, as translated in Immanuel Kant, *Practical Philosophy*, p. xvii.
6. This is Rousseau's contribution to the great debate over the nature of evil that arose out of the Lisbon earthquake, to which Voltaire famously contributed in *Candide*.
7. Smith ridiculed the notion that the right to private property in any way cast suspicion on the state's right to tax its subjects. See *Lectures on Jurisprudence*, p. 324, and my discussion of Smith and Hume on property rights in *On Adam Smith's Wealth of Nations*, Part IV.

8. Kant saw this quite clearly: the first two *Discourses* and the *Nouvelle Héloise*, he said, "which present the state of Nature as a state of innocence . . . should serve only as preludes to [Rousseau's] *Social Contract*, his *Émile*, and his *Savoyard Vicar* so that we can find our way out of the labyrinth of evil into which our species has wandered through its own fault. Rousseau did not really want that man go back to the state of nature, but that he should rather look back at it from the stage which he had then reached" (Kant, *Anthropology*, p. 244 [Ak 326]).

Kant is hardly unique in this reading: it is by now a standard interpretation of Rousseau. However, a number of the Rousseau enthusiasts in the late eighteenth century missed the distinction between the state of nature and the state of society in their master's work—with disastrous results.

9. See note (o) (the fifteenth of Rousseau's notes) to Rousseau's *Second Discourse* (FSD 221–222).

10. A qualification. In its ancient sense, "politics" can cover our social lives as a whole, not just the nature of our governments, and Rousseau, in his concern for what it is to be a "citizen," continues to conceive of politics in such a way. But that means it may be a bit misleading, in modern terms, to say that Rousseau worries about inequality and poverty only in relation to "politics." For Rousseau, amour propre can pervasively corrupt the way social status is conferred. Once we live in society, however, a great deal of our private attention will inevitably be taken up with concern about our social status, and if we are wrongly admired or despised, and especially if we are placed in relationships of psychological dependence on or mastery over other people, our private lives, and not just our relationship with our government, will be severely harmed. So it is not quite right to say that Rousseau is uninterested in the "private life" of the poor, but it is certainly true that his concerns do not extend to anything much in this area *except* their social status—he says little or nothing about the hardship entailed simply by living in need, working too hard, being inadequately educated, and so on. This stands in stark contrast to Smith's portrayal of the poor, as I will show later, and to the concerns of nineteenth and twentieth century distributivists.

I am indebted to Dan Brudney for pointing out to me the need to address this point and to him, as well as to Fred Neuhouser's rich recent work on Rousseau, for indicating how the point might best be addressed.

11. DPE 133; compare *Social Contract*, Book 1, Chapter 8. Kant was of course to transform this insight into the relationship between freedom and law from a political to a moral one.

12. *Discourse on Political Economy*, p. 147; compare *Social Contract*, Book 2, Chapter 11.

13. Himmelfarb, *Idea of Poverty*, p. 61.

14. Ibid., p. 62.
15. Ibid., p. 46.
16. Trattner, *From Poor Law to Welfare State,* p. 18.
17. See text to introduction, note 2.
18. Daniel A. Baugh, "Poverty, Protestantism and Political Economy," p. 80
19. Ibid., p. 83.
20. Ibid., p. 85.
21. *Wealth of Nations,* p. 29. Note that Smith here identifies *himself* with a person widely regarded as the lowest of the low.
22. The lower sort, said Bernard de Mandeville, "have nothing to stir them up to be serviceable but their Wants, which it is Prudence to relieve but Folly to cure" (*Fable of the Bees,* volume 1, p. 194). Want is necessary to motivate the poor: "[I]f nobody did Want no body would work." Mandeville here echoes William Petty, who thought the poor should be kept busy even if they merely moved "stones at Stonehenge to Tower-Hill, or the like; for at worst this would keep their mindes to discipline and obedience, and their bodies to a patience of more profitable labours when need shall require it," and anticipates Arthur Young, who declared in 1771 that "every one but an ideot knows, that the lower classes must be kept poor, or they will never be in-dustrious" (Baugh, "Poverty, Protestantism and Political Economy," pp. 77, 103, note 74). So wages must be capped and leisure hours restricted. The poor should work long hours for low wages, else they would lose the habit of working altogether. The common practice of "work[ing] for four days in order to drink for three, Saturday, Sunday and good St Monday being de-voted to pleasure" (Neil McKendrick, "Home Demand and Economic Growth," p. 183) was an evil one, and it illustrated well the addiction of the poor to idleness and to drink.

    Smith says, about this last practice specifically and about the notion, gen-erally, that the poor are idle, "Excessive application during four days of the week is frequently the real cause of the idleness of the other three, so much and so loudly complained of. Great labour, either of mind or body, continued for several days together, is in most men naturally followed by a great desire of relaxation, which . . . is almost irresistible. . . . If it is not complied with, the consequences are often dangerous, and sometimes fatal. . . . If masters would always listen to the dictates of reason and humanity, they have fre-quently occasion rather to moderate, than to animate, the application of many of their workmen" (WN 100).
23. Writings about the poor, in both Scotland and England, are permeated by the assumption that the poor tend to be people of inherent and ineradicable vices, prime among which is an addiction to alcohol. "The Scottish Poor Law," writes T. M. Devine, "was underpinned by a set of values and attitudes

which assumed that . . . [t]he poor were poor because of defects of character, idleness and intemperance. In this view, only the combination of a rigorous poor law, expansion of schooling and the spread of evangelical Christianity could save urban society from moral catastrophe" ("The Urban Crisis," pp. 412–413). In seventeenth century England, John Bellers recommended his proposals to help the poor by saying that they may remove "the Profaneness of Swearing, Drunkenness, etc. with the Idleness and Penury of many in the Nation; which evil Qualities of the Poor, are an Objection with some against this Undertaking, though with others a great Reason for it" (Clarke [ed.], *John Bellers*, p. 55; see also p. 52). For Daniel Defoe, the linked vices of indolence and alcoholism may be a racial trait, something peculiar to the English poor: "[T]here is a general taint of Slothfulness upon our Poor, there's nothing more frequent, than for an Englishman to Work till he has got his Pocket full of Money, and then go and be idle, or perhaps drunk, till 'tis all gone, and perhaps himself in Debt; and ask him in his Cups what he intends, he'll tell you honestly, he'll drink as long as it lasts, and then go to work for more. . . . [I]f such Acts of Parliament may be made as may effectually cure the Sloth and Luxury of our Poor, that shall make Drunkards take care of Wife and Children, spendthrifts, lay up for a wet Day; Idle, Lazy Fellows Diligent; and Thoughtless Sottish Men, Careful and Provident . . . there will soon be less Poverty among us" ("Giving Alms No Charity," pp. 186–188).

These views continued into the next century. Both when the original act for the protection of Friendly Societies was proposed in 1793 and when it was amended in 1819, the debate turned considerably on whether such societies contributed to or detracted from alleviating the alcoholic tendencies of the poor. (From a 1793 Board of Agriculture report: "[B]enefit clubs, holden at public houses, increase the number of those houses, and naturally lead to idleness and intemperance" [quoted in Gosden, *Friendly Societies*, p. 3]).

24. See also *Lectures on Jurisprudence*, p. 363. On p. 540, Smith traces the tendency toward drunkenness among the poor to lack of education: a person "with no ideas with which he can amuse himself," he says, will "betake himself to drunkenness and riot."

25. Henry Fielding was but one of many writers in the eighteenth and nineteenth centuries who worried about the blurring of ranks consequent on the lower order's consuming luxury goods: "[T]he very Dregs of the People," he wrote in 1750, "aspire . . . to a degree beyond that which belongs to them." Sir Frederick Eden's famous 1797 report "constantly complained of the mis-spending of the poor on unnecessary luxuries and inessential fripperies," and even Elizabeth Gaskell, writing in the mid-nineteenth century, felt compelled "to offer

some explanation of the extravagance of . . . working class wives" who in-
dulged in ham, eggs, butter, and cream (McKendrick, "Home Demand and
Economic Growth," pp. 167–168, 191–192). McKendrick writes that Smith's
contemporaries "complained that those becoming marks of distinction between the classes were being obliterated by the extravagance of the lower ranks;
that working girls wore inappropriate finery, even silk dresses" (p. 168).

26. Laqueur, "Bodies, Details, and the Humanitarian Narrative," pp. 176–177.

27. Nevertheless, there are a number of interesting and thoughtful studies of
Kant's politics. I recommend above all the works by Jeffrie Murphy, Susan
Meld Shell, Howard Williams, Onora O'Neill, and Allen Rosen listed in the
bibliography, along with the collection edited by Ronald Beiner and William
Booth. I contributed to this literature in *A Third Concept of Liberty.*

28. Further evidence for this might be found in the paucity of references to
traditional authorities on politics or jurisprudence in Kant's works. There is
no mention of Bodin, Montesquieu, Grotius, Pufendorf, or Vattel anywhere
in the *Metaphysics of Morals;* Grotius and Pufendorf are included in a list of
political thinkers in Kant's review of Hufeland's *Essay on Natural Right* and
mentioned contemptuously, along with Vattel, as overrated authorities in
Perpetual Peace.

   The only predecessor to Kant I have found who uses the phrase "distributive justice" in at all a similar way is Hobbes: "Distributive Justice, the
Justice of an Arbitrator . . . [is] the act of defining what is Just. Wherein, . . .
if he performe his Trust, he is said to distribute to every man his own: and
this is indeed Just Distribution" (*Leviathan,* I.15; see also Hobbes's criticism
of Aristotle's notion of distributive justice in *De Cive,* III.6). Hobbes is however *rejecting* the standard distinction between commutative and distributive
justice in this passage, so if Kant is relying on Hobbes, without noting that
Hobbes's usage is anomalous, that is yet more evidence that he did not know
or did not care about the standard literature of the natural law tradition.

29. And, stacking the deck against the proponent of a right of necessity, the
example Kant gives is one of a person "who, in order to save his own life,
shoves another . . . off a plank on which he had saved himself" (MM intro.,
appendix, ii; 60). The traditional defenders of the right of necessity would
not have agreed that this is a legitimate example of that right—Grotius, citing
Lactantius approvingly on precisely this case, explicitly says that one cannot
invoke the right of necessity in defense of actions that would endanger another's life (LWP 194–195) while Pufendorf describes, as a legitimate use of
the right, only an attempt to *keep* a fellow shipwreck victim *from* climbing
on to one's plank, which is quite a different matter, on his moral philosophy
as well as Kant's, from throwing off someone who is already on board (*On
the Duty of Man and Citizen,* I.5; 54; the cases Pufendorf gives at LNN II.vi.3,

299, are also subtly but importantly different from Kant's example)—and Kant does not even consider the possibility that the law of necessity was meant to allow only for measures that would save a life at the expense of other, lesser, laws of justice. This mischaracterization of the law of necessity again suggests a lack of familiarity with the jurisprudential tradition.

30. See, for instance, David Boaz, *Libertarianism*, pp. 47, 97.

31. *Metaphysics of Morals*, pp. 136, 172; *Conflict of Faculties* (Ak 92–93).

32. See also the Collins notes, in Kant, *Lectures on Ethics*, edited by Peter Heath and J. B. Schneewind, pp. 416, 455.

33. This thesis has a long pedigree. Brian Tierney, citing the medieval canonists' view that the rich owe their "superfluities" to the poor, explains this view by saying that "the canonists, lacking any subtle theories about capital accumulation and its possible effects on productivity . . . , assumed that there was a given amount of food and other goods available. A man who acquired more than was due to him was therefore necessarily depriving someone else of his fair share. He was literally guilty of theft" (Tierney, *Medieval Poor Law*, 37). As John Chrysostom, one of the early church fathers, wrote, "Tell me, . . . whence art thou rich? From whom didst thou receive it, and from whom [did] he [receive it] who transmitted it to thee? From his father and his grandfather. But canst thou, ascending through many generations, show the acquisition just? It cannot be. The root and origin of it must have been injustice. Why? Because God in the beginning made not one man rich, and another poor" (*Homilies on Timothy XII*, p. 447).

34. See Fleischacker, "Philosophy and Moral Practice" and "Values behind the Market."

35. Kant's analysis here stands in especially stark contrast with the almost exactly contemporaneous attack on state aid to the poor and eulogy to private charity by Joseph Townsend: "Nothing in nature can be more disgusting than a parish pay-table, attendant upon which . . . are too often found combined, snuff, gin, rags, vermin, insolence, and abusive language; nor in nature can any thing be more beautiful than the mild complacency of benevolence, hastening to the humble cottage to relieve the wants of industry and virtue, to feed the hungry, to cloath the naked, and to sooth the sorrows of the widow with her tender orphans; nothing can be more pleasing, unless it be their sparkling eyes, their bursting tears, and their uplifted hands, the artless expressions of unfeigned gratitude for unexpected favours" (*A Dissertation on the Poor Laws*, p. 69). The rich benefactor is Christ, dispensing "unexpected favours" (grace) to his or her unworthy but suitably grateful recipients. One can hardly imagine a view more nauseating to Kant.

36. Compare the famous passage about the naturally sympathetic person in the first chapter of the *Foundations of the Metaphysics of Morals* (G 398).

37. Collins notes, p. 417. In this last passage, Kant is also worried that the pleasures of flattery with which charity is rewarded may lead people to perform acts of charity in the place of other, less pleasurable moral acts, or to expect similar flattery for moral acts that are not normally rewarded in such a way. The sentimental understanding of charity may thereby corrupt the entire moral realm.

I should say that these insights into how charity can degrade the recipient and corrupt the giver seem to me superb. I often find it all too tempting to suppose that writing a check here or there to a good cause or emptying my pockets to a beggar excuses my other sins and transforms me into a wonderful human benefactor. We should not suppose that our relatively easy gifts of material goods are the most important of our moral duties—or that there is anything especially wonderful about addressing human problems in this voluntary way rather than trying to arrange larger, political solutions to those problems. As long as we are careful to recognize that Kant is *not* saying that virtuous action should be a miserable experience (Schiller's claim that Kantian virtue requires one to hate being good was a caricature, as is now widely recognized), we may find a rich and still highly relevant set of moral insights in Kant's animadversions on charity.

38. And an obligation that can be made an equal one—in absolute terms, as a proportion of income, or as a proportion of disposable income. The last of these kinds of equality allows for progressivity in taxation.

39. *Lectures on Ethics,* p. 236; see also Collins notes, p. 455.

40. See especially §83 (but the word appears often and seems to carry the same technical meaning on each appearance. Werner Pluhar has collected the instances of it in the index to his translation, *Critique of Judgment,* p. 493).

41. Douglas, "Dissenting Opinion," pp. 244–246.

42. There has been much speculation that *Theory of Moral Sentiments,* pp. 232–234, inserted into Smith's revisions of the work for the final 1790 edition, is a comment on the French Revolution. Given that we have no letters by Smith mentioning the revolution, nor so much as a comment on it reported in his name, and given also that the revisions were completed by November 18, 1789—a month before the Jacobin Club was formed—I see little reason to believe this.

43. Notoriously, he says that revolution is absolutely prohibited by morality in both his 1793 essay on "Theory and Practice" (collected in Kant, *Practical Philosophy*) and his 1797 *Metaphysics of Morals,* yet he expresses a vicarious enthusiasm for the French Revolution in his 1798 *Conflict of the Faculties* (Ak 85).

44. After this book was in production, I was alerted to the fact that Kant's immediate follower, Fichte, did state the notion explicitly, and Fichte may de-

serve equal billing with Babeuf as the inventor/discoverer of modern distributive justice. (My thanks here to a colleague who wishes to remain anonymous.) From within an approach to political philosophy extremely similar to Kant's, Fichte argued that the right not to be in poverty was on the same level, and justified by the same reasons, as the right to property itself:

> To be able to live is the absolute, inalienable property of all human beings. We have seen that a certain sphere of objects is granted to the individual solely for a certain use. But the final end of this use is to be able to live. . . . [Hence a] principle of all rational state constitutions is that everyone ought to be able to live from his labor, . . . and the state must make arrangements to insure this. . . . [A]ll property rights are grounded in the contract of all with all, which states: 'We are all entitled to keep this, on the condition that we let you have what is yours.' Therefore, if someone is unable to make a living from his labor, he has not been given what is absolutely his, and . . . the contract is completely canceled with respect to him. (Fichte, *Foundations of Natural Right*, p. 185).

Elsewhere, Fichte says that every "rational state" should institute a distribution of goods ensuring that all its citizens have an agreeable life, and that the share each citizen would have in this distribution "is *his own* by right." ("The Closed Commercial State," in Reiss, *Political Thought*, p. 90). Both of these writings appeared shortly after Babeuf's abortive uprising; Fichte is said to have been influenced by Babeuf (Reiss, *Political Thought*, p. 16). Both Babeuf and Fichte, riding the wave of egalitarianism brought on by the French Revolution, took earlier ideas about rights and used them to develop the notion that now goes under the name "distributive" or "economic" justice. Of the two, Babeuf was politically more important; Fichte was philosophically deeper and more rigorous, and he developed the argument for economic justice in strikingly cogent form.

45. Spence, "The Real Rights of Man" (read as a lecture in 1775 and published in 1795; reprinted in Spence, *Political Works*, p. 1); compare Ogilvie, *An Essay on the Right of Property in Land* (1782), as quoted in Noel Thompson, *Real Rights of Man*, p. 15.

46. Paine, *Rights of Man*, in *Writings*, pp. 484–502. Paine considered himself a disciple of Smith, calling for his proposals to replace the poor laws that he, like Smith, regarded as oppressive to the poor and limiting his proposals to institutions that could operate *outside* the market rather than suggesting any sort of state control over capital or labor. He is thus a forerunner of welfare-state liberalism rather than of socialism.

47. *Rights of Man,* in *Writings,* p. 488, at the top of the page and again at the bottom.

48. Assuming that they expect to have a retirement: the very notion is something Paine is essentially introducing here.

49. *Rights of Man,* in *Writings,* p. 489.

50. *Defense of Gracchus Babeuf,* pp. 83–84

51. Thomson, *Babeuf Plot,* p. 33. The summary was not written by Babeuf, although he endorsed it at his trial. He also said there, directly, "I have dared to entertain, and to advocate, the following doctrines: The natural right and destiny of man are life, liberty, and the pursuit of happiness. Society is created in order to guarantee the enjoyment of this natural right. In the event that this right is not so guaranteed to all, the social compact is at an end" (*Defense of Gracchus Babeuf,* p. 20).

3. From Babeuf to Rawls

1. For instance, William Thompson, *An Inquiry into the Principles of the Distribution of Wealth, Most Conducive to Human Happiness* (1824); George Ramsay, *An Essay on the Distribution of Wealth* (1836); John R. Commons, *The Distribution of Wealth* (1893); John Bates Clark, *The Distribution of Wealth* (1899).

2. Thompson, *Making of the English Working Class.*

3. Lees, *Solidarities of Strangers,* pp. 80–81.

4. Ibid., p. 165.

5. Charles Tilly, *Popular Contention in Great Britain,* p. 355.

6. Young, *General View of the Agriculture of the County of Suffolk,* as quoted in A. J. Peacock, *Bread or Blood,* p. 35; see also Lees, *Solidarities of Strangers,* p. 77.

7. Himmelfarb, *Idea of Poverty,* pp. 74–75. Himmelfarb describes Pitt's bill as including "rates in aid of wages, family allowances, money for the purchase of a cow or some other worthy purpose, schools of industry for the children of the poor, wastelands to be reclaimed and reserved for the poor, insurance against sickness and old age, a further relaxation of the law of settlement, and an annual poor law budget to be submitted to Parliament."

8. Lees, *Solidarities of Strangers,* pp. 73–74.

9. Ibid., pp. 161, 164.

10. *Griffith v. Osawkee,* as quoted in Abbott, *Public Assistance,* p. 6. Abbott writes that "every American poor law [from the 1790s on had] given the person who is in need a 'right to relief' " (8). This is not so clear, at least from the evidence she adduces for the point. She quotes an 1802 New Jersey judicial opinion, for instance, as saying that laws for relief of the poor were passed

"to prevent the charity of individuals being oppressed and exhausted by heavy burdens, and that an ample and ready relief might be afforded to the indigent." Here, public poor relief seems to be, as it had been in England, a substitute for private *charity*, not the satisfaction of a right. Similarly, the 1859 constitution of Kansas declared that relief would be given to those "who, by reason of age, infirmity or other misfortune, may have claims upon the *sympathy and aid* of society" (Abbott, *Public Assistance*, p. 5, my italics). Sympathy, not justice; charity, not rights fulfillment, was the basis of American poor law. This is not merely a detail about wording, moreover: the fact that the basis of poor relief was charity rather than justice meant that individual poor people could not sue for relief, that they could indeed even be penalized for accepting relief. Abbott discusses an 1811 case in which the Supreme Court of New Jersey held that a poor person could not recover the relief that had wrongly been withheld from him by a negligent overseer (eight dollars, accumulated over eight weeks) and a 1911 case in which the Iowa Supreme Court refused to allow a man whose feet had had to be amputated because of the stinginess of a local relief agency to recover damages (20–21). She also notes that many states, even in 1940, deprived those receiving relief of the right to vote (127, 220–223) and that some, at that late date, continued to lock "paupers" up in poorhouses (16). Finally, she points out that the "poor" covered by the American laws were often limited to those, in the words of an 1892 Wisconsin decision, "so completely destitute of resources, property, or means of security as to be unable to obtain the absolute means of subsistence" (17). "Public aid," wrote Judge Brewer, must be limited to "the helpless and dependent" (13). And even the helpless and dependent had no *right* to such aid; they merely had a legitimate claim on the "sympathy ... of society."

11. "In 1845 Norway made public relief a legal right of the aged, the sick, the crippled, lunatics, and orphans; the decisive responsibility in this field was entrusted to the municipal poor commissions simultaneously established. With the next decade Finland and Sweden enacted poor laws affirming the obligation of local authorities to care for their poor; moreover, both statutes established the right of the poor to appeal local decisions to higher authority. However, these reforms were only short-lived. Less than a generation passed before revisions of the poor laws again made aid to the poor an act of charity to which no legal right could be established, exception being made only for certain categories. . . . It was not until 1900 and 1922, respectively, that new Norwegian and Finnish poor laws re-established mandatory assistance to all those unable to provide for themselves. The Swedish Poor Law of 1918 was essentially similar although the right to assistance was confined to persons incapable of work; the local authorities were, however, free to aid also able-

bodied, unemployed persons in need" (George Nelson, *Freedom and Welfare*, p. 448).

12. See Lees, *Solidarities of Strangers*, pp. 160–161, for Cobbett and Hodgskin. The notion that the bourgeoisie wrongly deprive workers of the product of their own labor runs through Marx's writing.

13. Marshall, *Principles of Economics*, pp. 2–4.

14. Quoted in Mary Ann Glendon, *A World Made New*, p. 186. Roosevelt's belief that the poor had a right to aid ran deep. He developed it at an early point in his career and expressed and acted on it often; see Thomas Greer, *What Roosevelt Thought*, pp. 11–14, 27–30.

15. Perhaps the apparent Hegelianism here is not a coincidence: Hegel's dialectical account of history was in good part inspired by the movement from radicalism to reaction in the French Revolution, and both the birth of distributive justice and the reaction against it were very much products of that revolution.

16. Townsend, *Dissertation on the Poor Laws*. Himmelfarb discusses Burke, Colquhoun, and Malthus in *Idea of Poverty*, pp. 66–73, 77–78, and 100–132.

17. Townsend, *Dissertation on the Poor Laws*, p. 36. "It seems to be a law of nature," he says, "that the poor should be to a certain degree improvident, that there may always be some to fulfil the most servile, the most sordid, and the most ignoble offices in the community" (35).

18. Himmelfarb, *Idea of Poverty*, pp. 28–31.

19. Himmelfarb points this out as regards Burke (ibid., pp. 70–71).

20. Young, quoted in K. D. M. Snell, *Annals of the Labouring Poor*, p. 111.

21. Snell, *Annals of the Labouring Poor*, p. 111.

22. Social Darwinists in England and America never advocated genocide (at most they favored sterilizing some of the unfit, which was indeed practiced in the United States into the 1970s; see Stephen Jay Gould, *The Mismeasure of Man*, pp. 164, 335–336). Their intellectual cousins in Germany, of course, both advocated and carried out genocide.

23. On Mandeville and "the utility of poverty," see Baugh, "Poverty, Protestantism and Political Economy," pp. 76–78.

24. Richard Hofstadter, *Social Darwinism in American Thought*, p. 21. Hofstadter writes that it was impossible in America "to be active in any field of intellectual work in the three decades after the Civil War without mastering Spencer" (p. 20).

    Hofstadter's book is still the outstanding work on Spencer's reception; it also provides an excellent overview of Spencer's thought. For a close, careful interpretation of Spencer's view of justice by a contemporary philosopher, see Miller, *Social Justice*, Chapter 6.

25. F. A. P. Barnard, quoted in Hofstadter, *Social Darwinism*, p. 18.

26. Hofstadter, *Social Darwinism*, p. 26.

27. Ibid., p. 27, summing up *Social Statics*, pp. 311–396.

28. His follower William Graham Sumner similarly looked forward to the end of poverty, if evolution was allowed to work its wonders: "Let every man be sober, industrious, prudent, and wise, and bring up his children to be so likewise, and poverty will be abolished in a few generations" (Hofstadter, *Social Darwinism*, p. 47). The social evolutionists hoped for the end of poverty as much as other progressives of their day; they simply believed that there had to be a "lost generation" or two of unfit people who died out if humanity was to overcome poverty. This is not terribly unlike the Marxist-Leninist belief that there needs to be a period of violent revolution followed by a period of dictatorship before humanity can achieve a world of peace, true community, and the satisfaction of needs. When we consider the eugenic programs of sterilizing people with subnormal IQs, let alone the horrific crimes of the Nazis, we may today think it obvious that Spencer and his followers had no spark of humanity in them. But that is no more true of all of them than it is of all Marxist-Leninists; in both cases it is probably fairest to say that there were more humanitarian and less humanitarian ways of understanding the ideology.

29. Hofstadter, *Social Darwinism*, p. 29.

30. Ibid., p. 30.

31. Spencer, *The Man versus the State*, p. 369; see also p. 364.

32. For his views on the poor rates, see, for instance, his speech in Leeds of December 18, 1849, against removing the poor rates from their property-tax base, which assumes the legitimacy of the poor rates throughout and contains this remarkable echo of William Cobbett: "the poor have the first right to a subsistence from the land" (John Bright and James Rogers [eds.], *Speeches of Richard Cobden*, pp. 419–420). On Cobden's attitude toward the 1834 Poor Law, and on his complicated commitment to "laissez-faire" in general, see W. D. Grampp, *Manchester School of Economics*, pp. 103–105. On his reaction to the cotton famine, see Wendy Hinde, *Richard Cobden*, pp. 311–312, 316n. Cobden also made common cause with the Chartists for a time, supported restrictions on child labor, and "was throughout his life a vigorous advocate of popular schools for working-class children" (J. A. Hobson, *Richard Cobden*, p. 392). On the other hand, he opposed trade unions and laws that restricted working hours—all in the name of a view, which he seems to have held quite sincerely, that limitations on free trade would hurt the working classes. Ian Bowen has, I think, captured Cobden's ambiguous relationship to working-class causes particularly well: "Cobden's own ideas were, at bottom, more radical than those of many later liberals. They differ from later liberalism because he was not faced with an inescapable choice—between

attack or defense of a ruling capitalist system. It is rather hard now to state his exact position, for in his day both capitalism and Socialism were partners in opposition. The ruling classes were . . . the landlords whom he routed" (Bowen, *Cobden*, p. 63; see also the whole of Chapter 5, from which this passage is taken).

33. William Cunningham, "Free Trade," p. 92.

34. See Thompson, *Distribution of Wealth*, pp. 81–85, 89–90, 103–144, 173–178, 363–365, 600.

35. Some recent authors have argued, however, that there is a tradition of "left libertarianism" in which poverty programs are a part of the government's duty to protect freedom; see Peter Vallentyne and Hillel Steiner, *Left-Libertarianism and Its Critics* and *The Origins of Left-Libertarianism*.

36. See, for instance, Hayek, *Law, Legislation, and Liberty*, Chapters 1 and 2.

37. David Boaz, however, describes Spencer as "a towering scholar whose work is unjustly neglected and often misrepresented today" (Boaz, *Libertarianism*, p. 47). One wonders what he means by "misrepresented." It's hard to see how it could be a misrepresentation of Spencer to say that he wanted the poor to die out. Or is Boaz unaware of these aspects of Spencer—despite the fact that they run through Spencer's work?

38. Blaug, *Economic Theory in Retrospect*, p. 408; John Bates Clark, *The Distribution of Wealth*, pp. 5, 8, 9, emphasis added.

39. See Frank E. Manuel, *The New World of Henri Saint-Simon*, Chapter 31. Manuel is, however, quite cynical about Saint-Simon's commitment to Christianity.

40. Rawls writes, "[A] society in which all can achieve their complete good, or in which there are no conflicting demands and the wants of all fit together without coercion into a harmonious plan of activity, is a society in a certain sense beyond justice. It has eliminated the occasions when the appeal to the principles of right and justice is necessary" (TJ 281). He then says, in a footnote, that "[s]ome have interpreted Marx's conception of a full communist society as a society beyond justice in this sense." Rawls cites Robert Tucker, *Marxian Revolutionary Idea*, Chapters 1 and 2 as a source for this view. See also Allen Wood, *Karl Marx*, Chapter 9. Hume describes (limited) scarcity as a condition for justice in *Treatise of Human Nature*, pp. 487–495, and *Enquiries*, pp. 183–184.

41. The controversy is exhaustively and superbly surveyed in Norman Geras, "The Controversy about Marx and Justice." Geras himself believes that Marx had a conception of justice *malgré lui* (pp. 244–258); see also R. G. Peffer, *Marxism, Morality, and Social Justice*, Chapter 8.

42. Moreover, the claim that Marx himself opposed the entire notion of justice, if controversial, is not at all implausible; he certainly did rail against justice

and rights talk in some of his writings, and the claim that he could not have meant to throw out the notion of justice altogether is based mostly on inferences from passages that do not explicitly take back the critique of justice. Geras suggests that the debate between these two interpretations cannot be settled by looking at Marx's texts, that Marx may indeed be ambivalent—incoherent, even—on this matter ("The Controversy about Marx and Justice," pp. 233, 237, 265–267).

43. The first is filled in addition with vile anti-Semitic rhetoric: "Money is the jealous god of Israel, beside which no other god can exist. . . . The bill of exchange is the real god of the Jew. . . . As soon as society succeeds in abolishing the *empirical* essence of Judaism—huckstering and its conditions—the Jew becomes *impossible,* because his consciousness no longer has an object. . . . The *social* emancipation of the Jew is the *emancipation of society from Judaism*" (MER 50–52).

44. Wood, *Karl Marx,* Chapter 9. (Wood is criticized in Geras and Peffer; see note 41.) According to Wood, "Marx does believe that a communist revolution will introduce a new mode of production, and with it new standards of right and justice" (138). If my analysis is correct, however, Marx believes that communist revolution will get rid of the individualism essential to *all* notions of "right" and "justice." While it may bring in new evaluative standards of some sort, those standards will emphatically not be standards of "right and justice."

45. See discussion of Babeuf, Chapter 2, Section 4.

46. *Grundrisse,* in Tucker, *Marx-Engels Reader,* p. 222; compare "Jewish Question," ibid., pp. 44–46.

47. "Man is a species being, not only because in practice and in theory he adopts the species as his object (his own as well as those of other things), but—and this is only another way of expressing it—but also because he treats himself as the actual, living species: because he treats himself as a *universal* and therefore a free being" (MER 75; see also 33–34, which has a very helpful editor's note on the term). A side note of interest is that Marx here seems to adopt a Kantian notion of freedom whereby thinking in universal terms, and in particular treating oneself and others as instances of a universal, is essential to freedom.

48. As the *Communist Manifesto* says, under communism "the free development of each is the condition for the free development of all" (MER 491).

49. *Theory of Justice,* pp. 74, 104. Rawls has a tendency to "liberalize" Marx, to pull insights of Marx (often the ones I have been stressing) together with similar ideas he finds in Mill and Alfred Marshall; see *Theory of Justice,* p. 259 and "Fairness to Goodness," in *Collected Papers,* pp. 276–277.

50. And this seems plausible, but actually it is probably the weakest point in

Marxist thought, and one over which Marx's followers glided more blithely than Marx himself did. The fact that a society does something need not mean, as it is often taken to mean, that there is some ready way by which the human beings composing that society can change its direction, and Marx's own emphasis on the dialectical march of history implicitly recognizes that point. "Society" is not, strictly speaking, a human *creation:* it is not something that any individual human being or group of human beings can set out, deliberately, to make, and it may well be something that cannot be deliberately controlled in any significant respect. What we all do, separately and in groups, will undoubtedly help determine the shape of our society in the future, but that does not mean we can expect to shape our society *deliberately,* in accordance with any individual or jointly formed conscious intention or plan. Societies may well instead be what Friedrich Hayek, interpreting Smith and Hume, has called "spontaneous orders": collections of events and things that do have a discernible shape but whose shape arises from actions that do not intend that shape, whose shape can in fact not be predicted, much less planned, in any detail. If that is so—and I think Hayek is probably right about this—then we cannot expect straightforwardly to design social forms that meet our hopes and ideals; at best, we can try to modify the forms within which we live, attending as we do to how our reforms might most successfully become an ongoing part of the way those forms already work.

51. On Marx's critique of morality, see Wood, *Karl Marx,* Chapter 10. Again, I would go further than Wood. Wood argues that some aspects of bourgeois morality are salvageable from a Marxist perspective (pp. 153–156) and says "[T]here is . . . some reason to say (as Engels does) that in future society there will be an 'actual human morality' in place of the false, ideological moralities of class society" (156). It seems to me that "human morality" would be something of a contradiction in terms for Marx himself. It belongs to the nature of anything regarded as a *morality* that it stands over us in a nonhuman, and dehumanizing, way. So while Marx would surely agree that "kindness, generosity, [and] loyalty" would be respected in communist society, as Wood says (154), he would probably not expect these or other qualities to be treated as *moral* ones—and that shift in terminology is meant to reflect a deep shift in our entire attitude toward these qualities, and toward the evaluation of one another's behavior.

Rather different views of Marx and morality can be found in Peffer, *Marxism, Morality, and Social Justice,* Chapters 4–7; Gerald Cohen, *If You're an Egalitarian, How Come You're So Rich?,* Chapter 6; and Dan Brudney, *Marx's Attempt to Leave Philosophy,* pp. 337–347.

52. Thompson, *Distribution of Wealth,* p. xvii.

53. See note 13.
54. See, especially, Bentham, "Anarchical Fallacies."
55. J. J. C. Smart describes precritical ethical agents and Kantians as suffering from "rule worship"; see Smart, "Outline of a System," p. 10.
56. Bentham, "Anarchical Fallacies," p. 495.
57. Smart, "Outline of a System," p. 73
58. Sidgwick, *Methods of Ethics*, p. 274. I will show later how close this language is to the language John Rawls uses to set up his central problem in *A Theory of Justice*. Rawls was a great admirer of Sidgwick; see his introduction to *Methods of Ethics* and *Theory of Justice*, pp. 22, 58, 92.
59. Hutcheson, *Inquiry into the Original of Our Ideas of Virtue*, III.viii.
60. "Anarchical Fallacies,"p. 493; see also Bentham, *Principles of Morals and Legislation*, pp. 2–3.
61. See the literature cited in Harry Frankfurt, "Equality as a Moral Ideal," p. 138, note 7. Frankfurt discusses the argument critically. A version of the argument can already be discerned in William Thompson's *Distribution of Wealth*, Chapter 1, Section 4.
62. Mill, *Utilitarianism*, p. 42.
63. "Outline of a System," p. 37; compare Rawls, *Theory of Justice*, p. 23.
64. Actually, almost all of it fell into one of the latter three categories. The reactionaries occupied—and continue to occupy—an important part of the political spectrum but had only a handful of respected intellectual defenders.
65. This sentence is also the opening line of the blurb for *Theory of Justice*, which Rawls himself presumably wrote. Both the opening and the closing lines of the blurb characterize the book as an alternative to utilitarianism.
66. A large question raised by this shift in orientation is the degree to which the concept of justice as a whole, not simply the concept of "distributive justice," is altered once it is conceived as, in general, about distribution. Of course, one might regard even what used to be called "commutative justice" as a matter of distribution—a distribution of rights, perhaps, and of punishments for rights violations—but this is not how premodern theorists of justice tended to understand it. A state that conceives of itself primarily as *safeguarding* a society or natural order is likely to act quite differently from a state that conceives of itself primarily as *distributing* goods or rights throughout society. D. D. Raphael has an interesting discussion of shifts in the general notion of justice in the last chapter of his *Concepts of Justice*.
67. Alternatively, we might say that it has been reinterpreted such that all people are deserving and no one is any more deserving than anyone else. But then desert is separated from anything remotely like Aristotelian "merit."
68. Smart, "Outline of a System," pp. 32, 73.
69. Samuel Scheffler stresses this point in the course of a deep exploration of

the relationship between Rawls and utilitarianism: see his *Boundaries and Allegiances,* Chapter 9, especially pp. 150 and 164.

70. Rawls adds some further qualifications to this definition on pp. 302–303; see also his reformulations in *Political Liberalism,* p. 271, and *Justice as Fairness,* pp. 42–47.

71. See Mill, *Utilitarianism,* Chapter 5, pp. 45–46, or Marx, "Critique of the Gotha Program," in Tucker, *Marx-Engels Reader,* p. 528.

72. For a sample of the voluminous literature on these topics, see Thomas Nagel, *Equality and Partiality,* Chapters 7 and 8; Frankfurt, "Equality as a Moral Ideal"; Cohen, *If You're an Egalitarian,* Chapter 8; and Fleischacker, *Third Concept,* Chapter 10.

73. Dworkin, "Equality of Welfare" and "Equality of Resources," first published in *Philosophy and Public Affairs* 10 (1981), reprinted in Dworkin's *Sovereign Virtue.*

74. Cohen, "Equality of What?" Cohen, probably the most persuasive contemporary Marxist, has argued that Marxism must now engage in normative discourse of a kind it had some reason to eschew when it could plausibly maintain that the fall of capitalism was historically inevitable. From this normative perspective, Cohen has also criticized Rawls for tolerating far too much inequality in the name of justice; see *If You're an Egalitarian,* Chapters 6–9.

75. Sen, "Equality of What?" pp. 157–158.

76. Ibid., p. 158.

77. Ibid., p. 161.

78. Nussbaum, "Nature, Function, and Capability."

79. See "Women and Cultural Universals," the first chapter of Nussbaum, *Sex and Social Justice,* and the essays cited before her first note to that chapter on p. 377.

80. "[The capabilities approach] strongly invites a scrutiny of tradition as one of the primary sources of . . . unequal abilities" (ibid., p. 34).

81. Ibid., p. 40.

82. See Charles Beitz, *Political Theory and International Relations,* and Thomas Pogge, *Realizing Rawls.*

83. Michael Green has suggested to me that Nozick should be understood, not as attacking the very notion of distributive justice, but as himself having a conception of distributive justice. Nozick does remark that the "complete principle of distributive justice," by his lights, should "say simply that a distribution is just if everyone is entitled [by the principles of just acquisition and just exchange] to the holdings they possess under the distribution" (ASU 151). But this procedural conception of distributive justice is at best a van-

ishing case of the notion. Nozick defines justice almost entirely in terms of what the premodern world had called "commutative justice"; his "distributive justice" is then satisfied whenever commutative justice is satisfied. One feature that modern and premodern notions of distributive justice have in common, however, is that they are *supplemental* to commutative justice, which in the modern case means that existing property rights do not exhaust the rightful claims a person may make to possess certain goods. By limiting the interest of justice in distribution strictly to *how* distributions arise rather than *what* they look like, Nozick disengages himself from the entire modern tradition according to which it is a condition of just distribution for some goods to wind up in the hands of the needy. That is of course Nozick's point: to say what the distribution of goods should look like is to have what he calls a "patterned" principle of justice, and he rejects such principles. To count nonpatterned principles of justice as conceptions of distributive justice is to strip the concept of most of its content, however; certainly none of the premises I gave in the introduction to this book are relevant to such a conception, nor does it resemble any of the other conceptions that come under the modern concept.

84. Jan Narveson says that he was motivated to write a book on libertarianism in good part because Nozick presented no proper foundation for the doctrine; see Narveson, *Libertarian Idea,* pp. xi–xii.

85. Kymlicka, *Liberalism, Community and Culture,* especially Chapters 8 and 9.

86. Tamir, *Liberal Nationalism,* pp. 53–56, 107–111.

87. Tully, "Struggles over Recognition and Distribution," p. 470.

88. Ibid. Tully's concern with "recognition" derives from Charles Taylor's influential exploration of the political claims made by cultural subgroups in his "Politics of Recognition."

For debate over whether the currently popular focus on recognition contributes to or distracts from the pursuit of distributive justice, see Iris Young, "Displacing the Distributive Paradigm," in *Justice and the Politics of Difference*; Brian Barry, *Culture and Equality,* pp. 264–279; and Nancy Fraser and Axel Honneth, *Recognition or Redistribution?*

89. See Daniels, *Just Health Care,* and Allen Buchanan et al., *From Chance to Choice.*

90. The protection against poverty that I favor is, however, substantial. It would include nutrition, shelter, health care, education (including job training), and a significant amount of leisure. I lay out the conditions I consider necessary for freedom, and therefore something that all governments should guarantee, in *Third Concept,* Chapters 10 and 11.

Epilogue

1. Fleischacker, *Ethics of Culture,* especially Chapters 3 and 4. Cohen worries interestingly about the way we imbibe moral outlooks in childhood in *If You're an Egalitarian,* Chapter 1.
2. Wittgenstein, *Philosophical Investigations,* §§65–67.
3. The phrase is Kant's, used several times in his 1793 essay on "Theory and Practice" (in *Practical Philosophy*). See my discussion of the phrase, in connection with Rawls, in *Third Concept,* Chapter 10.

Bibliography

Abbott, Edith. *Public Assistance* (2 vols.). Chicago: University of Chicago Press, 1940.

Anderson, Benedict. *Imagined Communities.* London: Verso, 1983.

Andrews, Edward Derning, and Faith Andrews. *Work and Worship: The Economic Order of the Shakers.* Greenwich: New York Graphic Society, 1974.

Aquinas, Thomas. *The Political Ideas of St. Thomas Aquinas.* Edited by Dino Bigongiari. New York: Hafner Press, 1953.

———. *Summa Theologiae.* Blackfriars translation. Edited by T. Gilby and T. C. O'Brien. New York: McGraw-Hill, 1966.

Aristotle. *Nicomachean Ethics* and *Politics.* In *The Complete Works of Aristotle,* edited by Jonathan Barnes. Princeton, NJ: Princeton University Press, 1984.

Arthur, Anthony. *The Tailor-King: The Rise and Fall of the Anabaptist Kingdom in Münster.* New York: St. Martin's Press, 1999.

Augustine. *City of God against the Pagans.* Edited and translated by R. W. Dyson. Cambridge: Cambridge University Press, 1998.

[Babeuf, "Gracchus"]. *The Defense of Gracchus Babeuf before the High Court of Vendome.* Edited and translated by John Anthony Scott. Amherst: University of Massachusetts Press, 1967.

Baldwin, J. W. *Medieval Theories of the Just Price.* Philadelphia: American Philosophical Society, 1959.

Barry, Brian. *Culture and Equality: An Egalitarian Critique of Multiculturalism.* Cambridge, MA: Harvard University Press, 2001.

Baugh, Daniel A. "Poverty, Protestantism and Political Economy: English Attitudes toward the Poor, 1660–1800." In *England's Rise to Greatness,* edited by Stephen Baxter. Berkeley: University of California Press, 1983.

Beaumarchais, Pierre Augustin Caron de. *The Barber of Seville and the Marriage of Figaro.* Edited and introduced by John Wood. Baltimore: Penguin, 1964.

Beiner, Ronald, and William Booth, eds. *Kant and Political Philosophy.* New Haven, CT: Yale University Press, 1993.

Beitz, Charles. *Political Theory and International Relations.* Princeton, NJ: Princeton University Press, 1979.

Bentham, Jeremy. "Anarchical Fallacies." In *The Works of Jeremy Bentham,* edited by John Bowring. New York: Russell and Russell, 1962.

———. *An Introduction to the Principles of Morals and Legislation.* New York: Hafner, 1948.

Blaug, Mark. *Economic Theory in Retrospect.* 5th ed. Cambridge: Cambridge University Press, 1996.

Boaz, David. *Libertarianism: A Primer.* New York: Simon and Schuster, 1997.

Bowen, Ian. *Cobden.* London: Duckworth, 1935.

Braudel, Ferdinand. *Capitalism and Material Life, 1400–1800.* Translated by M. Kochan. New York: Harper and Row, 1967.

Bright, John, and James Rogers, eds. *Speeches of Richard Cobden.* London: Macmillan, 1870.

Broadie, Sarah, and Christopher Rowe, eds. and trans. *Aristotle: Nicomachean Ethics.* Oxford: Oxford University Press, 2002.

Brooks, Roger, trans. *Peah.* Volume 2 of *The Talmud of the Land of Israel: A Preliminary Translation and Explanation.* Edited by Jacob Neusner. Chicago: University of Chicago Press, 1990.

Brudney, Dan. *Marx's Attempt to Leave Philosophy.* Cambridge, MA: Harvard University Press, 1998.

Buchanan, Allen, Dan W. Brock, Norman Daniels, and Daniel Wikler. *From Chance to Choice: Genetics and Justice.* Cambridge: Cambridge University Press, 2000.

Chrysostom, John. *Homilies on Timothy XII.* In *A Select Library of the Nicene and Post-Nicene Fathers,* edited by Philip Schaff. New York: Christian Literature Co., 1894.

Cicero, Marcus Tullius. *De finibus bonorum et malorum.* Trans. H. Rackham. Cambridge, MA: Harvard University Press, 1967.

———. *De Officiis.* Translated in *On Duties,* edited by M. T. Griffin and E. M. Atkins. Cambridge: Cambridge University Press, 1991.

Claeys, Gregory, ed. *Utopias of the British Enlightenment.* Cambridge: Cambridge University Press, 1994.

Clark, John Bates. *The Distribution of Wealth.* New York: Macmillan, 1899.

Clarke, George, ed. *John Bellers: His Life, Times and Writings.* London: Routledge and Kegan Paul, 1987.

Cohen, Gerald. "Equality of What? On Welfare, Goods, and Capabilities." In *The Quality of Life,* edited by Martha Nussbaum and Amartya Sen. Oxford, UK: Clarendon, 1993.

————. *If You're an Egalitarian, How Come You're So Rich?* Cambridge, MA: Harvard University Press, 1998.

Commons, John R. *The Distribution of Wealth.* New York: Macmillan, 1893.

Crossan, John Dominic, and Richard Watts. *Who Is Jesus?* Louisville, KY: Westminster John Knox, 1996.

Cunningham, William. "Free Trade," *Encyclopedia Britannica.* 11th ed. Vol. 11.

Daniels, Norman. *Just Health Care.* Cambridge: Cambridge University Press, 1985.

Defoe, Daniel. "Giving Alms Not Charity." In *The Shortest Way with the Dissenters and Other Pamphlets.* Oxford: Oxford University Press, 1927.

Desroche, Henri. *The American Shakers.* Translated by J. K. Savacool. Amherst: University of Massachussetts Press, 1971.

Devine, T. M. "The Urban Crisis." In *Glasgow,* edited by T. M. Devine and G. Jackson. Manchester, UK: Manchester University Press, 1995. Vol. 1.

Douglas, William O. "Dissenting Opinion." *Wisconsin v. Yoder.* 406 US 205 (1972).

Dworkin, Ronald. *Sovereign Virtue.* Cambridge, MA: Harvard University Press, 2000.

Fichte, Johann Gottlieb. *Foundations of Natural Right.* Edited by Frederick Neuhouser. Translated by Michael Baur. Cambridge: Cambridge University Press, 2000.

Fleischacker, Samuel. *On Adam Smith's Wealth of Nations: A Philosophical Companion.* Princeton, NJ: Princeton University Press, 2004.

————. *The Ethics of Culture.* Ithaca, NY: Cornell University Press, 1994.

————. "Philosophy and Moral Practice: Kant and Adam Smith." *Kant-Studien,* 82:3 (1991): 249–269.

————. *A Third Concept of Liberty.* Princeton, NJ: Princeton University Press, 1999.

————. "Values behind the Market: Kant's Response to the *Wealth of Nations.*" *History of Political Thought* 17:3 (1996): 379–407.

Fowle, T. W. *The Poor Law.* Littleton, CO: Fred B. Rothman and Co., 1980. (Originally published 1893.)

Frankfurt, Harry. "Equality as a Moral Ideal." In *The Importance of What We Care About.* Cambridge: Cambridge University Press, 1988.

Fraser, Nancy, and Axel Honneth. *Recognition or Redistribution?* London: Verso, 2003.

Furet, François. *Revolutionary France, 1770–1880.* Translated by A. Nevill. Oxford: Basil Blackwell, 1992.

Geertz, Clifford. *Local Knowledge.* New York: Basic Books, 1983.

Geras, Norman. "The Controversy about Marx and Justice." In *Marxist Theory,* edited by Alex Callinicos. Oxford: Oxford University Press, 1989.

Geremek, Bronislaw. *Poverty: A History*. Translated by Agnieszka Kolakowska. Oxford: Blackwell, 1994.

Glendon, Mary Ann. "Rights in Twentieth-Century Constitutions." *University of Chicago Law Review* 59 (1992): 519–538.

———. *A World Made New: Eleanor Roosevelt and the Universal Declaration of Human Rights*. New York: Random House, 2001.

Gosden, P. H. J. H. *The Friendly Societies in England 1815–1875*. Manchester, UK: Manchester University Press, 1961.

Gould, Stephen Jay. *The Mismeasure of Man*. New York: W. W. Norton, 1981.

Grampp, W. D. *The Manchester School of Economics*. Stanford, CA: Stanford University Press, 1960.

Gray, A. *The Socialist Tradition: From Moses to Lenin*. London: Longmans, Green, and Co., 1946.

Greer, Thomas. *What Roosevelt Thought*. East Lansing: Michigan State University Press, 2000.

Griswold, Charles. *Adam Smith and the Virtues of Enlightenment*. Cambridge: Cambridge University Press, 1998.

Grotius, Hugo. *The Law of War and Peace*. Translated by F. W. Kelsey. Indianapolis, IN: Bobbs-Merrill, 1925.

Haakonssen, Knud. *Natural Law and Moral Philosophy*. Cambridge: Cambridge University Press, 1996.

Harrington, James. *The Commonwealth of Oceana and a System of Politics*. Edited by J. G. A. Pocock. Cambridge: Cambridge University Press, 1992.

Hayek, Friedrich. *Law, Legislation, and Liberty*. Chicago: University of Chicago Press, 1973. Vol. 1.

Herzog, William. *Jesus, Justice, and the Reign of God*. Louisville, KY: Westminster John Knox Press, 2000.

Himmelfarb, Gertrude. *The Idea of Poverty*. New York: Alfred A. Knopf, 1984.

Hinde, Wendy. *Richard Cobden: A Victorian Outsider*. New Haven, CT: Yale University Press, 1987.

Hobbes, Thomas. *De Cive: the English version entitled, in the first edition, Philosophicall rudiments concerning government and society*. Edited by Howard Warrender. Oxford: Clarendon, 1983.

———. *Leviathan*. Edited by C. B. Macpherson. Harmondsworth, UK: Penguin, 1968.

Hobson, J. A. *Richard Cobden: The International Man*. London: T. Fisher Unwin, 1919.

Hofstadter, Richard. *Social Darwinism in American Thought*. Philadelphia: University of Pennsylvania Press, 1944.

Hont, Istvan, and Michael Ignatieff, eds. *Wealth and Virtue*. Cambridge: Cambridge University Press, 1983.

Hume, David. *Enquiries.* 3rd ed. Edited by L. A. Selby-Bigge and P. H. Nidditch. Oxford, UK: Clarendon Press, 1975.

———. *Treatise of Human Nature.* 2nd ed. Edited by L. A. Selby-Bigge and P. H. Nidditch. Oxford, UK: Clarendon Press, 1978.

Hutcheson, Frances. *Inquiry into the Original of Our Ideas of Virtue.* New York: Garland, 1971.

———. *A Short Introduction to Moral Philosophy.* Glasgow: R. Foulis, 1747.

———. *A System of Moral Philosophy.* London: A. Millar, 1755.

Irwin, Terence, ed. *Nicomachean Ethics.* Indianapolis, IN: Hackett, 1985.

Israel, Jonathan. *The Dutch Republic: Its Rise, Greatness, and Fall, 1477–1806.* Oxford, UK: Clarendon, 1995.

Jouvenel, Bertrand de. *The Ethics of Redistribution.* Indianapolis, IN: Liberty Fund, 1990.

Kamtekar, Rachana. "Social Justice and Happiness in *The Republic:* Plato's Two Principles." *History of Political Thought* 22:2 (2001): 189–220.

Kant, Immanuel. *Anthropology from a Pragmatic Point of View.* Translated by Victor Lyle Dowdell. Edited by Hans Rudnick. Carbondale: Southern Illinois University Press, 1978.

———. *The Conflict of the Faculties.* Translated by Mary Gregor. Lincoln: University of Nebraska Press, 1979.

———. *Critique of Judgment.* Translated by Werner Pluhar. Indianapolis, IN: Hackett, 1987.

———. *Foundations of the Metaphysics of Morals.* Translated by L. W. Beck. New York: Macmillan, 1959.

———. *Lectures on Ethics.* Translated by Louis Infield. Indianapolis, IN: Hackett, 1963.

———. *Lectures on Ethics.* Translated by Peter Heath. Edited by Peter Heath and J. B. Schneewind. Cambridge: Cambridge University Press, 1996.

———. *The Metaphysics of Morals.* Translated by Mary Gregor. Cambridge: Cambridge University Press, 1991.

———. *Practical Philosophy.* Edited and translated by Mary J. Gregor. Introduction by Allen Wood. Cambridge: Cambridge University Press, 1996.

Kraut, Richard. *Aristotle: Political Philosophy.* Oxford: Oxford University Press, 2002.

Kymlicka, Will. *Liberalism, Community and Culture.* Oxford, UK: Clarendon, 1989.

Laqueur, Thomas. "Bodies, Details, and the Humanitarian Narrative." In *The New Cultural History,* edited by Lynn Hunt. Berkeley: University of California Press, 1989.

Lees, Lynn. *The Solidarities of Strangers: The English Poor Laws and the People, 1700–1948.* Cambridge: Cambridge University Press, 1998.

Locke, John. "Draft of a Representation Containing a Scheme of Methods for the Employment of the Poor." In *Political Writings of John Locke,* edited by David Wootton. New York: Mentor, 1993.

———. *Two Treatises of Government* (reprinted frequently).

MacIntyre, Alasdair. *Whose Justice? Which Rationality?* Notre Dame, IN: University of Notre Dame Press, 1988.

Maimonides, Moses. *Mishneh Torah.* Hebrew (reprinted frequently). [Translated as *Code of Maimonides.* New Haven, CT: Yale University Press, 1949–1972. 22 volumes.]

Mandeville, Bernard de. *The Fable of the Bees, or Private Vices, Publick Benefits.* Edited, with a commentary, by F. B. Kaye. Oxford, UK: Clarendon Press, 1924.

Manuel, Frank E. *The New World of Henri Saint-Simon.* Cambridge, MA: Harvard University Press, 1956.

Manuel, Frank E., and Fritzie P. Manuel, eds. and trans. *French Utopias.* New York: Free Press, 1966.

Marshall, Alfred. *Principles of Economics.* 7th ed. London: Macmillan, 1916. (Originally published 1890.)

Marshall, T. H. *The Right to Welfare.* New York: Free Press, 1981.

McKendrick, Neil. "Home Demand and Economic Growth." In *Historical Perspectives: Studies in English Thought and Society,* edited by N. McKendrick. London: Europa Publications, 1974.

Mill, John Stuart. *Utilitarianism.* Edited by George Sher. Indianapolis, IN: Hackett, 1979.

Miller, David. *Social Justice.* Oxford, UK: Clarendon Press, 1976.

More, Thomas. *Utopia.* Translated by Paul Turner. Harmondsworth, UK: Penguin, 1965.

Morley, Henry, ed. *Ideal Commonwealths.* New York: The Co-operative Publication Society, 1901.

Murphy, Jeffrie. *Kant: the Philosophy of Right.* New York: St. Martin's Press, 1970.

Nagel, Thomas. *Equality and Partiality.* Oxford: Oxford University Press, 1991.

Narveson, Jan. *The Libertarian Idea.* Philadelphia: Temple University Press, 1988.

Nelson, George, ed. *Freedom and Welfare.* Westport, CT: Greenwood, 1953.

Nozick, Robert. *Anarchy, State, and Utopia.* New York: Basic Books, 1974.

Nussbaum, Martha. *The Cosmopolitan Tradition.* New Haven, CT: Yale University Press, forthcoming.

———. "Duties of Justice, Duties of Material Aid." *Journal of Political Philosophy* 8:2 (2000): 176–206.

———. "Nature, Function, and Capability: Aristotle on Political Distribution." In *Oxford Studies in Ancient Philosophy,* edited by Julia Annas and Robert H. Grimm. Supplementary volume, 1988. Oxford: Oxford University Press, 1988.

———. *Sex and Social Justice.* New York: Oxford University Press, 1999.

O'Neill, Onora. *Constructions of Reason.* Cambridge: Cambridge University Press, 1989.

Paine, Thomas. *The Writings of Thomas Paine.* Edited by Moncure Daniel Conway. New York: G. P. Putnam, 1894. Vol. 2.

Peacock, A. J. *Bread or Blood: A Study of the Agrarian Riots in East Anglia in 1816.* London: Victor Gollancz, 1965.

Peffer, R. G. *Marxism, Morality, and Social Justice.* Princeton, NJ: Princeton University Press, 1990.

Plato. *The Republic.* Edited by Giovanni Ferrari. Translated by Tom Griffin. Cambridge: Cambridge University Press, 2000.

Plutarch. *Tiberius Gracchus.* In *Plutarch's Lives,* translated by Bernadotte Perrin. Cambridge, MA: Harvard University Press, 1959.

Pocock, J. G. A. *The Machiavellian Moment.* Princeton, NJ: Princeton University Press, 1975.

Pogge, Thomas. *Realizing Rawls.* Ithaca, NY: Cornell University Press, 1989.

Pufendorf, Samuel. *On the Duty of Man and Citizen.* Translated by M. Silverthorne. Edited by J. Tully. Cambridge: Cambridge University Press, 1991.

———. *The Law of Nature and Nations.* Translated by C. H. Oldfather and W. A. Oldfather. Oxford, UK: Clarendon Press, 1934.

Ramsay, George. *An Essay on the Distribution of Wealth.* Edinburgh: A. C. Black, 1836.

Raphael, D. D. *Concepts of Justice.* Oxford, UK: Clarendon Press, 2001.

Rawls, John. *John Rawls: Collected Papers.* Edited by Samuel Freeman. Cambridge, MA: Harvard University Press, 1999.

———. *Justice as Fairness: A Restatement.* Edited by Erin Kelly. Cambridge, MA: Belknap Press of Harvard University Press, 2001.

———. *Political Liberalism.* New York: Columbia University Press, 1993.

———. *A Theory of Justice.* Cambridge, MA: Belknap Press of Harvard University Press, 1971.

Reid, Thomas. *Active Powers.* Cambridge, MA: MIT Press, 1969.

Reiss, H. S., ed. *The Political Thought of the German Romantics.* New York: Macmillan, 1955.

Roemer, John. *Theories of Distributive Justice.* Cambridge, MA: Harvard University Press, 1996.

Rosen, Allen. *Kant's Theory of Justice.* Ithaca, NY: Cornell University Press, 1993.

Rosen, Mark. "The Outer Limits of Community Self-Governance in Residential Associations, Municipalities, and Indian Country." *Virginia Law Review* 84 (1998): 1053–1144.

Rousseau, Jean-Jacques. "A Discourse on Political Economy." In *The Social Contract and Discourses,* translated by G. D. H. Cole. London: J. M. Dent, 1973.

————. *First and Second Discourses.* Translated by R. Masters and J. Masters. Edited by R. Masters. New York: St. Martin's Press, 1964.

Salter, F. R., ed. *Some Early Tracts on Poor Relief.* London: Methuen and Co., 1926.

Scheffler, Samuel. *Boundaries and Allegiances.* Oxford: Oxford University Press, 2001.

Schneewind, Jerome. *The Invention of Autonomy.* Cambridge: Cambridge University Press, 1998.

Sen, Amartya. "Equality of What?" In *Tanner Lectures on Human Values,* edited by S. McMurrin. Cambridge: Cambridge University Press, 1980. Vol. 1.

Shell, Susan Meld. *The Rights of Reason.* Toronto: University of Toronto Press, 1980.

Sidgwick, Henry. *The Methods of Ethics.* Introduction by John Rawls. Indianapolis, IN: Hackett, 1981.

Simmons, A. J. *The Lockean Theory of Rights.* Princeton, NJ: Princeton University Press, 1992.

Slack, Paul. *English Poor Law, 1531–1782.* London: Macmillan, 1990.

Smart, J. J. C. "An Outline of a System of Utilitarian Ethics." In Smart and Bernard Williams, *Utilitarianism: For and Against.* Cambridge: Cambridge University Press, 1973.

Smith, Adam. *An Inquiry into the Nature and Causes of the Wealth of Nations.* Edited by R. H. Campbell, A. S. Skinner, and W. B. Todd. Oxford: Oxford University Press, 1976.

————. *Lectures on Jurisprudence.* Edited by R. L. Meek, D. D. Raphael, and P. G. Stein. Oxford: Oxford University Press, 1978.

————. *Theory of Moral Sentiments.* Edited by D. D. Raphael and A. L. Macfie. Oxford: Oxford University Press, 1976.

Snell, K. D. M. *Annals of the Labouring Poor.* Cambridge: Cambridge University Press, 1985.

Spence, Thomas. *The Political Works of Thomas Spence.* Edited by H. T. Dickinson. Newcastle upon Tyne, UK: Avero Publications, 1982.

Spencer, Herbert. *The Man versus the State.* New York: Appleton, 1893.

————. *Social Statics.* New York: Augustus M. Kelley, 1969. (Originally published London: John Chapman, 1851.)

Tamir, Yael. *Liberal Nationalism.* Princeton, NJ: Princeton University Press, 1993.

Taylor, Charles. "The Politics of Recognition." In *Multiculturalism,* edited by Amy Gutmann. Princeton, NJ: Princeton University Press, 1994.

Thompson, E. P. *Customs in Common: Studies in Traditional Popular Culture.* New York: New Press, 1991.

————. *The Making of the English Working Class.* Harmondsworth, UK: Penguin, 1980.

Thompson, Noel. *The Real Rights of Man*. London: Pluto Press, 1998.

Thompson, William. *An Inquiry into the Principles of the Distribution of Wealth, Most Conducive to Human Happiness*. New York: Augustus Kelley, 1963. (Originally published London: Longman, Hurst, 1824.)

Thomson, David. *The Babeuf Plot*. London: K. Paul, Trench, Trubner, 1947.

Tierney, Brian. *Medieval Poor Law*. Berkeley: University of California Press, 1959.

Tilly, Charles. *Popular Contention in Great Britain, 1758–1834*. Cambridge, MA: Harvard University Press, 1995.

Townsend, Joseph. *A Dissertation on the Poor Laws*. Berkeley: University of California Press, 1971. (Originally published 1786.)

Trattner, Walter. *From Poor Law to Welfare State*. 5th ed. New York: Free Press, 1994.

Tuck, Richard. *Natural Rights Theories*. Cambridge: Cambridge University Press, 1979.

Tucker, Robert, ed. *The Marx-Engels Reader*. New York: W. W. Norton, 1978.

———. *The Marxian Revolutionary Idea*. New York: W. W. Norton, 1969.

Tully, James. "Struggles over Recognition and Distribution." *Constellations* 7:4 (2000): 469–482.

Vallentyne, Peter, and Hillel Steiner, eds. *Left-Libertarianism and Its Critics*. New York: Palgrave, 2000.

———. *The Origins of Left-Libertarianism: An Anthology of Historical Writings*. New York: Palgrave, 2000.

Vitoria, Francesco de. "On the American Indians." In *Political Writings*, edited by A. Pagden and J. Lawrence. Cambridge: Cambridge University Press, 1991.

Vries, Jan de, and Ad van der Woude. *The First Modern Economy: Success, Failure, and Perseverance of the Dutch Economy, 1500–1815*. Cambridge: Cambridge University Press, 1997.

Williams, Howard. *Kant's Political Philosophy*. Oxford, UK: Blackwell, 1983.

Winch, Donald. *Riches and Poverty*. Cambridge: Cambridge University Press, 1996.

Wittgenstein, Ludwig. *Philosophical Investigations*. Translated by G. E. M. Anscombe. New York: Macmillan, 1958.

Wood, Allen. *Karl Marx*. London: Routledge and Kegan Paul, 1981.

Wood, Gordon. *The Radicalism of the American Revolution*. New York: Random House, 1991.

Woodhouse, A. S. P., ed. *Puritanism and Liberty*. London: J. M. Dent and Sons, 1974.

Young, Iris. *Justice and the Politics of Difference*. Princeton, NJ: Princeton University Press, 1990.

Index

Harvard University Press is a member of Green Press Initiative (greenpressinitiative.org), a nonprofit organization working to help publishers and printers increase their use of recycled paper and decrease their use of fiber derived from endangered forests. This book was printed on 100% recycled paper containing 50% post-consumer waste and processed chlorine free.